Saving the Overlooked Continent

American Protestant Missions in Western Europe, 1940-1975

To Alfons Lammers

SAVING the OVERLOOKED CONTINENT

HANS KRABBENDAM

American Protestant Missions in Western Europe 1940-1975

LEUVEN UNIVERSITY PRESS

This book appears in the peer-reviewed series
KADOC Studies on Religion, Culture & Society

Cover: a cartoon by James Emerson Russell published in *United Evangelical Action*, 15 January 1946, 13. The illustration reminded its readers that the starving population in Europe needed religion even more than food to survive.

ISBN 978 94 6270 257 8
eISBN 978 94 6166 365 8
D/2020/1869/61
https://doi.org/10.11116/9789461663658
NUR: 704

CONTENTS

ACKNOWLEDGEMENTS

The publication of a manuscript is reason for rejoicing; dispersed data have found a home in a coherent book. Looking back, the solitary researcher realizes he has been on a path not unlike a pilgrimage, where the journey undertaken in writing the book has been as important as the destination, and where he has been joined along their route by others in a collective enterprise. As pleased as I am that the book is now ready to enter the public domain, I reflect on the many friends, colleagues, and professionals who have blessed my road with clever questions, helpful suggestions, stimulating arguments, and useful sources. One feels almost sorry to have reached the destination!

My thank-you-list begins with my former colleagues at the Roosevelt Study Center (now Roosevelt Institute of American Studies - RIAS) in Middelburg, the Netherlands. For 25 years I worked in the company of Kees van Minnen, Leontien Joosse, Giles Scott-Smith, Dario Fazzi, and many visiting researchers. They created a stable and stimulating environment for research in Middelburg's magnificent Abbey, and there we had countless formal and informal conversations about the topic of this book.

But ideas need evidence and most of the source material for the book had to be gathered elsewhere. The unique collections of the Billy Graham Center Archives at Wheaton College, Illinois, in the United States, were crucial for uncovering this story. For anyone visiting the Center, Bob Shuster and his staff professionally coordinate the appropriate materials and help researchers to efficiently mine them. I am grateful to them for their friendly service.

I found a similar welcome at the Evangelical Alliance in London, where the staff gave me free access to browse their abundant collections on the British evangelicals and their international relations. At the archives of the German Evangelical Alliance in Bad Blankenburg, the Rev. Werner Beyer opened the doors to surprisingly rich and detailed information. Both of these depositories deeply anchored my story in Europe. Historian John G. Turner was exceptionally generous in sending me his research materials on the activities of Campus Crusade for Christ in Europe. His notes enabled me to fill in a missing piece of the religious puzzle.

As important as these paper collections were, they could not yield the complete account. For that I needed the personal experiences of missionaries, most importantly Dr. Robert Vajko and Ms. Sarah Page. They helped me get a picture of life in the field, that corrected many of my outsider assumptions.

While collecting these data, I had the good fortune to be a part of an American-European research cohort doing exciting projects on transnational evangelicalism. The group started at Keele University and met annually for five years at European venues where we shared ideas, sources, insights, and jokes. These meetings were true academic highlights. Uta Balbier, the late Paul Boyer, Heather D. Curtis, Darren Dochuk, Emma Long, Eileen Luhr, John Maiden, Melani McAlister, Steven Miller, Kendrick Oliver, Andrew Preston, Axel Schaefer, Timothy Stoneman, David Swartz, Daniel Williams and others, made up the core of this intellectually stimulating and warm-hearted group. Their deep understanding of transatlantic religious processes boosted my research immensely and gave rise to a series of articles that explored specific themes and laid the groundwork for this book. A complete list of these early building block articles can be found in the bibliography.

Bruce and Tizzy Kuklick offered me hospitality in the United States. They always managed to keep me from taking myself too seriously, offering new perspectives, critical feedback, and a steady stream of humor and companionship. Closer to home, George Harinck was a constant fellow-traveler along my path. A friend and co-organizer of many successful events, he never lost interest in the subject nor faith in its goal. I am sure we will continue to explore together.

Once the first draft was written, I could turn to Ms. Michael Strange, whose extraordinary editorial gifts transformed a manuscript written by a non-native speaker into a clear and gentle English text. My gratitude is boundless.

By then, I had arrived at the Catholic Documentation Center at the Radboud University in Nijmegen, the Netherlands. This new environment welcomed me and my curious project, and helped me see it in a new perspective. I thank everyone who made me feel at home in this strong and caring academic community. It feels safe to work under the supervision of the able and amiable

Natalia Grygierczyk, the innovative director of the University Library. She gently encouraged me to deliver the end result.

Finally, every story's beginning stems from a time before its meaning and order emerge. I vividly remember this moment of conception, though it was more than three decades ago. In 1987, Alfons Lammers, then Chair of American History at Leiden University, told the story of Billy Sunday to a group of interested undergraduate history majors. The tale was soon to become one of the chapters in his book on American evangelists, *Helden van het geloof: Amerika in de greep van de dominees* (Heroes of the Faith: America Gripped by the Preachers). I fell under the spell of this inspiring teacher and awoke to the fascinating phenomenon of American evangelism, making American religious history the topic of my master's thesis. As I have witnessed – with equal parts familiarity and bewilderment – successive waves of religious interventions from America wash ashore in Europe, the relevance of the topic has only been enhanced. The original fascination has never left me. That I am able to add to the larger story several decades later, testifies to the power of the original mustard seed. I gratefully dedicate this book to the sower.

INTRODUCTION

In the fall of 1946, a team of four American evangelists toured the Netherlands under the banner of Youth for Christ. They spoke to 65,000 mostly young people at 42 rallies, and counted among their successes 3,500 decisions for Christ. A Protestant minister in the Netherlands expressed his admiration for the power of this American religious injection: "The Youth for Christ team has done more in six weeks than our Dutch Reformed Church has done in all of its history."[1] This jubilant response was shared by some ministers and contradicted by others who felt that the jazzy presentation of the gospel was an insult to the Christian tradition. Both sides agreed that this religious impulse could only have originated in North America.

Two years later Oswald J. Smith, pastor of the People's Church in Toronto and champion of missions, returned from a six-week European trip and addressed his constituency, "Let us pray and let us work (so) that Europe, one of the greatest of all mission fields, may be evangelized before it is forever too late."[2] Smith's call for action indicated the sense of urgency in the plans to re-Christianize Europe. These two examples of intense religious expectations on both sides of the Atlantic marked a shift in the North-American-European religious balance after World War II that few people noticed, then and now.

This book pinpoints this shift and explains the motives and aims of American Protestants in their drive to influence the religious future of Europe after

1 *Youth for Christ Magazine*, January 1947, 55.

2 Oswald Smith, "The Miracle of Youth for Christ in Europe," *People's Magazine* (first quarter 1949), 21.

World War II. It uncovers the means used to achieve these ends and assesses the results, including the structural American religious presence in Europe. This phenomenon created a landmark in the history of Christendom as this enduring American campaign to evangelize Europe reversed the direction of Western missions for the first time. This new direction, however, went through the same phases of mission enterprises elsewhere, including discovery, mobilization, institutionalization, and indigenization. Similarly, the results went beyond the original expectations.

The American missionary impulse in Europe after World War II directly reflected developments in the sending and receiving countries, and matched the military, economic, and political programs, which had positioned the United States as the dominant partner in Europe and it's new reference culture. As a consequence Europe also imported the internal competition among American Protestants. Theological tensions between modernists and traditionalists, and organizational competition between churches and independent (mostly evangelical) parachurch associations offered a slate of options that triggered civic and ecclesiastical responses in Europe. But behind the competing religious networks was also a considerable overlap in goals and means. Of course the three branches of American Protestantism (mainline, evangelical, fundamentalist) were boughs from the same trunk. The organizational divisions marked boundaries, but could not erase a tradition of shared ideas and practices. Many evangelicals were part of mainline or modernist bodies, many ideas of the fundamentalists echoed in evangelical churches. The formal organizational structure of ecumenical modernists was closer to the fundamentalists than it was to the informal organizational structure of the evangelicals. These similarities and overlaps among religious contenders have changed the interpretation of American Protestantism as a two-party structure that pitted progressives against conservatives, while the latter group was also bitterly divided.[3]

In this constellation, the newly organized "evangelicals" came to occupy center stage, combining historical antecedents and modern mobilization skills into a global identity. After their successful distancing from the fundamentalists, they aspired to bask in the middle of the religious spectrum and filled most missionary positions.[4] At times the tripartite competition in this volume may generate some bewilderment, especially for those who are not versed in the intricacies of American Protestantism, and this puzzlement will increase over time as the relative positions shift. But that is exactly the charm of this story: It reveals the historical dynamism and the mixed feelings

3 Douglas Jacobsen and William Vance Trollinger, Jr., eds., *Re-Forming the Center: American Protestantism, 1900 to the Present* (Grand Rapids, MI: Eerdmans, 1998). Discussion forum in *Church History* 71.2 (June 2002): 368-390.

4 Grant Wacker, *America's Pastor: Billy Graham and the Shaping of a Nation* (Cambridge, MA: Harvard University Press, 2014), 5-31.

of recognition and alienation that many Europeans experienced when they encountered American missionaries on their own turf. Taking into account that there is not one overarching narrative about religious history but many, distinguishing the three traditions makes sense from a European perspective. Although the three groups differed in emphasis, means, translation, visibility, and provoked divergent responses, they came from a clear location overseas.

But even more important for understanding the meaning of this American missionary enterprise is the fact that Europe was the battleground. Statistical overviews reveal that the present evangelical strongholds are in Africa and Asia, especially when Pentecostal affiliations are taken into account. An estimated half of the 800 million affiliated with the evangelical-Pentecostal movement reside in Africa, a quarter in Asia, ten percent each in Latin and North America, and only 2 percent in Europe. It is exactly these statistics that make Europe a most interesting subject for scholarly research. The numbers draw attention to the basic structure of religion in society, and open up an opportunity to learn as much from the busts as from the booms in evangelicalism. Also, the structural inclusion of Western Europe in the American missionary enterprise immediately after World War II was a prime example of the reverse movement of missionary activities, and helped inaugurate the truly global and multidirectional phase of this undertaking.[5]

This story combines the fields of historical transatlantic relations and religious studies. It adds a chapter to the transatlantic corpus on the mutual perceptions Americans and Europeans had of each other regarding intentions and interventions. The late Lamin Sanneh of Yale University encouraged his readers to think about the significance of missionaries as cultural mediators: "Departments of American Studies, for instance, are innocently oblivious of the significance of the missionary movement for developments on the home front. How much more so were the agents and personalities who manned the machinery of the enterprise abroad and presided over its field expansion."[6] Similarly, missiological researchers call for more cultural context to explain the patterns of religious contact and confrontation. While the interest in missionaries is rising, the story of missionaries in Europe has yet to be told in full. A survey of the activities of American evangelists in Europe is indispensable to clarify the trends in transnational religion in the Western world. This analysis of the timing and the shape of this religious exchange sophisticates the debate

5 Mark Hutchinson and John Wolffe, *A Short History of Global Evangelicalism* (Cambridge: Cambridge University Press, 2012), 209-243.

6 Lamin Sanneh, *Translating the Message: The Missionary Impact on Culture* (Maryknoll, NY: Orbis Books, 2009), 12.

about the pace, process, and particularities of religion in the streams of modernization, globalization, and secularization.[7]

The first chapter sets the historical stage for the postwar missions. The confessional strategy of American missionaries in Europe began in the middle of the nineteenth century and was the first sign of a shift in the direction of religious influence that, until that time, had been from Europe to the United States. Still, in the next few decades European ministers who accompanied or followed the millions of immigrants to America greatly outnumbered the occasional American missionaries traveling to Europe. American missionaries most commonly came to Europe to support Protestant denominations in Catholic or Eastern Orthodox countries, or to establish mission posts on the Continent in the Anglo-Saxon holiness tradition. These activities remained small-scale until the last quarter of the century when evangelists like Dwight Moody and holiness preachers such as Robert Pearsall and Hannah Whitall Smith successfully courted and awed European audiences. Evangelists Oswald Smith and Frank Buchman (of the Moral Rearmament Movement) followed Moody and the Smiths in the first half of the twentieth century, but none of them settled in Europe permanently. In addition to these mass evangelists, small missionary organizations set up shop in Europe.

The number of American missionaries had grown steadily after the American Civil War. Mission-minded Americans flocked to the African and Asian continents and eventually surpassed the number of European missionaries. By 1911, almost eight thousand Americans were involved in Protestant missions outside their own continent, against twelve thousand Europeans. After World War I two-thirds of Protestant missionaries came from North America, which marked a quantitative shift among Western Protestants. In the interwar years Europe's Protestant position changed from an equal to a junior partner

7 Sociologist Rodney Stark explained the growth of postwar missions simply by contrasting the energetic Americans to inert Europeans, whose state support systems discouraged social activities. See his, "Efforts to Christianize Europe, 400-2000," *Journal of Contemporary Religion* 16:1 (2001): 105-123. His analysis only considers one (supply) factor, which acts as the basis for his strikingly optimistic expectation about the results; Stefan Paas, "Evangelistic Mission in Europe: Seven Historical Models," in Gerrit Noort, Kyriaki Avtzi, and Stefan Paas, eds., *Sharing Good News: Handbook on Evangelism in Europe* (Geneva: World Council of Churches Publications, 2017), 21-35; Brian Stanley, "Mission to the World: Changing Perspectives in American Protestantism, 1910-2010," in Larry Eskridge and Edith L. Blumhofer, eds., *Saving the World? The Changing Terrain of American Protestant Missions, 1910 to the Present* (University of Alabama Press, forthcoming). See David W. Ellwood, *The Shock of America: Europe and the Challenge of the Century* (Oxford, UK: Oxford University Press, 2012); Mary Nolan, *The Transatlantic Century: Europe and America, 1890-2010* (Cambridge: Cambridge University Press, 2012). See Anne Deighton's review of Elwood's book in the *Journal of American Studies* 47 (August 2013): 861; Ruud Janssens, "I would Rather Go to Europe than go to Heaven," in Michael J. Wintle, ed., *Imagining Europe: Europe and European Civilisation as Seen from its Margins and by the Rest of the World, in the Nineteenth and Twentieth Centuries* (Brussels: Peter Lang, 2008), 123-145.

status in the evangelical enterprise and the post-World War II period witnessed a second, qualitative shift when Europe turned from a sending to a receiving region. By 1971 the numbers of American missionaries had swelled to 34,000 of the 52,500 Protestant missionaries in the world.[8]

The new missionary enterprise began with American Protestants' material assistance to Europe. This pattern had been created by American relief efforts during and after the Great War and was repeated after World War II. Millions of dollars in relief flowed from prosperous America to war-torn Europe. Americans rebuilt churches, established care centers for refugees, and assisted displaced families living below the poverty line. These actions were considered a priority and they helped to alleviate immediate need. By 1950 the necessity for this material assistance ended, temporary American Protestant workers returned home, and a growing number of evangelical missionaries entered Europe. Their numbers would swell from a few score in 1948 to more than 3,700 in 1985 (in addition to thousands of Mormons and Jehovah's Witnesses). They stayed much longer than the initial postwar relief workers, and were succeeded by fresh recruits.[9] Recently historians of religion have analyzed evangelical efforts to reach out beyond national borders to achieve global transformation as a testimony to evangelical flexibility, and have taken note of the challenges these developments created for maintaining a stable identity among evangelicals. An underreported part of this history, mainly on the level of individual states, shows the strength of internal opposition from fundamentalists and the Calvinist confessional right to evangelical outreach.[10]

8 Mark A. Noll, *The New Shape of World Christianity* (Grand Rapids, MI: Eerdmans, 2002), 80. Dutch missiologist Jan Jongeneel contrasted the innovation of William Carey's (interdenominational) missionary societies separate from the church with the church-led continental missionary operations. European thinkers about missions criticized the activism and idealism of American missionaries as too aggressively pressuring the transformation of the political and social order. The (Anglo-Saxon) Kingdom-concept contrasts with the (European) church-centered goal. European resistance was not only about power, but also about goal and means. "European-Continental Perception and Critiques of British and American Protestant Missions," *Exchange* 30.1 (2001): 103-124.

9 R. Pierce Beaver, "Distribution of the American Protestant Foreign Missionary Force in 1952," *Missionary Research Library, Occasional Bulletin* 4.10 (13 July 1953), 1-3 and Samuel Wilson, ed., *Mission Handbook: North American Protestant Ministries Overseas*, 13th edition (Monrovia, CA: MARC, 1986).

10 Crawford Gribben, *Evangelical Millennialism in the Trans-Atlantic World, 1500-2000* (Basingstoke: Palgrave Macmillan, 2011); Mark Hutchinson and John Wolffe, *A Short History of Global Evangelicalism* (Cambridge: Cambridge University Press, 2012); Brian Stanley, *The Global Diffusion of Evangelicalism: The Age of Billy Graham and John Stott* (Nottingham: Inter-Varsity Press, 2013); Stefan Paas, "The Making of a Mission Field: Paradigms of Evangelistic Mission in Europe," *Exchange* 41 (2012): 44-67. Paas correctly notes the connections between home and foreign missions in the expectation of civilizing effects of personal conversion. At the receiving European side, the arrival of American and other missionaries was not a complete surprise, as a number of committed Christian intellectuals had been doubting the completion of the process of Christianization of the continent.

OVERVIEW OF AMERICAN PROTESTANT MISSIONARIES IN WESTERN EUROPE, 1958-1985

	1958	1962	1964	1968	1968	1972	1975	1979	1985
				OV	NAT				
France	57	107	35	267	264	372	416	652	716
Italy	31	68	23	139	79	171	190	248	308
Portugal	24	33	11	31	58	37	53	109	168
Belgium	24	25	13	24	33	83	158	226	175
Spain	23	37	15	102	39	202	228	346	438
Austria	17	18	14	73	23	145	165	250	250
Ireland	11		2	32	9	11	55		
Germany	37	117	34	279	275	391	445	616	661
Great Britain	19	3	14	82	40	139	170	504	445
the Netherlands	8	22	12	38	59	45	151	124	159
Switzerland	8	20	15	32	41	66	79	70	74
Scandinavia	7	14	11	34	28	52	77	131	123
General Europe	11	8	27	3			153	301	
	266	475	207	1160	951	1714	2187	3429	3818

Sources: Missionary Research Library, *Directory of North American Protestant Foreign Mission Agencies*, 4th edition, 1960; "North American Protestant Foreign Mission Agencies," fifth edition 1962; "North American Protestant Foreign Mission Agencies," sixth edition 1964; "North American Protestant Ministries Overseas," 8th edition, 1968; Edward R. Dayton, ed., *Mission Handbook: North American Protestant Ministries Overseas*, 10th edition (Monrovia, CA 1973); Edward R. Dayton, ed., *Mission Handbook: North American Protestant Ministries Overseas*, 11th edition (Monrovia, CA 1976); *Mission Handbook: North American Protestant Ministries Overseas*, 12th edition (Monrovia, CA 1980); Samuel Wilson, ed., *Mission Handbook: North American Protestant Ministries Overseas*, 13th edition (Monrovia, CA 1986).
Note that 1964 lists the number of organizations active in each country; and 1968 lists the number of overseas missionaries (North Americans) [OV] and nationals (from the country listed) [NAT].

The presence of American religion in postwar Europe is usually taken to be one of the instruments deployed to combat Communism in the context of the Cold War. Though Cold War concerns did occupy the minds of religious leaders in the West, it was not the main, nor the only motive for their activities. Billy Graham's frequent anti-Communist references might lead one to such conclusions, but it was concern for access to the mission fields rather than Communism per se that stimulated American evangelists to go global.[11]

These voices had been muffled by the mix of national and religious identifications in Europe between 1850 and 1940. Stefan Paas, *Church Planting in the Secular West: Learning from the European Experience* (Grand Rapids, MI: Eerdmans, 2016).

11 Mark Silk, *Spiritual Politics: Religion and America Since World War II* (New York: Simon and Schuster, 1988); Eric R. Crouse, "Popular Cold Warriors: Conservative Protestants, Communism, and Culture in Early Cold War America," *Journal of Religion and Popular*

The main argument of this book is that concern for pluralism at home and abroad propelled American Protestants into missions in Europe and by doing so framed Europe as a secular place in contrast to the United States. Representatives of American mainline churches assumed the responsibility to restore religious institutions in Europe as a safeguard against fascism and Communism. Evangelicals felt that these established churches allowed too much theological pluralism and threatened the core of Christianity, while simultaneously blaming the liberal ecumenical organizations for not being pluralist enough to create space for their evangelical programs. As part of a new religious network in the making (they founded the National Association of Evangelicals in 1943), they feared being driven from the religious market by more liberal Christians who had joined together nationally in the Federal (after 1950 National) Council of Churches and internationally in the World Council of Churches. Fundamentalist organizations were even more hostile to ecumenist operations. They blamed evangelicals for being soft and organized their own channels. Once the new missionaries landed in European nations, they encountered state protection of the established churches that restricted new missionary activity. Missionaries had to legitimatize their presence in Europe both towards their constituency and towards Europeans. It took considerable time to recruit and train missionaries capable of creating stable outposts and an alternative transnational network. The result of their voluntaristic efforts in the 1950s was more diversity and prestige by keeping both the established and the free churches on board.

At the end of the 1960s, the evangelicals' fear of being excluded had subsided thanks to their own quantitative expansion and the declining position of their opponents, both mainstream and fundamentalist. Their visible growth led to European recognition of evangelicalism as a third force in Christendom – next to Roman Catholicism and mainstream Protestantism. This new situation changed evangelical strategy from opposition to the established churches to cooperation with them. Their success created a dual identity: believers

Culture 2 (Fall 2002): 1-18; Dianne Kirby, ed., *Religion and the Cold War* (New York: Palgrave Macmillan, 2003); Andrew Preston, "The Death of a Peculiar Special Relationship: Myron Taylor and the Religious Roots of America's Cold War," in John Dumbrell and Axel Schäfer, eds., *America's Special Relationships: Foreign and Domestic Aspects of the Politics of Alliance* (New York and London: Routledge, 2009), 202-216; Andrew Preston, *Sword of the Spirit, Shield of Faith: Religion in American War and Diplomacy* (New York: Alfred A. Knopf, 2012); Alexander Stephan, ed., *The Americanization of Europe: Culture, Diplomacy, and Anti-Americanism after 1945* (New York: Berghahn, 2006); Jonathan P. Herzog, *The Spiritual-Industrial Complex: America's Religious Battle against Communism in the Early Cold War* (New York: Oxford University Press, 2011). The exception is Carl McIntire, whose main aim was to roll back Communism. See Markku Ruotsila, *Fighting Fundamentalist: Carl McIntire and the Politicization of American Fundamentalism* (New York: Oxford University Press, 2016).

belonged to their national churches and to international movements. In order to achieve this combination they needed new institutions and a public voice.

In the 1970s traditional believers in Europe felt bolstered by the successes of their American fellow evangelicals and proceeded to adopt American styles and organizations and to build new institutions in response to the cultural and often secular shifts that had occurred in the 1960s. In turn, by the mid-1970s, American evangelicals broadened their horizons by openly embracing a structural involvement in society. By this time the American protestant presence in Europe had been well-established, which concludes the narrative of this book. Of course, the story did not end here. The 1980s was a decade of reorientation among protestant believers, which led in the following decade to a branching of evangelicals into three major groups which shared little theological cohesion: open or progressive, reformed, and charismatic evangelical. Eventually, in the twenty-first century, this new constellation resulted in more cordial contacts and cooperation of evangelical and ecumenist Protestants with Roman Catholics. This result stood in sharp contrast to the hopes and fears that had held sway in the immediate postwar period. Only a close analysis of the process of American Protestants creating a presence in Europe can explain this paradoxical result.[12]

Relevance

In addition to the relevance the topic of evangelicalism has to the globalization of American Protestantism, this book also contributes to mission history by adding an overlooked, but increasingly important, story of its confrontation with secularized and non-protestant Western areas. This exploration adds to the debate among historians and social scientists about the motives, means, and direction of religious expansion and decline in Europe and North America, without falling in the trap of dichotomies of religious and secular societies or conservative-progressive movements.[13]

Thomas Berg correctly indicated that the troubled relationship between evangelicals and the mainline churches was not only a domestic American phenomenon, but also an international one. International prospects triggered the combativeness of evangelical missions in the late 1940s, even as the missions made efforts to maintain connections to the mainline churches

12 Stanley, *Global Diffusion*, 235-247. He mainly describes the Anglo world.

13 Peter Berger, Grace Davie, and Effie Fokas, *Religious America, Secular Europe? A Theme and Variations* (Aldershot/Burlington VT: Ashgate, 2008). The authors indicate that massive evangelicalism is the main difference between Europe and the United States (p. 11) On a much larger scale Charles Taylor's *A Secular Age* (Cambridge: The Belknap Press of Harvard University Press, 2007) explores the competition between transcendence and immanence in Western culture and uncovers the connections and tensions between these positions, which sometimes led to intellectual monopolies.

where many evangelicals were harbored. This evangelical-ecumenical tension reached a climax in the 1960s, but turned around slowly towards a convergence in the 1970s. This shift was a result not only of the relative growth of evangelicals, but also of their growing diversity within the subculture. In this decade the Majority World gained access to the leadership, challenged Western domination in religious institutions (mostly targeting the United States), and emphasized contextual thinking and social and economic issues. As we will see, the Europeans mediated between American and non-Western interests, a project that advanced evangelical diversity. The overlap with similar trends in ecumenical history made it harder for evangelicals to categorically reject their former antagonists. Only by looking at the activities of American Protestants in Europe one can understand the radical change from mutual rejection in explicitly hostile rhetoric to mutual cooperation in irenic terms.[14]

To understand this remarkable shift, one needs to begin by examining American protestant perceptions of Europe. The mainstream Protestants were excited by the postwar prospects of transatlantic cooperation as the foundation for a truly global ecumenism and invested much in staff, aid, and organizational resources to strengthen their European partners. The conservative Protestants saw Europe as the keeper of the keys to the colonies and on a more theoretical level, as the prime example of what had gone wrong in history when people had abandoned traditional religion.

This narrative divides conveniently into four periods characterized as the discovery of Europe as a mission field in the late 1940s, the launch of mission programs in the 1950s, the creation of alternative networks in the 1960s, climaxing in the 1970s followed by diversification. In the 1980s the consolidation of the New Religious Right, the arrival of televangelists and increasing media competition significantly changed both religious communication and transatlantic perceptions.

The core time frame for this research is 1940-1975, the period of the "new evangelicalism" that fueled so much of the missionary fervor for Europe. It follows the shifting interaction between evangelicals, the more conservative believers – usually labeled fundamentalist – and the more liberal variation in the mainline churches. Other groups such as Pentecostals, who tried and

14 Thomas C. Berg, "'Proclaiming Together?' Convergence and Divergence in Mainline and Evangelical Evangelism 1945-1967," *Religion and American Culture* 5 (1995): 49-76. This brings in the relation between religion and empire as analyzed by Jay Riley Case, *An Unpredictable Gospel: American Evangelicals and World Christianity* (New York: Oxford University Press, 2012), 3-15; Brian Stanley, *The Bible and the Flag: Protestant Missions and British Imperialism in the Nineteenth and Twentieth Centuries* (Leicester: Apollos 1990); Andrew Porter, *Religion Versus Empire? British Protestant Missionaries and Overseas Expansion, 1700-1914* (Manchester: Manchester University Press, 2004); Norman Etherington, ed., *Missions and Empire* (Oxford: Oxford University Press, 2008), and Michael G. Thompson, *For God and Globe: Christian Internationalism in the United States Between the Great War and the Cold War* (Ithaca, NY: Cornell University Press, 2015).

eventually found inclusion in the evangelical mainstream, and members of new religious movements, such as Mormons and Jehovah's Witnesses, who often acted in similar ways to evangelicals, only enter this analysis periodically when they intersected with the strategies of the three major groups. The same incidental references are made to transatlantic theological exchanges, which fall outside the scope of this study, unless these had a direct impact on behavior.[15]

Most religion scholars agree that evangelicals faced two periods of differentiation in a global setting. Between 1943 and 1957 they untied their connections to the fundamentalists, and between 1957 and 1974 they consolidated their position and created a consensus, one that would unravel again after 1974. In the late 1970s, a new wave of immigration in Europe mostly out of former colonies changed the religious dynamics once again and by the 1980s satellite connections enabled a new religious phenomenon – American televangelists – to inaugurate a new phase of global transnational religion and this again changed the agenda of missionary agencies. This final episode is left to others as it deals with new sets of phenomena.

Missiologists provide a second reason for ending the story in the mid-1970s. Up until that decade most protestant missionary activities targeted either Christians from a different branch (mostly Catholics and Orthodox) or lapsed Protestants (through revivals). In both instances the message counted on some kind of recognition of doctrine or narrative and the hope to persuade others to abandon false ideas. In the background, a third type of mission framework loomed, which positioned the Christian faith as an ideological counterpart to secularism. In the 1990s, however, this sense of common ground evaporated and gave rise to a new post-ideological culture, which in combination with the dismantling of Soviet-dominated Europe, changed the religious dynamics in Europe dramatically. In these years neo-Pentecostal mission groups entered the European field in great numbers, which again shifted the goals and methods.[16] All these developments built on the more pluralistic situation that American missionaries had helped create in Europe.

Sociologist Grace Davie identified three fundamental factors that set the 1970s apart as the inauguration of a new era. These factors were the economic depression that ended the expectation of constant growth, the turn to more market and less state (embodied by Margaret Thatcher and Ronald Reagan), and new challenges to the secular state from as different courses as Pope John

15 Wilfried Decoo, "Mormons in Europe," in Terryl L. Givens and Philip L. Barlow, eds., *The Oxford Handbook of Mormonism* (New York: Oxford University Press, 2015), 543-557; Johnnie Glad, "Proclaiming the Message: A Comparison of Mormon Missionary Strategy with Other Mainstream Christian Missions," *International Journal for Mormon Studies* 2 (2009): 142-168; David Martin, *Pentecostalism: The World Their Parrish* (Oxford: Blackwell, 2002).

16 Brian Stanley, *The Global Diffusion of Evangelicalism: The Age of Billy Graham and John Stott* (Nottingham: Inter-Varsity Press, 2013), 28; Paas, "Evangelistic Mission in Europe."

Paul II and the Ayatollah Khomeini. The strength of the market and of religion became visible in 1989 when the Communist state-run block crumbled and religious impact on (international) politics increased.[17]

The focus on competing perspectives of American Protestants corrects a one-dimensional secularization thesis and helps to understand the multidirectional nature of religious expansion and decline in Europe and North America. While some scholars contrast secular Europe with religious America, others see a more sophisticated spectrum and a trend towards more convergence. This second interpretation corresponds with the growing awareness of both continents being part of a global development, which among other things includes the globalization of American evangelicalism. This discussion is bound to benefit from a study of the moments when actual contact took place between American Protestants and Europeans. The result of this process was a connection between transatlantic evangelical believers as well as a growing alienation between Europeans and Americans. The evangelicals' use of market and business thinking shaped their activities and the message with which they attempted to reach Europeans in the three decades after World War II.[18]

Scholars now recognize that American evangelicals followed in the tracks of the mainstream Protestants in seeking cooperation with the federal government, expressing an agenda for the nation's course, and of representing American Protestantism to Europeans. As American evangelicals became aware of the issue of national security and wanted to restore the nation's religious and moral foundation, they paradoxically embraced the state but kept their distance from the supranational institutions that they associated with Catholics and liberals. They appreciated pluralism more than their fundamentalist brothers, but this pluralism had its limits. Concern with national security and an appreciation for America's exceptional past, privileged the con-

17 This book will not focus on the prosperity gospel, Pentecostals-Charismatics, or televangelists. These groups have received sufficient treatment elsewhere. Similarly, it will only pay attention to activities of new religious movements from American soil, when they entered the discussion as competitors to Protestants in filling Europe's spiritual vacuum. Grace Davies, "Religion, Territory, and Choice: Contrasting Configurations, 1970-2015," in McLeod and Hempton, *Secularization*, 309-326.

18 David Martin, *On Secularization: Towards a Revised General Theory* (Farnham, UK: Ashgate, 2005); Callum G. Brown and Michael Snape, eds., *Secularisation in the Christian World: Essays in Honour of Hugh McLeod* (Farnham, UK: Ashgate, 2010); Katharina Kunter and Jens Holger Schjørring, eds., *Europäisches und globales Christentum: Herausforderungen und Transformationen im 20. Jahrhundert: Challenges and Transformations in the 20th Century* (Göttingen: Vandenhoeck & Ruprecht, 2011); Abigail Green and Vincent Viaene, eds., *Religious Internationals in the Modern World: Globalization and Faith Communities since 1750* (Basingstoke: Palgrave Macmillan, 2012).

servative forces among the evangelicals (as well as in the mainline churches), while liberal evangelicals were marginalized.[19]

Initially the fear of a non-evangelical monopoly was a dominant motive for evangelicals to identify Europe as a mission market. This anti-monopoly attitude explains their emphasis on Roman Catholic areas, their reluctance to cooperate with established churches, and their occasional alliances with ecumenists. This resulted in the creation of more space for Christian pluralism – the condition, but not necessarily the engine, for evangelical growth in Europe.

After the establishment of an evangelical presence in Europe, the speed of secularization in Europe in the 1970s turned the tables in the relationship of the evangelicals to the established churches. New waves of individualism, consumerism, and anti-institutionalism gave evangelicals an advantage. The link between religion and conservative politics in America, the continuing fragmentation within the evangelical family, and the competition for attention from assertive televangelists, however, prevented further penetration despite the broadening horizons. In the United States as well as in Europe, the evangelical movement had to reinvent and restyle itself in order not to lose its attraction. Focusing in this way enriched the effect of the waves of religious exchange, influenced the dynamic nature of cultural perceptions, intensified the growing impact of globalization which was visible in consumer styles and media use, and allowed for the persistence of transnational networks.

Terms, Methodology, and Sources

Most of this book deals with evangelicals who were and are a heterogeneous and ever-changing group. Evangelicalism is first of all a theological concept that carved a new identity for conservative Christians in the United States in the 1940s, an identity that dwelled on the dominant religious, social and political position of their predecessors in the nineteenth century and earlier in protestant history.[20]

One of the main features of evangelicalism is its Anglo-American core, even though it shared many parallels with European reformed and pietist tra-

19 Axel Schaefer, ed., *American Evangelicals and the 1960s* (Madison: University of Wisconsin Press, 2013); David R. Swartz, *Moral Minority: The Evangelical Left in an Age of Conservatism* (Philadelphia: University of Pennsylvania Press, 2012).

20 The literature on Evangelicalism is immense. I follow the widely accepted four core beliefs presented by David Bebbington: the centrality of Christ's atonement, the authority of the bible, the need of conversion, and the urge for activism, with the addition of Hutchinson and Wolffe that evangelicalism empowers those who miss individual autonomy, leading to a popular movement, that feels part of a higher cause. The features of the modern American variant are given by Darren Dochuk, "Evangelicalism," in Philip Goff, ed., *Blackwell Companion to Religion in America* (Chichester: Blackwell Publishing, 2010), 540-558.

ditions. In geographical terms it is not restricted to the US, but is also found in the English commonwealth nations. Recognition of the global spread of evangelicalism has not yet resulted in books that look beyond the Anglo-American world. This is even true in the impressive collection of essays collected by David Hempton and Hugh McLeod, that extent the scope to include Germany and adds some references to other European nations. Gradually, scholars add case studies from other nations, such as in a recent collection by John Corrigan and Frank Hinkelmann on the Netherlands, Belgium, Germany, Switzerland, Austria, and Poland, and a special issue on evangelicals in the Low Countries.[21]

The geographical focus of this book is Western Europe, even though it does not pretend to be comprehensive. Though there are many local and regional varieties, the point of departure is the American perspective that approached Western Europe as a coherent field, with regional variations. Fortunately a number of country studies tracing the presence of American missions in Europe have been published. Most of them were conducted by (former) practitioners who analyzed the performance of a single missionary agency with the goal of understanding the quality of their operations. Some studies seek to address more theoretical questions about intercultural exchange. As these are often the only public sources available, they are valuable. Granted that each country had a distinctive internal religious structure and a set of negotiated international relations, still, two main target areas stand out for American evangelicals. One focus was on the Catholic South including Belgium and France as confessional targets. Another concentrated on lapsed or nominal Protestants in need of a revival, mostly in Germany, Holland, and the Lutheran North.[22] In both cases, the missionaries tried to correct wrong

21 David Hempton and Hugh McLeod, eds., *Secularization and Religious Innovation in the North Atlantic World* (New York: Oxford University Press, 2017); John Corrigan and Frank Hinkelmann, eds., *Return to Sender: American Evangelical Missions in Twentieth Century Europe* (Zürich: LIT-Verlag, 2019); Special issue "Evangelicals in the Low Countries," *Trajecta* 26.2 (2017).

22 Dale G. Vought, *Protestants in Modern Spain* (South Pasadena, CA: William Carey Library, 1973); James C. Enns, "Saving Germany: North American Protestants and Christian Mission to West Germany, 1945-1974" (PhD. Dissertation, Cambridge University, 2012); Allen V. Koop, *American Evangelical Missionaries in France, 1945-1975* (Lanham, MD: University Press of America, 1986); William L. Wagner, *North American Protestant Missionaries in Western Europe: A Critical Appraisal* (Bonn: Verlag für Kultur und Wissenschaft, 1993); David E. Bjork, *Unfamiliar Paths: The Challenge of Recognizing the Work of Christ in Strange Clothing: A Case Study from France* (Pasadena: William Carey Library, 1997); Hilkka Mäläskä, *The Challenge for Evangelical Missions to Europe: A Scandinavian Case Study* (South Pasadena, CA: William Carey Library, [1970]); Marion F. Martin, "The Conservative Baptist Mission in Italy: Past Achievements, Future Opportunities" (D. Miss. Dissertation, Deerfield, IL: Trinity Evangelical Divinity School, 1994); Sipco Vellenga, *Een ondernemende beweging. De groei van de evangelische beweging in Nederland* (Amsterdam: VU University Press, 1991).

expressions of true Protestant religion and were able to refer to some common understanding of the Christian faith. The United Kingdom is a special category, being the closest religious partner to North America, a sender as well as receiver of evangelical messages, and an intermediary to the mainland. In the course of the increasing decline of organized religion in Europe during the fourth quarter of the twentieth century it is valid to ask whether and for how long these two approaches – confessional change and revival of nominal Christians – continued as separate tracks before an ideological confrontation with neo-paganism emerged, only to be followed later by inclusive post-Christian efforts.[23]

Organizationally, there are three types of agencies to investigate. Seen from an American perspective these were denominational agencies, voluntary agencies, and network organizations. Denominational missions were the first and oldest agencies, including the Baptists, Methodists, and Presbyterians, with the strongest force being the Baptists.[24] The second category held the growing family of interdenominational or non-denominational associations. Among the hundreds of associations, Youth for Christ, The Evangelical Alliance Mission and the Greater Europe Mission occupied the strongest positions in the emerging network in Europe.[25] The mortar between these individual bricks was provided by the third category, the umbrella organizations such as the National Council of Churches, the National Association of Evangelicals, and the American Council of Christian Churches, and their respective missionary satellites, under which were included the three branches in American Protestantism: mainline, evangelical, and fundamentalist. Billy Graham played a leading role as figurehead of American evangelical religion, both as an evangelist and as an international organizer. His campaigns linked American and European believers and drew unprecedented media attention, but they could not have succeeded without the rank-and-file American missionaries and European believers, who were in turn shaped by a multiplicity of religious agencies.[26]

The main actors in this plot are students, ministers, missionaries, journalists, and some government officials, in at least three subcultures on both sides of the Atlantic – a good indication of the variety of sources needed to explore the key components. These tend to be scattered and include interviews,

23 Paas, "Making of a Mission Field," 62-63.

24 Scott W. Sunquist and Caroline N. Becker, eds., *A History of Presbyterian Missions 1944-2007* (Louisville, KY: Geneva Press, 2008).

25 Jon P. DePriest, *Send the Light: TEAM and the Evangelical Mission* (Bloomington, IN: AuthorHouse, 2007); Hans Finzel, ed., *Partners Together: 50 Years of Global Impact - The CBFMS Story* (Wheaton, IL: Conservative Baptist Foreign Mission Society, 1993).

26 Vernon Mortenson, *God Made it Grow: Historical Sketches of TEAM's Church Planting Work* (Pasadena, CA: William Carey Library, 1994); W.H. Fuller, *People of the Mandate: The Story of the World Evangelical Fellowship* (Grand Rapids, MI: Baker Book House, 1996).

reports, newsletters, and publications on missionaries in Europe. This documentation reveals an image of Europa in prophetic brochures, missionary fairs, concerts, festivals, publications, private correspondence, and reflective interviews. As the evangelicals competed with people from both the mainstream and the fundamentalists, the two opposing sides shed light – sometimes contrasting and sometimes similar – on evangelicals. A great variety of these sources can be accessed at the archives at the Billy Graham Center at Wheaton College, in Wheaton, Illinois. The papers of Carl McIntire at Princeton Seminary Library represent the separatist fundamentalist side, and records of the National Council of Churches in the United States in Philadelphia, and individual denominations document the plans and responses of both flanks.

European sources on American religious activities in Europe are even more fragmented. Depositories of the World Council of Churches in Geneva, the Evangelical Alliance in London, the Deutsche Evangelische Allianz in Bad Blankenburg, Evadoc – the Protestants-Evangelisch Archief- en Documentatiecentrum in Leuven, Belgium, and of the Historical Documentation Center for Dutch Protestantism in Amsterdam, hold records revealing national circumstances and responses. Although these depositories offers only a small selection of sources on American missions in Western Europe, these are sufficient to help balance the story and prevent it from tilting too much towards the American side.

It takes a research group rather than a single individual to create a comprehensive overview of the penetration in specific European countries. Fortunately, there is a growing British and continental European historiography on American religion abroad that is based on the growing collection of archives of European evangelical organizations. In combination, they offer building blocks for the construction of a more complete European story.[27]

Research on American Protestants in Europe reveals that their activities have both a national and a transnational character. The research opens a window on the shifts in power relations, communication channels, competition, and cooperation. Indeed, the missionary activities did export American issues to Europe, as well as new vocabularies, instruments, agendas, and institutes. In the thirty years under scrutiny, transatlantic relations became more intense, allowing pluralism to increase while old traditions were shaken. As old enemies disappeared and new ones emerged, alliances shifted, and new identities were articulated.

27 John Corrigan and Frank Hinkelmann, eds., *Return to Sender: American Evangelical Missions in Twentieth Century Europe* (Zürich: LIT-Verlag, 2019); special issue "Evangelicals in the Low Countries," *Trajecta* 26 (2017): 169-360.

DISCOVER!

EMERGING RELIGIOUS INTEREST IN EUROPE, 1780-1940

European-American Religious Relations before and after the American Revolution

When the Puritans set sail from England, some after a period of refuge in the Dutch Republic, they turned their backs on Europe and embarked on an "errand in the wilderness" in the New World. They rejected Europe's diluted religion, but maintained the ideal of a privileged church that protected true religion in close cooperation with the state. They hoped Europe would learn from them. Three hundred years later the American religious landscape consisted of colors in all shades, and the moment for America to turn once again towards Europe had come.

During the European settlement of North America in the seventeenth and eighteenth centuries the formal relationships of Protestant churches in Europe with their counterparts in America slowly gave away to informal ones.[1] Trade companies that had the authority to regulate religious affairs, such as the Dutch West India Company, had invited these churches to the New World, and when the companies' power waned, association between church and

1 Edwin S. Gaustad, *Proclaim Liberty Throughout All the Land: A History of Church and State in America* (New York: Oxford University Press, 2003); Mark A. Noll, *The Old Religion in a New World: The History of North American Christianity* (Grand Rapids, MI: Eerdmans, 2002); Patricia Bonomi, *Under the Cope of Heaven: Religion, Society, and Politics in Colonial America* (New York: Oxford University Press, 1986).

motherland was often voluntary.[2] In states that required membership in an established church as a condition for public office, congregational structures made the relationship with European ecclesiastical authorities weak.

European ecclesiastical traditions framed the ecclesiastical rules in the New World, but most authority resided in local or regional hands. Central authority was difficult to enforce. Local autonomy was the guiding principle of congregational and Presbyterian Church government, but many other churches acted as associations and worked bottom-up, taking care of their own buildings, training, and congregational life without outside assistance.[3] Poor quality of imported clergy and a growing need for more clerics fanned a desire among church leaders to take education into their own hands and establish seminaries in the New World. Church life was often weak. In the seventeenth and early eighteenth centuries the colonies complained more about neglect by the motherland than they did about an overbearing interference. Many European religious groups had escaped repressive regimes and cut official ties with European ecclesiastical authorities. Uniform application of church rules proved hard when dissidents could easily survive in neighboring states.

Some colonial governments in North America took the initiative to improve the number and level of the clergy, but the overall results were disappointing and associations took it upon themselves to fill the need for leaders. The Church of England had a hard time keeping a strong position among the colonists. Dissenters outnumbered regular Anglicans everywhere. Many talented Calvinists flocked to New England. The other sects explicitly prevented the residence of an English bishop in the American colonies in the late eighteenth century.[4] This attitude grew even stronger after the American Revolution. The early success by the Society for the Propagation of the Gospel in Foreign Parts in expanding the size and influence of the Anglican Church through legal protection and church plantings was annulled by the anti-British mood of the Revolution. Only its organizational model of voluntary organi-

2 Dirk Mouw, "Dutch Clergy in Colonial North America," in Leon van den Broeke, Hans Krabbendam, and Dirk Mouw, eds., *Transatlantic Pieties: Dutch Clergy in Colonial America* (Grand Rapids, MI: Eerdmans, 2012), 1-34. Even when the Massachusetts Bay charter was revoked in 1684, the New England Congregational churches remained independent from England, Harry S. Stout, *The New England Soul: Preaching and Religious Culture in Colonial New England* (New York: Oxford University Press, 1986), 111-112; Jon Butler, *New World Faiths: Religion in Colonial America* (New York: Oxford University Press, 2008), 63-66, 113-114.

3 Sydney Ahlstrom, *A Religious History of the American People* (New Haven, CT: Yale University Press, 1970), 189, 193; Bonomi, *Under the Cope of Heaven*, 82-85.

4 Gaustad, *Proclaim Liberty*, 16-19; Bonomi, *Under the Cope of Heaven*, 30-33. The Anglicans depended on British print culture, but had to rely on lay people. Jeremy Gregory, "Transatlantic Anglican Networks, c.1680-c.1770: Transplanting, Translating and Transforming the Church of England," in Jeremy Gregory and Hugh McLeod, eds., *International Religious Networks* (Woodbridge: The Boydell Press/Ecclesiastical History Society, 2012), 127-142.

zation continued.[5] In sum, colonists maintained some relationship with European churches, but by the eighteenth century, apart from the Anglicans, most churches began to create their own regulatory bodies in the colonies, borrowing continental structures, but increasingly making their own decisions, and expanding their scope of activity.[6]

As the revolutionary spirit spread in conjunction with a growing pluralism and revivals, resistance to old authoritative structures mounted. The cultural climate in the young republic turned away from European sources for religion. Historian Mark A. Noll explained:

> With tradition, hierarchy, and deference to historical precedent discredited by the ideology of the Revolution, religious thinkers in the national period made do with what was left in their efforts to preserve Christian doctrine and inspire Christian practice. The materials at hand were commonsense moral reasoning, narratives of republican liberation, and the bible. With all thought of a Christian establishment washed away by the republican tide, believers knew it depended upon themselves and the direct ministrations of the Holy Spirit to do what had to be done. An extraordinary mobilization of the churches was the result.[7]

After the American Revolution, liberalism in its various forms divided churches in the old world from those in the new world. American churches gradually adapted to the legal separation of church and state, joined the forces of progress, democracy and pragmatism, and resisted the social restrictions that European church authorities legitimized.

Nevertheless, informal transatlantic contacts continued to flow. Among the strongest were the pietist circles, believers who prized a personal deepening of faith. This type of believer traveled frequently and actively looked for other believers across denominational and national boundaries. Many of them had been chased out of their own countries and looked for companions. Since the 1780s, a European network of pietist believers, with strongholds in

5 A. G. Roeber, "The Waters of Rebirth: The Eighteenth Century and Transoceanic Protestant Christianity," *Church History* 79.1 (2010): 40-76. Also voluntary organizations promoting international Protestant ties favored the British cause during the War of Independence and revealed the strength of nationalist feelings and British superiority. It lacked the communication channels. See Katherine Carté Engel, "The SPCK and the American Revolution: The Limits of International Protestantism," *Church History* 81.1 (March 2012): 77-103. Both conclude there was no stable transnational Protestant community in the late eighteenth century, but that Western Christians found ways to overcome their divisions and get out into the world, by the victory of interior transformation over sacramental grace (59-60). Roeber showed that since the mid eighteenth century Protestants sought the means for a unified front against Catholics beyond their denominations.

6 Noll, *Old Religion*, 50; Jon Butler, *New World Faiths: Religion in Colonial America* (New York: Oxford University Press, 2008), 113-116.

7 Mark Noll, *America's God: From Jonathan Edwards to Abraham Lincoln* (New York: Oxford University Press, 2002), 444.

England and Germany, not only corresponded with each other, but also actively cooperated to reach other Europeans with the evangelical message, managed to initiate social work, and to prosper before nationalism disrupted these contacts and forced many of them to seek refuge in America.[8] This pietist network prepared the spirit for action.

This stream towards America met there with planned activities in the revival tradition. Both trends created the contrast of an active (Anglo)America compared to a passive Europe. The desire and efforts to make the religious revival a repetitive experience catapulted Anglo-Americans into the lead in transatlantic protestant cooperation. This first wave of Anglo-American revivals in the 1730s-40s had created a tension with the Calvinist ideas that were considered too passive and negative to help believers grow. Revivals promised spiritual growth even to a point of perfection. This perception of contrast was an important element of the future engagement with Europe. This mode of representation cast the two continents in opposing terms: passive versus active, receiving versus sending, waiting versus advancing. Many revivalist activists definitely separated from the main church bodies, followed thirty years later by a similar Calvinist exodus. The rapid expansion of revivalism was facilitated by the spread of its idea of conversion across boundaries of space, race, age, gender, and denomination. The appeal of a personal identification of the believer with the person of Jesus Christ expressed in sermon and song transcended the older church boundaries. While the forces against this activism, both ecclesiastical and civic, were stronger in continental Europe than in the Anglo-American world, the genie had left the bottle and would gain power in the twentieth century.[9]

This new constellation allowed some religious tables to be turned. Several oppressed or marginalized minorities in European countries, such as Quakers, Baptists and Methodists, turned into regional majorities in America. For some liberty-lovers, America's freedom proved excessive, and they turned to counter measures. The shape and fate of the immigrant church depended on the timing of the move. Religious immigrants faced a broad spectrum of options: to abandon the church altogether, to join an American church, to continue the old church, to establish a parallel denomination, or to begin a new religious community. The seemingly wide-open American space allowed

8 P.N. Holtrop, *Tussen Piëtisme en Réveil. Het 'Deutsche Christentumsgesellschaft' in Nederland, 1784-1833* (Amsterdam: Rodopi, 1975), 18; R.H. Martin, "The Pan-Evangelical Impulse in Britain 1795-1830: With Special Reference to Four London Societies" (Ph. Dissertation, Oxford, UK, 1974); Jonathan Strom, Hartmut Lehmann, and James Van Horn Melton, eds., *Pietism in Germany and North-America, 1680-1820* (Farnham, UK: Ashgate, 2009); Nicholas M. Railton, *No North Sea: The Anglo-German Evangelical Network in the Middle of the Nineteenth Century* (Leiden: Brill, 2000), 16-17, 41, 127, 166, 192-193, 249-254.

9 Mark Hutchinson and John Wolffe, *A Short History of Global Evangelicalism* (Cambridge: Cambridge University Press, 2012), 46-52, 86-100.

room to grow, and the great distances created buffers between competing groups. Significantly, race and ethnicity stimulated diversity and pluralism, and the absence of a strong confessional conservatism allowed innovative experiments. Accepted traditions proved vulnerable and faced decline when they did not participate in the revivals – a hallmark of American Protestantism. In the classic words of historian Sidney Ahlstrom: "Only through that convulsive outburst of piety did 'American Evangelical Protestantism' become aware of itself as a national reality and alive to its culture-shaping power."[10] Nevertheless, not all Protestants embraced revivalism. The German Reformed at Mercersburg and other groups rejected revivalism, and its individualistic expression.[11]

This shift in power between established and dissenting or minority denominations had consequences for society. Protected churches, such as the Anglican (Episcopal) Church, bred stability, supported good citizenship, and discouraged individualism. The church mirrored the social hierarchy of the world. Since wealth was based on land, property ownership meant Anglicans stayed where they had settled. Along with some exceptional itinerant Anglicans, radical believers (Quakers and Baptists) promoted a more egalitarian society, and were more mobile than those staying close to the European established churches.

A general restlessness, caused by moral pressures and the high expectation of a conversion experience, along with the availability of abundant space, facilitated the formation of dissenting groups. This combination of opportunity and distinct religious desires encouraged mobility. The pressure to accept salvation and actively pursue a new life spurred many Methodists to move away from areas with slavery. Strong support for domestic missions in the United States inside the Methodist organizations, which employed three thousand staff, provided the impulse necessary to arrive first in new areas in order to secure the spread of Biblical holiness. The Methodist organization was impressive. It used the untapped resource of women and created an informal religious empire that fanned a growing optimism to reform society and redeem the world. For this purpose they sought global partners.[12]

Methodist missionaries active in Europe proclaimed the established churches dead in the period of the American Civil War. Historian David Hempton concludes: "In this way American Methodism's European missions, though not particularly successful, confirmed Methodists' belief in the religious and cultural superiority of American Protestantism over the dead and formal reli-

10 Ahlstrom, *Religious History*, 6.

11 James D. Bratt, ed., *Antirevivalism in Antebellum America: A Collection of Religious Voices* (New Brunswick, NJ: Rutgers University Press, 2006).

12 David Hempton, "International Religious Networks: Methodism and Popular Protestantism, c.1750-1850," in Jeremy Gregory and Hugh McLeod, eds., *International Religious Networks* (Woodbridge: The Boydell Press/Ecclesiastical History Society, 2012), 143-164.

gions of old Europe."[13] While Methodism attracted the lower economic classes in the United States and the United Kingdom, it failed to reach the working class in continental Europe.

Competition did not necessarily harm the religious establishment. The drive of (denominational) religious activism overlapped with the Protestant establishment's deeply felt responsibility for raising the moral foundation, advancing educational standards, and improving social conditions in the nation and outside.[14] The mass immigration wave in the nineteenth century intensified the religious relations with Europe and prepared the phase of American religious reciprocity.

Immigrant Churches and Transatlantic Connections in the Nineteenth Century

A major target of this benevolent agenda was the immigrant masses, especially those who were considered a threat to the Protestant establishment. Dedicated Protestant emigrants from Europe to America often wanted either to preserve their heritage or to cleanse it of corruption. The first category depended on Europe for clergy and literature; the second group had no interest in maintaining ties with the corrupted churches in the countries they had left and whose authorities had jailed their itinerant preachers.[15]

Conservative immigrant churches kept their distance from the other American churches, as they wished to prevent quick assimilation. But by doing so they condemned themselves to a sectarian position. In America a choice to maintain the (European) tradition led to tension with public opinion, that celebrated democratic rule, accepted pluralism, and advocated individual choice. The result of maintaining the European traditions was the opposite for churches in Europe. Independence came at the cost of weakened impact on society, education, politics, and culture.[16] The leadership in immigrant denominations outside the established churches such as German

13 S. Scott Rohrer, *Wandering Souls: Protestant Migrations in America, 1630-1865* (Chapel Hill, NC: The University of North Carolina Press, 2010); David Hempton, *Methodism: Empire of the Spirit* (New Haven, CT: Yale University Press, 2005), 152-153, 159-161, 166-167; Hempton, "International Religious Networks," 157: Methodism's high expectation of success in foreign missions was triggered by the astonishing domestic growth.

14 William R. Hutchison, ed., *Between the Times: The Travail of the Protestant Establishment, 1900-1960* (Cambridge: Cambridge University Press, 1989), 303-305; David Sehat, *The Myth of American Religious Freedom* (New York: Oxford University Press, 2011), 4.

15 Dag Thorkildsen, "Revivalism, Emigration and Religious Networks in Nineteenth-Century Norway," in Jeremy Gregory and Hugh McLeod, eds., *International Religious Networks* (Woodbridge: The Boydell Press/Ecclesiastical History Society, 2012), 165-182.

16 Noll, *Old Religion in a New World*, 24-25.

Mennonites and Dutch Christian Reformed believers, among other, decided to protect themselves from liberal progressivism and millennial, Biblicist, evangelicalism. Their departure from Europe was the ultimate rejection of their native culture, which they had hoped to reform. Now they sustained this reform impulse in a different location. Their adherence to formal confessions and to ethnic cohesion was the main buffer to quick assimilation.[17]

These church leaders weighed the means to preserve their identity. In their new setting they encountered countless examples of new ideals, such as the promotion of education, acceptance of diversity, encouragement of social activism, all of which could either strengthen or weaken their groups. Mennonite groups split when patriotism threatened their pacifist identity. Similarly Missouri Synod Lutherans and Dutch Calvinists resisted entanglement with the state and rejected the pressure to seek unity with other immigrant churches. Isolation and lack of power placed them at the margins of the host society. Initially this caused no problem, but the tensions accumulated when their outsider status weakened their chance at success in keeping the next generations attached to the subculture in competition with other churches. To hold onto the next generation, they adopted American organizational means, such as fund raising, specialist societies, rhetorical styles, and social programs. The younger generation then expanded these means and adopted the agenda of other American churches as well.[18] From this position, either in isolation or on a slow path to accommodation, these churches had a minimal influence on the church in the fatherland, except that representatives of the American churches attended synods and assemblies, in order to confirm their orthodoxy, promote emigration, or to fend off competition.

An example from Swedish immigrant churches presents an outline of the process of alienation from European roots. Mass migration in the three decades after the Civil War brought six hundred thousand Swedes to the United States. The orthodox atmosphere in the immigrant Lutheran churches in the 1880s surprised Swedish visitors in America. Whereas the state church in Sweden offered space to various wings, the more homogeneous immigrants narrowed the boundaries of acceptance and were stricter in doctrine and behavior. The visitors regretted or even openly condemned this sectarian division, the isolation, and the lack of education of the clergy in the immigrant churches, and advised prospective emigrants not to join them. Earlier lack of support for these churches made the immigrant churches critical, even hostile to the authorities in Sweden. Also members of the main Lutheran church were

17 James D. Bratt, "Protestant Immigrants and the Protestant Mainstream," in Jonathan Sarna, ed., *Minority Faiths and the American Protestant Mainstream* (Urbana: University of Illinois Press, 1998), 111-113.

18 For instance in joining or mimicking organizations for schools, youth, women, missions, health care, see Hans Krabbendam, *Freedom on the Horizon: Dutch Immigration to America, 1840-1940* (Grand Rapids: Eerdmans, 2009), 111-125, 311-315.

critical of the church in Sweden, which remained subservient to the state.[19] By 1930, the English language had conquered a solid place in Augustana Lutheran congregations, but the Swedish tongue was still heard and spoken. In 1930, only 150 out of 1,250 congregations were exclusively English, but that year marked the turn to assimilation, when the subscription rate to the English-language church periodicals surpassed the Swedish ones. Adaptation to American religious practices and languages was even faster in free churches. Historian Arnold Barton concludes: "...the free church people, whether converted before or after emigration, made a cleaner break with the old country, not only geographically but ideologically. Indeed, emigration and conversion, based on free, individual choice, represented parallel processes of alienation from the past."[20]

Overall, formal transatlantic church relations weakened in the nineteenth century when American ecclesiastical bodies severed all official hierarchical ties with their European mother churches. Friendly visits to synods or return trips to their native lands, exchanges of religious newspapers and theological work helped to maintain transnational relations, but did not reestablish authority. It was often in the interest of the immigrant church to keep these lines of communication open to secure the flow of clergy and new members. But the celebrated freedom from the state that had inspired settlement in the United States, encouraged the independence of their own institutions from their homelands and sometimes triggered an anti-clerical attitude.[21] Strong pietist expectations and strict confessional boundaries tied many Protestant immigrant communities together to escape the temptations that could arise from too much freedom (lack of discipline, worldliness, individualism, materialism). These conservative immigrant churches maintained the closest links with the home country, but mainly to support the free church model which strengthened congregational autonomy in the old country. Toleration for authoritative interventions from the old country in the immigrant churches diminished as the congregations gained a sense of achievement and strength and had to respond autonomously to the challenges of the new country.[22]

19 H. Arnold Barton, *A Folk Divided: Homeland Swedes and Swedish Americans, 1840-1940* (Carbondale, IL: Southern Illinois University Press, 1994), 52-55, 106.

20 Barton, *Folk*, 256, 333.

21 Orm Overland, "Religion and Church in Early Immigrant Letters," in Todd Nichol, ed., *Crossings: Norwegian-American Lutheranism as Transatlantic Tradition* (Northfield, MN: Norwegian Historical Association, 2003), 42-43, 46.

22 Jon Gjerde, "The Perils of 'Freedom' in the American Immigrant Church," and Vidar L. Haanes, "Pastors for the Congregations," in Todd Nichol, ed., *Crossings: Norwegian-American Lutheranism as Transatlantic Tradition* (Northfield, MN: Norwegian Historical Association, 2003), 3-29 and 93-118, esp. 105.

Social Action and Cooperation

As the perceived evils of slavery, alcohol abuse, and prostitution cross national borders, moral crusaders had to do the same to attempt to stop their spread. With intensifying communication, civic groups in different parts of the world learned from each other, and created international formal and informal networks to engage in social reform. The battle against alcohol abuse and human trafficking were closely linked to religious values that considered them as the most visible forms of public immorality. The scope of these activities was the "World," a term showing nothing if not ambition and high expectations, and the churches often acted in alliance with humanitarian causes to elevate medical or educational standards and state-supported interventions against these problems.

Immigrant churches with social aspirations could not keep out the forces of change. They felt the pull of the mainline liberal reform tradition. In America religious growth could only happen thanks to the early and active presence of a variety of Christian groups with high ideals and a myriad of ideas seeking a global outlet. Religious historian Marc A. Noll identified two motives in exporting American religious ideas and practices outside the continent: one is sacrificial integrity and the other is self-seeking compromise.

This mix of motives moved Robert Baird, the first missionary to (Catholic) Europe, in 1834. This Presbyterian minister combined a trip to support French Protestants with a promotional campaign for a temperance organization. His tour was a sign of evangelical America's sense of superiority. European countries, such as Sweden and of course the United Kingdom, which were the most sympathetic towards revivalism, also embraced this moral crusade. It was European demand rather than American initiative that led to the adoption of American styles of communication, methods of persuasion, and means of organization for moral causes in Europe.[23] National organizations overlapped transnational ones. Domestic American reform organizations exchanged ideas, strategies, funding, and cooperation with similar groups especially with the British. The overlap between these mission organizations broadened the horizon and ambitions of the nationally oriented groups. They found partners abroad, not only in Europe but also in the colonies, as they realized that the interconnectedness of the nation and the world asked for a

23 Sidsel Eriksen, "Drunken Danes and Sober Swedes? Religious Revivalism and the Temperance Movements as Keys to Danish and Swedish Folk Cultures," in B. Strath, ed., *Language and the Construction of Class Identities: The Struggle for Discursive Power in Social Organization, Scandinavia and Germany after 1800* (Gothenburg: Gothenburg University, 1990), 55-94; Harry G. Levine, "Temperance Cultures: Concern about Alcohol Problems in Nordic and English-Speaking Cultures," in Malcolm Lader, Griffith Edwards, and D. Colin Drummond, eds., *The Nature of Alcohol and Drug Related Problems* (Oxford: Oxford University Press, 1992), 15-36.

global approach and interdenominational cooperation.[24] This combination of multiple goals was visible in interdenominational Christian Endeavor youth societies as a meeting point for those wishing to recruit missionary candidates and instill proper behavior in the next generation and keep them within the church. Protestants in other countries adopted these American success formulas. Magazines and books widely transmitted the models and the message. Some denominations founded similar youth groups, yet the interdenominational groups had the most effect abroad.

Since the realization of this social agenda needed joint action and visible results, American Protestants actively pressed for unity among denominations worldwide. The first Anglo-American initiative to explore cooperation took place in the summer of 1846, in London, the capital of the world's leading power. John Angell James, an independent minister in Birmingham, called for an Evangelical Alliance and involved American Presbyterian colleagues. Seventy-four Americans crossed the ocean to participate in this conference and made up about nine percent of the total body. Their hope was that this outside venue would help them conquer their internal tensions, especially over the issue of slavery. This purpose failed, as Methodist and Baptist denominations in the United States split over slavery nonetheless. The Americans rejected the European pressure to exclude slave owners from their ranks, which forced them to have to withdraw from the organization and set up a national one. The dream of unity was terminated, but would return after the Civil War. The Evangelical Alliance meeting in New York in 1873 lead to a series of events that mounted to the ecumenical highlight in Edinburgh in 1910. The many visits by American ministers to Europe kept this ideal going through personal contacts.[25]

The transport and communication revolution of the 1830s and 1840s enabled Americans to experience the interdependence of the world. Interest in foreign events grew steadily in the second half of the nineteenth century spurred by trade, migration, and tourism. Missionaries and moral reformers joined transnational networks and modernized international operations, organizationally and financially.[26] It was the age of the founding of numerous international organizations: formal ones to regulate the mail, rail, and tele-

24 Ian Tyrrell, *Reforming the World: The Creation of America's Moral Empire* (Princeton: Princeton University Press, 2010), 75-76.

25 Ian Randall, "American Influence on Evangelicals in Europe: A Comparison of the Founding of the Evangelical Alliance and of the World Evangelical Fellowship," in Hans Krabbendam and Derek Rubin, eds., *Religion in America: European and American Perspectives* (Amsterdam: VU University Press, 2004), 263-274; John Wolffe, "Transatlantic Visitors and Evangelical Networks, 1829-1861," in Jeremy Gregory and Hugh McLeod, eds., *International Religious Networks* (Woodbridge: The Boydell Press/Ecclesiastical History Society, 2012), 183-193.

26 Tyrrell, *Reforming*, 7 and chapter 1.

graph, and private/civic ones to consult about science, labor, or combinations of the two to solve common problems of public health and city planning.

The same connections allowed the first American religious export, Mormonism, to reach Europe in 1837 where it was especially successful in the United Kingdom and Scandinavia. As this religious movement drained converts "Homeward to Zion," which was in North America, its presence in Europe remained small. Only after World War II did the church broaden Zion to include places where Mormons lived.[27] It was a particular case of a widespread American missionary sentiment.

After the Civil War a new generation would rejuvenate the mission movement. They defined an ambitious end: to convert the world in one generation.[28] Their aim would return again as a battle cry in the next century, echoing the changing date of the apocalypse, and appealing to young, highly motivated, qualified workers at the growing centers of higher education, thus emphasizing the practical value of education. Hence this generation greatly stimulated the missionary impulse of the 1890s and the involvement of students (such as the Young Men's Christian Association and the Student Volunteer Movement), leading to a structural professionalization that invested in consolidation, education, and specific gender roles.[29] By the 1880s, American and European missionaries had created a transnational network sharing ideas, institutions, and means by which they worked towards a Christian empire.[30] A leading historian of transnationalism, Ian Tyrrell, identifies this decade as pivotal:

27 Philip Jenkins, *Mystics and Messiahs: Cults and New Religions in American History* (New York: Oxford University Press, 2000), 50-69; Johnnie Glad, "Proclaiming the Message: A Comparison of Mormon Missionary Strategy with other Christian Missions," *International Journal of Mormon Studies* 2 (Spring 2009): 142-168. Despite the many differences between the Christian tradition and Mormonism, the missionary movement shares the message that something is wrong with Christianity in Europe. Missions are key to the membership, inculcates the young with the content of the faith and effectively disciplines them by completely absorbing their time and energy. By standardizing the procedures and expecting the young adults to participate for one or two years they crank out the numbers. The targets were set in number of baptisms, which proved a level of success, but obscured the exiting of many converts despite these structures. The practice of sending short-term young single missionaries abroad began after World War II. The dress code, celebrations, and the book of Mormon set Mormons apart as Americans and hindered smooth indigenization. Jan Scripps, *Sojourner in the Promised Land: Forty Years among the Mormons* (Urbana: University of Illinois Press, 2000), 270; William Mulder, *Homeward To Zion: The Mormon Migration from Scandinavia* (Minneapolis: University of Minnesota Press, 2000); Tyrrell, *Reforming*, 228-233; G. R. Chard, "A History of the French Mission of the Church of Jesus Christ of Latter-day Saints, 1850-1960" (MA thesis, Logan, Utah: Utah State University, Merrill-Cazier Library, 1965) and Keith C. Warner, "History of the Netherlands Mission 1861-1966" (thesis, 1967).

28 Tyrrell, *Reforming*, 61.

29 David P. Setran, *The College 'Y': Student Religion in the Era of Secularization* (New York: Palgrave, 2007).

30 Tyrrell, *Reforming*, 49-73.

> The revival of missions had global aspirations and included a highly important European role. While Asians were key targets, continental Europe was also a candidate for evangelism, and alliances with European evangelicals were as vital as those with people in Europe's colonies because an evangelized Europe would renew the Christian values of European empires and rebound to the benefit of all colonies.[31]

The American efforts, however, were more targeted to recruit missionaries than to evangelize the Europeans themselves. As a result of growth in prosperity and missionary zeal, Americans began catching up in the missionary enterprise with Europe, first in financial contributions, then in numbers. Americans rose to become equal partners thanks to the introduction of progressive efficiency methods directed by laymen.[32]

The movement abroad increased the direct confrontation between Christianity and other world religions to the point that a few Hindi missionaries entered the United States in the 1880s. These encounters encouraged some liberal Christians to seek common ground with other religions. But more commonly, young missionary workers began to identify with the causes, problems, and disasters of their brethren and sisters abroad. They invested heavily in philanthropy and raised their voices against unjust structures that caused racial discrimination, imperialistic exploitation, or random violence. But despite this criticism, optimism abounded. Missionaries and their constituencies at home believed that personal contacts would advance their global goal of a harmonious world and that cooperation with governments advanced a global moral empire.[33]

American Church Plants in Europe

The impulse for Protestant missions to work in Europe was generated in part by a sense of strength, self-confidence, sometimes even superiority of the churches in the new republic. An example can be found in the March 1829 *Magazine of the Protestant Dutch Church* that announced that the Presbyterian Church of the United States had opened correspondence with the Reformed Church in France and that the Synod of the Dutch Church had followed their example, in the Netherlands. The magazine reported similar British efforts to

31 Tyrrell, *Reforming*, 60.

32 See for instance the election of John Mott as chairman of the Missionary conference in Edinburgh in 1910 and American leadership in the formation of the International Missionary Council in 1921.

33 Tyrrell, *Reforming*, 187. The impact of Bishop Charles Brent on Roosevelt and Taft and of Mott on Wilson offer evidence of the close personal impact of champions of missions on U.S. presidents. This paved the way towards state interference on behalf of missions, and missionaries engaging in diplomatic services (196).

strengthen Reformed churches on the Continent.[34] American Protestants in the 1830s considered themselves the most advanced Christians in Western civilization and perfectively equipped for the world's conversion to that faith. They believed that civil arrangements in a liberal state found a religious parallel with the "Protestant form of organization."[35] Civil liberty led to pluralism, which they welcomed.

Mark Noll's book *The New Shape of World Christianity* accounts for the successful transfer of American Protestant religion as a result of internal features:

> American voluntaristic, conversionistic religion has certainly exerted an influence elsewhere. The more important reality, however, is not that world Christianity is being driven by American activity. It is, rather, that forms of conversionistic and voluntaristic Christianity have flourished where something like nineteenth-century American social conditions have come to prevail – where, that is, social fluidity, personal choice, the need for innovation and a search for anchorage in the face of vanishing traditions have prevailed.[36]

Noll, rejecting the term hegemony because it suggests explicit use of power to dominate, proposes the friendlier metaphor of the template. He argues that when a culture is moving towards a more politically and economically liberal situation, its citizens feel drawn to adopt religious arrangements from the United States, because these have proven to function best in a liberal democracy.

A clear sign of America's growing prestige in Europe was the establishment of American churches on the continent, which opened new perspectives for transnational flow. The first American church was an Episcopal church in Paris. The congregation had met in private places since the 1830s, formalized its existence in September 1858, and consecrated the "Church of the Holy Trinity," a 500-seat edifice strategically located in the Rue Bayard, close to the Champs Elysee, in 1864. This congregation functioned as a combined ecumenical meeting place for clergy of the Greek and Russian Orthodox churches, and for the Anglican and Roman Catholic churches, and had the mission "to represent that primitive faith and order and simplicity of worship which characterize our Branch of the True Vine."[37] A decade later, the number of American preaching stations in Europe had grown to six. They maintained close cooper-

34 *Magazine of the Protestant Dutch Church*, 3 (March 1829): 374-375.

35 Andrew Walls, *The Missionary Movement in Christian History* (Maryknoll, NY: Orbis Books, 1996), 223-224.

36 Mark A. Noll, *The New Shape of World Christianity: How American Experience Reflects Global Faith* (Downers Grove, IL: IVP Academic, 2009), 53-59, 116.

37 *The Church Journal* (New York), October 7 and November 4, 1863. Quote from May 18, 1864. http://anglicanhistory.org/Europe/paris_articles1863.html. Visited September 4, 2019.

ation with the 172 British chaplaincies, five of which were connected to embassies, 18 had consulates, and 74 were for British citizens everywhere, organized either by the Society for the Propagation of the Gospel, or by the Colonial and Continental Church Society supervised by the bishops of London and Gibraltar. After the British government cut funding for churches at diplomatic posts, American Episcopalians joined in to avoid duplication and to show unity. Visiting Americans very much liked the chance to worship in Anglican services, but were somewhat put off by the "no less than nine separate prayers for the sovereign, the royal family and the Government of the country."[38] The concession to offer one prayer for the United States's president was not enough to inspire them to merge all operations, but cooperation with the British branch of the church nonetheless increased with the growing presence of Americans in Europe. Even so, this American church in Paris faced a dual goal of connecting with other churches and strengthening its own profile. The merger in 1849 of three missionary organizations into the American and Foreign Christian Union formulated its purpose diffusing and promoting "the principles of Religious Liberty, and a pure and Evangelical Christianity, both at home and abroad, wherever a corrupted Christianity exists."[39] Its anti-Catholic agenda was clear. When in the late nineteenth century other associations entered the mission field and diverted funds for this purpose, the Union concentrated its effort on sponsoring the American Protestant churches in Paris and Berlin.

American Mass Evangelism and Holiness Preaching in Europe

In the slipstream of American denominations, global reform organizations, humanitarian groups, independent agencies, and American preachers staged mass events in Europe. They came in two variations: as mass evangelists and as holiness preachers. Among traditional Christians the experience of conversion trumped any other religious moment.[40] The campaigns launched by former Chicago shoe salesman Dwight Moody and his singing companion Ira Sankey between 1873 and 1875 in the United Kingdom, brought this tradition to the attention of all Europe. Moody had been part of a previous revival in 1857. His use of laymen's prayer meetings, his cooperative methods, his simple colloquial explanation of the gospel – driven home by Sankey's powerfully emotional songs – made him a celebrity. He reached mass audiences in urban centers with his democratized message of salvation on both sides of the ocean.

38 J.P. Justin, "The American Church in Europe: A Letter to William Bacon Stevens," *The Church Journal* (New York), 24 December 1874.

39 "Records of the American and Foreign Christian Union," Presbyterian Historical Society (PHS), RG 118, Philadelphia, USA.

40 Noll, *New Shape*, 52-53.

Simultaneously, another American worked the hearts and minds of European Christians: Robert Pearsall Smith (1832-1898). Smith was a Quaker glass manufacturer from Germantown, Pennsylvania, turned lay holiness preacher. He had come under the influence of Wesleyan holiness preachers, and became one himself after the death of a son. He had a personal history of nervous breakdowns as well as holiness experiences. His European tour complete with lodging in aristocratic mansions, and house parties brought him international fame, but careless liaisons with female followers soon destroyed his reputation.[41] While Moody continued to draw attention in numerous secular and religious European newspapers, Smith and his wife stayed under the radar of the press. Both contributed to raising European expectations about their American brethren.

In the late nineteenth and early twentieth centuries, a spirit of tolerance was still present among American conservative Christians, but tensions simmered. The British Baptist holiness preacher F.B. Meyer, for instance, did not reject Pentecostalism, but neither did he embrace it. He kept quiet about his social gospel activities in England lest his American brethren be upset, and in general, withstood the trend to advocate separation from theological liberalism. This was very much in line with Dwight Moody's centrist endeavors.[42] Seeing himself as being on the same footing with the working class, Moody didn't hesitate to raise critical issues such as low wages and a larger role for women in the church.[43] He attracted an estimated two million attendees at his events in the 1870s and 1880s.

In the same period, America's elite embarked on religious tourism to examine their roots.[44] Henry R. Elliot, the secretary and treasurer of the Evangelist Company, organized an eight-week trip in the summer of 1895 for one hundred travelers, who each paid $400 to see the sites of European Calvinism. They were to visit the Presbyterians in Ireland and see the battlefield where the Protestants beat the Catholic King James II in the seventeenth century, and

41 Hans Krabbendam, "Zielenverbrijzelaars en zondelozen. Reacties in de Nederlandse pers op Moody, Sankey en Pearsall Smith, 1874-1878," *Documentatieblad voor de Nederlandse Kerkgeschiedenis na 1800* 34 (May 1991): 39-55; Karl Heinz Voigt, *Die Heiligungsbewegung zwischen methodistischer Kirche und landeskirchlicher Gemeinschaft: die "Triumphreise" von Robert Pearsall Smith im Jahre 1875 und ihre Auswirkungen auf die zwischenkirchlichen Beziehungen* (Wuppertal: Brockhaus, 1996), 39-132.

42 Ian Randall, "A Christian Cosmopolitan: F.B. Meyer in Britain and America," in George Rawlyk and Mark A. Noll, eds., *Amazing Grace*, 157-182.

43 David W. Bebbington, "Moody as a Transatlantic Evangelical," in Timothy George, ed., *Mr Moody and the Evangelical Tradition* (London: Continuum Books, 2005), 75-91.

44 *The Evangelist's Presbyterian pilgrimage: sailing per specially chartered steamer Berlin of the American line, June 26th, 1895: visiting the chief centers of Presbyterian interest in Ireland, Scotland, England, Germany, Belgium, and Holland* [New York: The Evangelist Company, 1895]. The organizer Henry R. Elliot (1849-1906) had just taken on the editorial responsibilities of the *(New York) Evangelist* in 1894 and soon thereafter became editor of the *Church Economist*.

then move on to the scene of the brave Scottish Covenanters, to Edinburgh the capital of pan-Presbyterianism (and the "most beautiful city" in the world), and to the Presbyterian presence in major cities, eventually travelling to Paris to visit the McAll mission and to remember the tragic fate of the Huguenots. Then they went to Geneva, the Presbyterian Mecca, finishing up with a final leg of the tour through Germany and Holland. The benefits of the tour lay in finding pride in the Presbyterian heritage in Europe, as the trip prospectus explained in a brochure: "Certainly nothing could be imagined that would leave on the mind a more correct or more vivid and inspiring sense of the value and dignity of the Presbyterian Church. It would equip a minister or office-bearer of the church with a new zeal, and double his efficiency. As a preparation for the ministry, it would be of the greatest value."[45]

The purported value of this trip stood in strong contrast to the report by the Rev. Walter W. Moore, the president of Union Theological Seminary in Virginia, who seven years later quoted British sources acknowledging that America held the future, not Europe. Moore disapproved of the new education bill that taxed all British subjects to support Anglican schools and thought that it undermined non-conformist religion at the same time. "The folly of the Anglicans in this matter will hasten the fall of the Established Church in England."[46] The cathedrals drew believers to the medieval style of worship that saw outward adherence as more important than inward conviction. Moore quoted with approval a jubilant report about the advance of the Huguenots in France, to whom he ascribed a virtual revival.

> Where in the world could be found so promising a mission field – one ready to yield such rich returns? Where could be found people so eager to listen to the preaching of the gospel, and to have their children taught its lessons? As well as promising, France is a most important mission field. The conversion, within the next few years, of some thousands of French people, would be of incalculable value to the religious and moral welfare of the world.[47]

These Presbyterian opinion makers showed an appreciation for Europe's religious past, but revealed the continent's enduring weakness in religious energy, and showed optimism about Europe's chance for revival.

Nevertheless, a rift among Protestants was building in response to the growth of science and modernism, and because of the penetration of naturalism inside the academy. All of these factors competed with a religious perspective. German liberal theology entered the mission fields and chipped away at

45 *The Evangelist's Presbyterian pilgrimage*, xi; Reports in *New York Times*, 26 June and 14 July 1895.

46 Walter W. Moore, *A Year in Europe* (3rd ed., Richmond, VA: The Presbyterian Committee on Publication, 1905), 51-53.

47 Ibid., 177-183 (British Education Bill) and 210-211 (Huguenot Revival).

the uniqueness of the bible. An academic approach represented by German scholars confronted Anglo-American activism. This division of labor between thinkers and doers proved divisive and one of the fields where it persisted was in the missions. Growing apocalyptic thinking increased the tension within missionary movements as some missionaries felt that slow progress in the mission field postponed the return of Christ.[48]

Similar tensions were felt at the great missionary conference held in Edinburgh in 1910. Europeans resented Anglo domination of mission enterprises. Here too the head competed with the heart, and faith missions carried the day with their stories of faith, strong inner motivation, and impressive results. Premillennialism gained ground and adopted "scientific" arguments. Mobilization and empowerment were the key elements in the drive to reach the entire world.[49]

The recruitment activities of the Student Volunteer Movement enormously increased the number of missionaries, allowing evangelicals to spread globally between 1880 and 1900. Historians Hutchison and Wolffe summarize the overall picture:

> Its secret lay in its ability to motivate by providing a unified, experiential religious worldview built around a personal sense of calling to ultimate ends. That unity was the coming together of evangelical experience from India to Chicago, the end product of evangelical experimentalism, whereby a doctrinal core was freed from European origins by being associated with the mobile personal self, attached to a historical imaginary which gave the believer a sense of safety, wherever they might be.[50]

The shared basis of a personal holiness experience created unity, motivation, and flexibility. This empowerment and appeal to missions, based on personal motivation, prepared the road for Pentecostalism.[51] By these actions, these leaders legitimized the American evangelical presence in Europe. Evangelical practices spread through conferences that reproduced and circulated pietist spirituality, crossed church boundaries and encouraged outreach to continental Europe.

48 Mark Hutchinson and John Wolffe, *A Short History of Global Evangelicalism* (Cambridge: Cambridge University Press, 2012), 139. The relative position of the state determined the popularity of post and premillennial ideas: a strong church in a weak state advanced postmillennial expectations and by contrast a weak church in a strong state premillennial.

49 Brian Stanley, *The World Missionary Conference: Edinburgh 1910* (Grand Rapids: Eerdmans, 2009).

50 Hutchinson and Wolffe, *A Short History*, 144.

51 Pentecostal revival erupted simultaneous in various places, not only in and from LA. New questions about healing, the place of doctrine, race relations, ratio and emotion. But for the time being, it remained at the margins of the evangelical debates. Gaston Espinosa, *William J. Seymour and the Origins of Global Pentecostalism: A Biography and Documentary History* (Durham, NC: Duke University Press, 2014).

America's urge to take over Britain's lead is illustrated by the activities of the Minneapolis Baptist minister William Bell Riley. His biographer William C. Trollinger uncovers the local, regional, and national influences on Riley and his initial internationalist agenda, albeit limited for the time being.[52] In the 1920s Riley founded the World's Christian Fundamentals Association (WCFA). He fully subscribed to the idea that the cause of the problems caused by Germany in the Great War was the modernist theological turn and the embrace of Darwinian evolutionism.[53] As it would in World War II, the Great War encouraged prophetic thinking, confirming the sense of urgency and pessimism of the premillennial ideas. Riley masterminded the amalgamation of anti-modernist theology with the prophetic movement in the World Conference on the Fundamentals of Faith, held in Philadelphia in the last week of May 1919. This was later hailed as the birthdate of the fundamentalist movement in America.

The word "World" in the title expressed universal ambitions, even if for the time being, the world was mainly the Anglo-Saxons and their colonies. Only one of the five WCFA committees reached beyond the nation's boundaries and it did that only indirectly. The Missions Committee encouraged the withdrawal from all mission agencies that allowed the staff to be "unconverted," or that accepted modernist views. Instead, it tried to divert the support to one of seven approved interdenominational missionary organizations. The WCFA peaked briefly in the early 1920s and then went into decline due to the incompatibility of the competing leaders many of who launched their own organizations. Moreover, they were not able to actually roll back modernism. They only exposed it; they made no provision for an alternative umbrella organization and limited their priorities to anti-evolution rhetoric from 1922 onwards.

The international activities of these first fundamentalist organizations were indirect at best, ineffective at worst. They responded both during the Great War and after, to the international aspirations of the ecumenical organizations, such as the Interchurch World Movement (IWM), which sought to overcome denominational strife by centralization, especially in the mission field.[54] Fundamentalists abhorred this idea and denounced this push for one church. Though they had little to fear from the IWM, which collapsed within

52 William Vance Trollinger, *God's Empire: William Bell Riley and Midwestern Fundamentalism* (Madison: University of Wisconsin Press, 1990), 33-61. The World's Christian Fundamentals Association was not as global as the first word suggested.

53 Trollinger, *God's Empire*, 34; Marsden, *Fundamentalism*, 141-64; Markku Ruotsila, *The Origins of Christian Anti-Internationalism: Conservative Evangelicals and the League of Nations* (Washington DC: Georgetown University Press, 2008), 43-50.

54 *World Survey by the Interchurch World Movement of North America*, 2 vols. (New York: Interchurch Press, 1920), "The world for Christ, not the world for a denomination, is the true missionary goal." (2:154) an equally strong encouragement to win the world for Christ (188). Already this report paid tribute to Europe as the origin of foreign missions and a strong influence, but indicated that Americans greatly outnumbered Europeans in missionary staff, and funding.

a year, its global aspirations nonetheless triggered their efforts to prevent the success of a global modernist movement.[55] They succeeded in forcing several denominations to withdraw from the IWM, but many other battles to purify the church of a weakness for modernism were lost, at least in Riley's Northern Baptist Convention. Riley's appeal for strict enforcement of doctrinal statements did not flourish. As we will see, these efforts were repeated in and after World War II based on the same, but now increased, fear of a modernist global church. But this time the counterforces were more successful in arranging a viable alternative.

American denominations invested their resources in Europe after the American Civil War. American Baptists reinforced British missionaries in Italy, and after World War I expanded their missions to Hungary, Rumania, Spain, and Yugoslavia, cooperating with German agencies. This cooperation was a result of a 1920 conference of Baptist national churches and agencies, which strengthened their involvement in (temporary) relief work. The Baptists claimed that they came to support indigenous church groups, not to act on their own accord.[56] As evidence of that attitude they showed that in 1939 the Italian Baptists had 49 churches and three thousand members, with only one American missionary couple to support the work.

Many free church missionaries with roots in Europe returned to their old countries as well. A Swedish historian estimated that there were some 2,745 American missionaries in Europe in 1895, serving congregations with 153,000 members.[57] In the second half of the nineteenth century newly formed denominations and religious movements such as the Methodists, Adventists, Mormons, and Jehovah's Witnesses moved from America to Europe with an abundance of missionary zeal. While the European intelligentsia rejected this diverse and chaotic religious catalog coming from America, a considerable number of lay people were charmed by its dynamism.[58]

55 Trollinger, *God's Empire*, 52-53; Marsden, *Fundamentalism*, 166.

56 For an overview of Southern Baptist missionary activities in Europe before 1940 see, Southern Baptist Convention, *Southern Baptists in Europe* (Richmond, VA: Foreign Mission Board of the Southern Baptist Convention, 1939).

57 Gunnar Westin, *The Free Church Through the Ages*, translated by Virgil A. Olson (Nashville, TN. Broadman Press, 1958).

58 Thomas A. Howard, *God and the Atlantic: America, Europe, and the Religious Divide* (New York: Oxford University Press, 2011). American writers also crossed the Atlantic in search of the Old World legacy for the New in all but religion. Goodness and simplicity, innocence and ignorance were the characterizations of the standard attitudes of the protagonists in the novels that were most affected by an actual European journey. Their interest and inspiration was more from the aesthetic and the material culture, the political arrangements, and the architecture than the religious structures. The inspirational force of European culture for American authors lasted about a century and a half till World War II. In religious aspects it was the grandeur of the Gothic architecture that impressed them more than anything else. They looked to historical sites, and not to the contemporary state of religion. See Klaus Lanzinger, *Jason's Voyage: The Search for the Old World in American Literature:*

Most church boards for foreign missions adopted the model of voluntary associations. Some American Presbyterians followed the guidelines from their European (Scottish) ancestors, but the mainstream Presbyterians, as Darryl Hart defines them, followed their own course "not as the daughter church to Old World sponsors, but as a Presbyterian expression without deliberate missionary strategy or oversight [from Europe]".[59] Presbyterians sent money and missionaries to Europe after World War I. In 1924 they made it explicit that work in Europe fell under the supervision of the Board of Foreign Missions, and subscribed to the same principle as the Baptists supporting only congregations that asked for assistance. It was not their intention to establish a mission outpost among the Europeans. A budget of $10,000 per year in the 1930s was sufficient.[60] The Presbyterian example showed that the growing internal division between fundamentalists and modernists prevented the formulation of one mission strategy. Some Presbyterians operated in the avant-garde of the ecumenical movement, others sided with the separatist side of the Presbyterian spectrum, and a third faction inspired by Karl Barth occupied a middle ground between the two flanks.[61]

Denominational missions met competition from interdenominational groups. The first conservative interdenominational mission organizations had settled in Europe after the Great War. Most of them were concerned with the Orthodox and Catholic regions of Europe and had a personal European connection, such as with the Estonian, Gans P. Raud. Born in 1882 into a Christian family, Raud traveled through Europe as an itinerant evangelist from 1904-1914, before coming to North America. In 1922 he founded a tuition-free training institute for missionaries to Europe, the American Seminary of the Bible, in Brooklyn, New York, where he served as president. His European Christian Mission, also called Gospel Mission Union, had ministries in Estonia, Ukraine and Germany, and after the war it expanded its operations to France, Spain, Austria, and Czechoslovakia.[62]

A second example of an independent agency settling in Europe during World War I is the Belgian Gospel Mission, created by Americans Ralph and Edith Norton who first provided relief and religion to British soldiers, and then

A Study of Melville, Hawthorne, Henry James, and Thomas Wolfe (New York: Peter Lang, 1989), 1-13.

59 D.G. Hart and John R. Muether, *Seeking a Better Country: 300 Years of American Presbyterianism* (Phillipsburg, NJ: P and R Publishing, 2007), 24.

60 See the historical overview of the Presbyterian Church in the USA in the report of the Board of Foreign Missions of the Presbyterian Church in the USA, "Work in Europe," [1948] United Presbyterian Church, col. 161B, box 3, Presbyterian Historical Society, Philadelphia.

61 Ibid., 208-221.

62 G. P. Raud, *A Life Lived for God: The Story of G.P. Raud, Founder of the Bible Christian Union* (New York: Bible Christian Union, 1955); John D. Boy, "Blessed Disruption: Culture and Urban Space in a European Church Planting Network" (PhD dissertation, City University of New York, 2015).

to Belgian troops in the Ypres region, continuing these contacts after the war. Their intention was to cooperate with the existing churches in evangelism, but when the Protestant churches failed to endorse fundamentalist bible positions, they decided to act alone to plant their own free churches and a bible school.[63] These initiatives were done on a small scale, depending on a lone person, who was, nevertheless able to find others through publications, conferences, and the circulation of staff.

After the Great War, American churches and associations launched new initiatives in relief. These activities raised the cost of the churches' programs while in the 1930s the economic crisis caused contributions to drop. Drought victims, unemployed, dislocated and destitute citizens flocked to the cities in search of aid, exhausting the coffers of the churches. The private sector was not strong enough to bear the burden of the relief effort and the state stepped in. This was more than an emergency measure; the New Deal energized people, recipients and administrators, and generated visible improvement despite its shortcomings. It was perhaps this service on behalf of the needy that made most clergy support the New Deal.[64]

Meanwhile, the modernist-fundamentalist tensions carried on within religious institutions and in public debates. Fundamentalist leaders interpreted the New Deal as the next step towards totalitarian suppression.[65] These conservative leaders equated the modernist embrace of the Social Gospel to the government's emphasis on economic planning. Even though they themselves pursued humanitarian relief, they were allergic to state organized social projects. The established Protestant churches suffered from growing institutional costs and the departure of disappointed conservatives. Newer independent groups gained leverage, presence, and appeal among the believers, most of whom believed that the organizations were carrying out their core purpose.

Underneath these activities a compelling question nagged at them: Why did the pressure of the times not lead to a revival? The missionary figures were unsatisfying as the number of North American missionaries fluctuated along with political and economic developments. The numbers dropped to 2,500 in 1936 compared to 13,555 missionaries in 1925. This initial drop was no doubt due to the economic depression, and the further drop of 3,000 between 1938 and 1945 was due to political instability. When peace and prosperity were re-

63 Aaldert Prins, "The History of the Belgian Gospel Mission from 1918 to 1962" (doctoral dissertation Leuven University, 2015); Phylis Thompson, *Firebrand of Flanders: The Gospel in Belgium Seen in the Life of Odilon Vansteenberghe* (Chicago: Moody Press, 1966), 49-60.

64 Samuel C. Kincheloe, *Research Memorandum on Religion in the Depression* (New York: Social Science Research Council, 1937; repr. 1972), 3.

65 Andrew Sutton, "Was FDR the Antichrist? The Birth of Fundamentalist Antiliberalism in a Global Age," *Journal of American History* 98.4 (March 2012): 1052-1074.

stored, the numbers returned to the earlier level of 15,000 in 1950.[66] It was not only a lack of funds that depressed the number. In fact, some denominations, such as the Pentecostals, collected an increasing amount of money for missions in the 1930s with only a temporary drop in 1931-33. The drop in numbers was a result of a return to normalcy after the explosion of activity immediately after World War I.[67] Significantly, the nineteenth century had set the stage for joint action, American bridgeheads, and the beginning of fundamentalist missions in continental Europe.

Frank Buchman's Appeal in Europe

But before the modernist-fundamentalist confrontation spread to Europe, there was another transatlantic religious figure from the United States in the person of Frank Buchman (1878-1961) who went along with the expectation of saving Europe, and who represented the immigrant connection. He was born into a Pennsylvania German Lutheran family, and schooled at a Lutheran Reformed Seminary in Philadelphia, where he gained experience in the social work that was so attractive to the new Protestant generation. He overextended himself in his work in a settlement house in Philadelphia, fell ill, and found inner healing at a religious conference in Keswick in the British Lake District. There he embraced the perfectionist notion of a "victorious Christian life."[68]

Buchman's personal religious experience connected the pietist strand in the Lutheran tradition with the Methodist holiness tradition and became a source of encouragement for others, mostly young men, to try the same. In the service of the Young Men's Christian Association at Pennsylvania State College he developed a program of personal attention to students entitled "soul surgery." He tried this system at other institutes as well, and exported it to YMCA and the Student Volunteer Movement posts in China and India.[69]

Buchman designed a five-step method that began with confidence in the messenger. This confidence then lead to a confession of sins, a conviction of the need for conversion, and a continuous propagation of this process to oth-

66 R. Pierce Beaver, "The Expansion of American Foreign Missionary Activities Since 1945,"*Occasional Bulletin of Foreign Missionary Activities* 5.7 (4 June 1954), 1; Robert T. Coote, "Finger on the Pulse: Fifty Years of Missionary Research," *The Free Library* 24.3 (1 July 2000): 98-105.

67 Robert T. Handy, "The American Religious Depression, 1925-1935," *Church History* 29 (1960): 3-16; Alison Collis Greene, "The End of the 'Protestant Era'?" *Church History* 80.3 (September 2011): 600-610; Heather D. Curtis, " 'God Is Not Affected by the Depression': Pentecostal Missions during the 1930s," *Church History* 80 (2011): 579-589.

68 See Hans Krabbendam, "The Transformers: Continuity and Change in the European Campaigns of American Evangelists Frank Buchman and Billy Graham, 1920-1960," *Journal of Religion in Europe* 7 (2014): 223-245.

69 Garth Lean, *Frank Buchman: A Life* (London: Constable, 1985), 73.

ers.[70] A subjective spiritual experience with dogma prevented him from getting entangled in the emerging modernist-fundamentalist debate. In 1921, an inner voice told him that he had a worldwide mission. As a result he began to focus on Europe, the springboard for his global project. He resigned from his paid position and lived off the generous donations of wealthy backers, never again to submit to a formal organization. In 1924, he began a world tour that ended in Europe where he met quite intentionally with the elite, whom he lectured in venues such as first class hotels and classic mansions. The royal family in Greece became charmed by his project and paved the way for his acceptance into the family networks of European aristocracy and royalty.[71]

This success of his European advance convinced Buchman that personal changes in the ruling class would inaugurate an era of global political reform. In 1934, he felt confident enough to announce a world-wide "Christian Revolution."[72] Politicians struggling with Europe's institutional stagnation eagerly took up the promise of direct reform.[73] Buchman's successes in the United Kingdom and South Africa, gave his enterprise a new name, the "Oxford Group," that trumpeted a respectable European concentration point for the powerful. In the 1930s Europe became the venue that inspired the formation of similar informal church groups. Subsequently all these groups were incorporated into the Oxford Group by international teams led by Buchman. This absorption paved the way for a series of mass meetings in European cities that resulted in the new slogan *Rising Tide* thus capturing the excitement of the movement. Its new mission acquired a new name: Moral Rearmament (MRA).[74]

Similar to his evangelical predecessors, Buchman charmed Europeans even more than he had Americans with his simple and direct call for change and with his pragmatic proof that personal change reconciled diehard adversaries. "Change" required only the personal courage to confess mistakes and seek redress. Yet it promised a huge return: a sense of moral superiority, a confirmation of individual autonomy through direct access to God's intentions, and the promise of making a contribution to the improvement of the

70 The Layman with a Notebook, *What is the Oxford Group?* (London: Oxford University Press, 1933). An anonymous self-description.

71 Daniel Sack, *Moral Re-Armament: The Reinventions of an American Religious Movement* (New York: Palgrave, 2009), 5. See the characterization by John M. Versteeg as "a holiness movement for the socially favored," *Christian Century* (23 January 1935).

72 Kevin Kee, *Revivalists: Marketing the Gospel in English Canada, 1884-1957* (Montreal and Kingston: McGill-Queen's University Press, 2006), 138-139; Frank D. Buchman, *Remaking the World* (London: Blandford Press, 1947), 4 (address in Oxford in July 1934).

73 He complimented Hitler for resisting communism in an interview in the August 26, 1936 *New York World Telegram*. This interview would haunt and discredit him as a fascist sympathizer.

74 Jarlert Anders, *The Oxford Group, Group Revivalism, and the Churches in Northern Europe, 1930-1945, with Special Reference to Scandinavia and Germany* (Lund: Lund University Press, 1995), 49; Sack, *Moral*, 100-101, 143-52.

world. The earlier progressive call for pacifism and disarmament, gave way to spiritual rearmament. An attractive aspect of the movement in the 1930s was its internationalism. This global perspective granted significant consequence to individuals' decisions, and built a bridge between different (often hostile) nations. Internationalism overcame divisions among religious groups, and through ecumenicity, changed hearts from the bottom-up.

Buchman believed in a Christian civilization, which needed to be mobilized in order to be livable. His inclusion of the high and mighty was evidence of his belief. He was an optimist who was convinced that all conflicts could be solved with proper mediation. To Buchman, Europe and the United States belonged together. He found no great contrast between the continents. Each warm reception in a European country confirmed his expectation that nations could be changed once they accepted his mediation. In order to be universal, Buchman increasingly moved away from recognizable evangelicalism and towards general Christian notions such as confession, charity, and hope. He presented a modernist expressive religion and paved the way for respectful engagement in personal and intimate conversations about religion outside the church walls.[75]

Moral Rearmament is an example of the universal claims of American Protestantism becoming explicit in Europe in the first half of the twentieth century. Buchman's group showed that interaction between the various components in the international Protestant community could create a rich flow across the Atlantic. The Buchman story revealed the standard ingredients: an emphasis on personal conversion, a strong male leadership, professional public relations devices and the use of modern communication techniques and popular culture, topped by serious warnings about the dangers of competing ideological systems, especially Communism. This spread ran parallel to the broadening of the audience. Buchman targeted the old European elite that longed for spiritual renewal, were part of international networks, possessed the money and language skills to communicate across borders, and were willing to host informal parties.

Buchman specialized in holiness training targeting political and economic elites. Practical and clear responses to his appeals for serious commitment to the faith encouraged him to widen his geographical horizon and expand his ideals in the hope of advancing a Social Gospel. But in the process he advocated faith as a means rather than a goal, that gradually secularized his message.[76] Buchman updated nineteenth-century holiness activities, but

75 The phenomenon of the expressive self, connected the Buchmanites to Pentecostals and charismatics, but there is no direct inspirational or personal line, see Sack, *Moral*, 76; Gaston Espinosa, *William J. Seymour and the Origins of Global Pentecostalism: A Biography and Documentary History* (Durham, NC: Duke University Press, 2014), 1-157.

76 David B. Marshall, *Secularizing the Faith: Canadian Protestant Clergy and the Crisis of Belief, 1850–1940* (Toronto: University of Toronto Press, 1992) quoted in Kee, *Revivalists*, 221.

believed that institutions obstructed direct spiritual communication. This rejection of institutions disabled the continuity of his movement and distanced him from the growing organizational schemes of both the mainline churches concentrated in the Federal and World Council of Churches, and the emerging alternative of a global evangelical organization.

Buchman's legacy for postwar Europe was that personal change was a real possibility, based on experience and not on theory.[77] His approach offered European Protestantism, which was in the process of declension, an alternative version of the relationship between public and private religion. The seriousness of this shift to personal experience would only become visible after World War II. When the religious constellations in Europe crumbled during and after the war, the second trend of revivalism came to the forefront, this time presented by Billy Graham. Graham shared with Buchman and many other American activists, the claim of universalism.

Reception in Europe

Europe's intelligentsia – both advocates of secularity and guardians of tradition – showed more apprehension than support for American evangelicalism. The latter category, especially in Britain and Germany, saw the French and American Revolutions as associated, and rejected both. They feared chaos and anarchy as a result of cutting the ties between church and state. In their opinion, religious liberty lead to religious confusion. Catholics found the arrangement in the United States dangerously relativistic. Believers' private judgments could easily lead to heterodoxy. Most Protestants judged the developments in America as a degeneration of European structures. They concurred in the verdict that religious freedom would result in indifference.[78]

Secular critics in Europe rejected religion as an obstacle encountered along the universal historical course to greater human freedom. They actually reached the same conclusion as their conservative opponents: the increase in religious enthusiasm moved America backward not forward in history. A second criticism of the lack of a central agency in America linked conservatives and secularists. French thinkers operated in a framework of unity (shaped both by a strong state and the overarching Catholic Church) and derided the American Revolution as a conservative Protestant rebellion leading to fragmentation. True liberation, they believed, came from a spiritual unity guided by science. In the Hegelian tradition, churches were to be subjected to the

77 James T. Kloppenberg, *Uncertain Victory: Social Democracy and Progressivism in European and American Thought, 1870-1920* (New York: Oxford University Press, 1988), 186-195.

78 Thomas A. Howard, *God and the Atlantic: America, Europe, and the Religious Divide* (New York: Oxford University Press, 2011), 28-84.

state or else they would become redundant. The more radical Marxists considered religiosity an opiate that dulled people and saw it as a result of the limitation of a bourgeois state. In this framework America was also an anomaly. A third objection to religion came from the revolutionaries of 1848 who believed that the churches blocked progress. They found evidence for this obstruction in the lack of intellectual development in America.[79]

The sense of European superiority was still paramount to Europeans in the early twentieth century. Dutch historian, Johan Huizinga in his 1918 book characterized American religion as, "All the easy credulity, the uncritical sense, the fantastic sensibility, the perpetuation of accepted biases, the naive sentimentality, as we know from the medieval spirit of the people, still characterize those of contemporary America."[80]

Yet there was also a growing positive trend in European views of American culture. British cultural critics of a conservative bent were more negative about American culture than their radical opponents, but wound up changing their tune in the late 1880s. In his book *Observing America*, Robert P. Frankel documents this shift in British observations between 1890 and 1950. These conservatives followed the assessment of the British diplomat James Bryce. But even Bryce emphasized the similarities between religious trends in the United States and the United Kingdom, at the same time as he admitted that Americans talked with more ease about religious convictions and experiences, were more expressive, generous, launched programs for all kinds of groups, and were more peaceful.

English visitors were generally more positive about American culture than mainland Europeans, though few explicitly singled out religion as a positive force. The most telling example is G.K. Chesterton. While one would expect appreciation from this Roman Catholic defender of family and traditional values, religion in America did not meet his approval. He disagreed with Clarence Darrow about the future of religion, but agreed with H.L. Mencken's disdain for the poisonous Puritan spirit, going so far as to propose the introduction of Thanksgiving Day in the United Kingdom: "to celebrate the happy fact that the Pilgrim Fathers left England."[81]

79 Howard drew two conclusions from this survey of European critics. First, he concluded that the presuppositions of these commentators prevented a fair investigation of religion in America because they offered economic explanations for religious phenomena. Second, they were not so much observers, but rather missionaries who wanted to secularize America. In their efforts to liberate Europe from the confines of religion, they could only feel puzzled by the resurgence of religion in America.

80 Johan Huizinga, *America: A Dutch Historian's Vision, From Afar and Near*, translated, with an introd. and notes, by Herbert H. Rowen (New York: Harper & Row, 1972), 208. This was a translation of Huizinga's 1918 book, *Mensch en Meenigte in Amerika*.

81 Robert P. Frankel, *Observing America: The Commentary of British Visitors to the United States, 1890–1950* (Madison: University of Wisconsin Press, 2007), 172.

European evangelical minority churches (many of which had an Anglo-American connection) were the most receptive to the message of American religious inspiration. In the late nineteenth century they reached out to each other because they were small and faced similar issues of evangelism, education, and attacks on religious freedom. Their distance to state connections made it easier for them to reach across borders.[82]

Prewar Patterns

The legacy of the nineteenth- and early twentieth-century American Protestant interest in Western Europe can be captured in four trends, to which the three branches of American Protestantism responded after World War II.

Within the first trend, the formally established churches in the United States related to their Protestant counterparts in Europe, but created their own institutions, independent synods, seminaries, and most important for the future, new associations for evangelism, missions and social reform. By 1830, these churches had ended any formal submissive relationship to their mother churches, and instead adopted a sense of superiority towards Europe that matched the self-confidence of the new Republic. In their scholarly orientation they remained attuned to Europe, but this was mainly an academic affair. Some interest in the old world reawakened with the increase in transportation, trade, and tourism. And the churches founded a number of congregations on the European continent that served American citizens. These churches joined hands with other denominations to export social activities and to cooperate in the missions. There were strong continuities into the twentieth century.

As a second trend, many ministers and believers in the free church tradition of America had left Europe to escape oppressive ecclesiastic regimes. During the nineteenth century many of these ethnic churches pursued a conservative agenda hoping to shield their flock from the assimilative pull of American society. This made them attractive to new immigrants, whose connection to the old-world legacy gradually weakened as their languages were forced out of use, the number of immigrants dropped, and new generations looked for allies in the American environment. The promotion of these immigrant churches growing out of oppressed minority churches in Europe, to the position of vibrant majority churches in their subcultures in America, fed a critical attitude towards the state churches in European countries.

Third, the American churches in the Arminian tradition, a tradition absent or weak in Europe (mostly Methodist and Baptist) were the most dynamic, outgoing, missionary-minded, and took the initiative to launch missions

82 Ian Randall, "Evangelicals and European Integration," *European Journal of Theology* 14.1 (2005): 17-26.

on the European Continent. They were moved by a sense of urgency. From a position of strength they supported their kin in Catholic Europe where their churches were tiny minorities. Anti-Catholicism was a strong incentive for missions within and outside America. Catholicism was considered a source of corruption, anti-republicanism, and authoritarianism.[83] From this generally evangelical tradition came holiness preachers and revivalists who tried to renew those whom they saw as stagnant believers from whatever church. Buchman served this purpose brilliantly by combining the promise of holiness with the hope of political harmony. His lack of institutional support and his drifting away from his evangelical moorings and (church) institutions, however, prevented the new movement from taking root. The informality of the holiness tradition did not need much organization or enduring traditions as it offered instantly applicable solutions. The organization of revivals was meant to bring people back into the church and therefore the organizers needed to find a basis on which to build cooperation with churches and associations.

A fourth trend included the new religious traditions from America moving to Europe. These ranged from close cousins of the Christian tradition (such as Adventists) to more distant ones (Mormons, Christian Scientists, and later Jehovah's Witnesses). These groups remain mostly outside the scope of this book, as they operated unilaterally in their attachment to formal American authority. However, they played a definite part in Europe as the most explicit representatives of American religion and as specialized competitors to the established organizations, providing alternatives to dissatisfied European believers. Sooner or later American Protestant groups had to respond to their activities. They needed to defend their own respectability and acceptability against these challengers.

The legacies of the nineteenth and early twentieth centuries were visible in motives, means, and in the effects of activities of American Protestants in Europe. American denominations wanted to strengthen kindred groups that were struggling, or to plant churches in Europe, where they were not yet represented. Newer religious movements actively proselytized Europe, as part of their universal expectations. All these groups harbored an element of belief in the superiority of an American construction of church and state, thought they had at least a competing truth, or that they were promising a higher spiritual level. Increasingly Americans who battled against theological liberalism associated their objections with Europe, which they regarded as a corrupted culture. They also targeted European immigrants as they prepared to settle in the United States.

83 Marjule Anne Drury, "Anti-Catholicism in Germany, Britain, and the United States: A Review and Critique of Recent Scholarship," *Church History: Studies in Christianity and Culture* 70.1 (March 2001): 98-131.

As to the means adopted, the main instruments they used to reach the goals were to send supportive colleagues, or fraternal workers, to organize associations which were supported by American backers (for moral issues such as temperance and abolition of slavery and prostitution or to revive youth), and – most visibly – to stage mass meetings and staff conferences. All three means would be employed after World War II.

What effects did these activities have on the religious landscape of Europe? In quantity the number of actual Americans actively working in Europe remained low. A high estimate is of some scores of workers, a large segment of which remained in Europe for only a short term. The voluntaristic individual, the sometimes anti-authority approach, and the inherently uphill struggle against powerful religious and civic establishments fragmented the effort. In their variety, they added new groups to the religious menu. There was also a new emphasis on youth, on mass events, on popular culture, all of which encouraged the idea of religion as personal choice. These three features especially would receive more emphasis after World War II as part of a structural approach. When the internal religious tensions of the modernist-fundamentalist competition erupted in America in the 1920s, each tradition turned to Europe to strengthen its cause. In this way Europe increasingly became the arena of America's religious competition and the recipient of America's religious energy.

EXPECT!
WARTIME PROSPECTS FOR POSTWAR EUROPE

Great Opportunities

In their struggle with modernity in the twentieth century, for better or worse, European nations had to confront the United States. Especially at moments of transition in years following a war, European leaders drafted plans with positive or negative American examples in mind. In the long run it was not America's military power that impressed European audiences the most, but American cultural examples. World War I established America's cultural dominance and throughout the twentieth century mass communication spread a message of political salvation.

Most European elites resisted these forces of cultural hegemony fearing that the masses would believe that the future was theirs, that they were entitled to prosperity as much as all other groups in society. Hollywood movies molded these aspirations in attractive visual form. Thanks to America's withdrawal from the international political arena (that is towards Europe) in the 1920s and early 1930s culture continued to spread these expectations.[1]

The economic depression of the 1930s did not kill these expectations, the Roosevelt Administration advanced economic liberalism and free trade as the most promising path to stable prosperity. For this goal it helped create inter-

1 David W. Ellwood, *The Shock of America: Europe and the Challenge of the Century* (Oxford, UK: Oxford University Press, 2012), 107-141; David Ekbladh, *The Great American Mission: Modernization and the Construction of an American world Order* (Princeton: Princeton University Press, 2010), 107, 298.

national institutions. During World War II these ideas matured. American bureaucrats and businessmen envisioned the postwar period as the greatest opportunity to apply American solutions to global problems, including the World Trade Organization, the Bretton Woods accord, and the United Nations. Religious leaders agreed. They shared the sense of crisis, the eagerness to create international networks and use of mass media to transform society. The YMCA after World War I, the Moral Rearmament movement in the interwar years, and the growing ecumenical organization after World War II were all part of this wave of building global institutions. These American initiatives provoked responses to these examples of modernization in Europe. Even though the key elements were political and economic, the cultural effects of these programs were immensely significant. The general message of salvation, the promises of rationalization and mass propaganda, and the emergence of a youth culture, all had parallels in American Protestant missions in Europe. The postwar episode of religious Americanization reveals that these private initiatives competed with each other and presented Europe with alternative choices.

Closest to the modernist agenda of other agencies was the liberal Protestant network, which had the strongest institutional ties with Europe, and the richest resources. The liberals responded efficiently to the pressing European emergency needs of the war since they had prepared their global organization in the past decades. The traditional Protestants concentrated first on domestic issues in the United States, but soon their missionary aspirations lead them to Europe. Both wings realized the major concerns of Europe as soon as the war began, and mobilized their forces to change a frightening scenario to a hopeful perspective. It was perhaps more the drive to make a new beginning, than a strong historical awareness that urged them to take on this task.

Modernist Hopes for Growing International Cooperation

As soon as the hostilities in Europe began in the fall of 1939, the American mainline churches sent observers overseas to gauge the impact of the war on religious relations. They noticed a dramatic change in the position of the churches in Central and Eastern Europe in relationship to the state, especially in Germany and Russia. In a Reformation Day message prepared for October that year the "Central Bureau for Relief of the Evangelical Churches in Europe" reported that the churches were stripped of their "Social Gospel" activities and had to resort to the Spiritual Gospel. The state had changed from a kind father who took care of the material needs of the church to a demonic power in opposition to the Christian faith. Civic authorities in these states took the resistance of the church to their policies as acts of rebellion.[2]

The ecumenical mission of the Protestant churches suffered as totalitarian states usurped them for their own power play. The Protestant minorities in France, Belgium, and Italy could hardly sustain their basic activities. The severance of free travel and lack of communication, the pressure of the economy, and the arrival of refugees paralyzed their own contribution to missions and outreach. Further to the east poverty and persecution threatened the existence of the Protestant church. In two-thirds of Europe, the church had lost its freedom to maintain its own educational and social institutions. They requested Americans for prayer and material help, especially for the many refugees.[3]

As the war went on, the expectation for Europe's future further deteriorated. The first rays of hope appeared in late 1943. From their sources of intelligence, ecumenical leaders Willem A. Visser 't Hooft, general secretary of the World Council of Churches, and Henry Smith Leiper, a former missionary in China and co-founder of the World Council of Churches, agreed that it was a matter of when, not if, the totalitarian regimes would collapse. Due to the loss of the churches' social function and autonomy in the war, these leaders envisioned an enormous political, social, and spiritual vacuum after the war, waiting to be filled. They put their hope in an active resistance movement, labor organizations, and the churches that had challenged the totalitarian pressures and counted on them as the pillars for reconstruction. The free West should encourage them by issuing a concrete and consistent call for a more just and peaceful world.

Visser 't Hooft feared that Russia would fill the space if the West failed to back up this opportunity for reform. He granted Russia (read the Communists) their place, but not a monopoly. Europe needed foremost a revival of Christian faith: "… the task of reChristianizing Europe is the task of the European churches themselves."[4] But they needed signals from the victorious countries in order to restore hope for the masses. Leiper saw an emerging cooperation in Europe among Catholics and Protestants, which was important as the war showed that churches were the conscience of the nation and therefore fulfilled a crucial public function. Sectarianism undermined this necessary spiritual unity. He believed he saw a thaw in the anti-religious attitude of Stalin. Euro-

2 For a comprehensive overview of the situation of the European churches under German occupation, see Jan Bank with Lieve Gevers, *Churches and Religion in the Second World War*, translated by Brian Doyle (London: Bloomsbury Academic, 2016), 163-295.

3 "European Protestantism at the Outbreak of War," [1939], 12 pp., in PHS, UPC 161B, box 3. A.H. Froendt, "The Christian Churches in the Field of Mercy," *Over There with the Churches of Christ* 21 (1940): 2-5, quoting from a report issued to the National Study Conference on the Study of the Churches in the International Situation, on February 27-29, 1940.

4 W.A. Visser 't Hooft, "Notes on the European Situation," *Christianity and Crisis* (13 December 1943).

pean churches were in need of help, but were no mission field. Proselytizing by American denominations would only weaken the church.[5] He strongly believed that the World Council of Churches should accept mutual aid as a crucial aspect of the new organizations: "for there could be no healthy ecumenical fellowship without practical solidarity."[6] Giving and receiving practical aid was the only way in which the church members really participated in the ecumenical movement.

In November and December 1944, A.L. Warnshuis, a third generation Dutch-American minister, former missionary to (Amoy) China and recently appointed foreign counselor to the Church Committee on Overseas Relief and Reconstruction, made a trip to Geneva. He returned to the United States with a high impression of the churches in Europe that had led "the opposition to those who wanted to destroy the basis of life."[7] The importance of the church had increased: "they now have a message, not only for the individual, but also for the community and the state and the nation... these churches are now more sure of themselves, as they have acquired experience in social action, and are no longer financially dependent on the state."[8]

This was not a pessimistic assessment of the religious condition in Europe, but an optimistic one. The recent suffering had strengthened the church by creating a unifying force, between Christians and non-Christians and among denominations. Warnshuis therefore strongly advised that Americans must not reintroduce denominational division by channeling aid via denominational ties. As he expected Europe to turn socialist, he sensed that Europeans feared both American and Russian economic imperialism. In a rather optimistic tone he found Europe to be the New World, where real changes could occur. He was confident that the church in Europe would play a central role

5 Henry Smith Leiper, "European Protestantism Tomorrow," *The Christian Century* (19 January 1944). Preserved in McIntire Papers Princeton, box 299 file 29. Samuel McCrea Cavert expressed the objective of the founding of an ecumenical training center as "a rebirth of dynamic Christianity in Europe."…. "The churches must speak to the world but they cannot do so with power until they have shown in their own life the reality of a fellowship which can bind peoples of diverse traditions, races and nations firmly together," in Henry Smith Leiper, ed., *Christianity Today: A Survey of the State of the Churches: Sponsored by the American Committee for the World Council of Churches* (New York: Morehouse-Gorham, 1947), 448-449 and 451.

6 Kenneth Slack, ed., *Hope in the Desert: The Churches' United Response to Human Need, 1944-1984* (Geneva: World Council of Churches, 1986), 9.

7 A. Livingston Warnshuis, "The Church Situation in Europe," National Lutheran Council, *News Bulletin Special*, 26 January 1945, 2, in PHS, UPC 161B, box 3. The American State Department supported this trip.

8 A.L. Warnshuis, *The Church's Battle for Europe's Soul* (New York: American Committee for the World Council of Churches, 1945), 18-19.

A. Livingston Warnshuis, author of a report on the condition of the church in war-struck Europe in 1945 (book cover).

in the reconstruction of the continent as it had stood up against the Nazis and had gained the confidence of the young generation.[9]

This assessment of Europe's religious strength led Warnshuis to caution Americans for "sympathetic understanding" that might be taken as condescending. Moreover, he warned "that American helpfulness would not be effectively given through the organization of small groups of separatist Christians, described as extensions of American Church denominations. In the struggle of these war years, such groups have either yielded to the governing powers and have been completely Nazified, or they have remained on the sidelines, exercising no influence upon the course of events." The "free churches have not been free, and the state churches have become free."[10] He believed in a new life for Europe's historic churches.

It was, as many other Americans realized, a grand opportunity: "... the discovery of how thoroughly paganized the masses in European countries have become has made evangelism a question of life and death for the churches. The opportunity now may be fleeing, and pagan forces temporarily made harmless will reappear in other forms unless they are overcome spiritually ... To give assistance in the reconstruction of the churches in Europe is to take part in the establishment of the Kingdom of Christ in the world."[11] In order to advance this goal and help Europe back on its feet, Warnshuis designed a plan to reconstruct Europe through this most important gesture of concerted action. All resources were pulled together internationally and then divided by the World Council's Department of Reconstruction and Inter-Church Aid according to national needs.

The first euphoria about the promise of opportunities subsided when American envoys discovered that the Protestant institutions in most of Europe had been more seriously weakened than they had anticipated. The burden of destruction, the loss of their social role, and the care for refugees multiplied the demands on their limited resources. The first wave of American liberators of Germany noticed the deep, deep despair in the country and numerous suicides. The mood was desperate, depressed by the wages of war, and with little hope of renewal.[12] Material aid not only saved physical lives, but also restored hope. Quick action was needed and as the richest partner in the WCC, the FCC

9 A.L. Warnshuis, "The Voice of the Martyrs," *Collier's Weekly*, 7 April 1945, 16-17; Warnshuis, *The Church's Battle*, esp. 16 and 18; Norman Goodall, *Christian Ambassador: A Life of A. Livingston Warnshuis* (Manhasset, NY: Channel Press, 1963), 129-146. The WCC adopted the European relief model of the European Central Bureau for Inter-Church Aid, headed by the Swiss theologian Adolf Keller. Warnshuis' biographer states that the WCC decided to merge with the IMC already in 1942 in order to create one world organization (p. 146).

10 Warnshuis, *The Church's Battle*, 27.

11 Ibid., 28.

12 Werner Sollors, *The Temptation of Despair: Tales of the 1940s* (Cambridge, MA: The Belknap Press of Harvard University Press, 2014), 6-9.

concentrated its combined relief efforts in one organization, the Church World Service in May 1946. Under its auspices 80 per cent of all relief goods from the United States – 3.4 million dollars in cash, and 5.4 million in food and clothing – entered Europe.[13]

Even though material aid was urgent, many Protestants in North America continued to entertain hopes for a spiritual renewal in Europe. The Presbyterian Church in the USA was one of the first to explicitly prepare a new course. In 1943 the foreign mission board of this church cancelled its older policy "that Europe is not to be considered foreign missionary ground for American Christians" and opened up specifically this possibility. The church's work in Portugal was the immediate result of this decision and supplemented the relief work.[14]

Mainline Hopes and Complexities: Material Aid and Spiritual Bonds

These mainline churches had to overcome their internal tensions between pacifists and realists before they could agree on a postwar strategy. Historian David A. Hollinger argued that the attack on Pearl Harbor effectively disabled the pacifist wing of the mainline churches, which cleared the way for the realists to include egalitarian and universalist ideals, that would roll back racism, imperialism, nationalism, and blatant capitalism, which were the structural obstacles to secure a "just and durable peace", as was the name of the commission that collected mainline Protestant ideas for the preparation of the postwar political order. Whatever their internal differences, the mainline Protestant leadership agreed that their churches could provide the principles that the United States needed to carry out its global responsibility. Their proposals echoed the anti-discrimination clauses and economic rights of the New Deal, which fanned the mistrust of a strong central power among many fundamentalists and evangelicals.[15]

13 Robert E. Stenning, *Church World Service: Fifty Years of Help and Hope* (New York: Friendly Press, 1996), 3-9.

14 Charles T. Leber, "Report on Europe," 20 January 1948, p. 2, PHS, UPC 161B, box 3. See for an overview: Duncan Hanson, "Europe," in Scott W. Sunquist and Caroline N. Becker, eds., *A History of Presbyterian Missions 1944-2007* (Louisville, KY: Geneva Press, 2008), 256-284.

15 David A. Hollinger, "The Realist-Pacifist Summit Meeting of March 1942 and the Political Reorientation of Ecumenical Protestantism in the United States," in David A. Hollinger, *After Cloven Tongues of Fire: Protestant Liberalism in Modern American History* (Princeton: Princeton University Press, 2013), 56-81; Matthew Avery Sutton, *American Apocalypse: A History of Modern Evangelicalism* (Cambridge: The Belknap Press of Harvard University Press, 2014), 232-262; Kevin M. Kruse, *One Nation Under God: How Corporate America Invented Christian America* (New York: Basic Books, 2015), 67-94.

The most urgent need during the war was the food supply. Food was not only a humanitarian need after the war, but also a strategic instrument in the war. A supply of food had to compensate for British military weakness, but as much as it was in the interest of the allies to stock food for military action, it was also necessary to restore the food supply in liberated areas. The United Nations Relief and Rehabilitation Administration (UNRRA) was surrounded by suspicion that its aid might go to the wrong people, former enemies or undeserving Russians, or to countries that could afford to buy food on the world market. At the receiving side, some European officials were wary of the strings attached. Also at the American side resistance mounted in the summer of 1946, from farmers, who wanted higher prices, consumers who wanted a stop to rationing, and from politicians smelling an election issue. But the political pressure of the Turkey and Greece crisis of early 1947 brought the food supply back on the agenda and inspired the Marshall Plan.[16]

As in wartime, relief was not only inspired by humanitarian concern, but it also served strategic ends in times of peace: bring Europe in the news, create sympathy for the organization in Europe, mobilize support, and establish fruitful contacts with European authorities to advance other levels of cooperation, and compete with other relief organizations.

The American campaigns to bring relief to Europe revealed the aspirations for the immediate postwar years. As early as September 1942, the Federal Council of Churches installed the Department of Reconstruction and Inter-Church Aid in order to renew church life in Europe.[17] From the very beginning the ideal was to collect the needs of the Protestant and Eastern Orthodox churches in Europe from the Geneva office and distribute the aid raised in the United States. Actually Dr. Samuel M. Cavert, General Secretary of the Federal Council of the Churches of Christ in America, asked all the denominations to trust the Inter-Church Aid committee to distribute their funds fairly, including those churches without connections to America. This seemed the most efficient way of bringing aid to Europe, because no other institution had access to the information about the most pressing needs. The question of distribution was left to the ecumenical councils in each country. The Department reviewed each proposal and transferred the approved projects to the churches who could render support.

It was the explicit purpose of the FCC to strengthen the churches already rooted in Europe, not to replace them. Programs took priority over buildings, but wooden structures in bombed-out areas were provided if no other meeting halls were available. Assistance consisted of bicycles for pastors to get around,

16 Ben Shephard, *The Long Road Home: The Aftermath of the Second World War* (London: The Bodley Head, 2010), 31-40, 56-57, 251-254.

17 Dr. Samuel M. Cavert, Memorandum on Policies and Objective of World Council of Churches in Reconstruction and Inter-Church Aid, 2 January 1946, PHS NCC RG 8, box 91 file Europe Committee.

salaries for severely underpaid clergy, funds for printing and training facilities, as well as material support for orphanages, retirement centers, and hospitals, for evangelization and social projects. There was special excitement for an ecumenical training center for Christian lay leaders, serving in the world. Later the committee added the direct care for the hungry and destitute to its mission. The board discovered that the national governments failed to provide the necessary care, which had grown more important ever since.

In April 1945 the American Committee for the World Council of Churches called for a great thank-offering on the Sunday after the peace in Europe was signed.[18] This initiative combined an expression of gratitude to fundraising for kindred institutions in Europe. Support for the impact of religion in Europe was necessary to prevent a next war. This joint activity enabled churches in Europe without partners overseas to receive aid. And it served to show that joint ecumenical action was better than separate denominational aid. For the sake of fair distribution the committee wanted interdenominational cooperation.[19] It feared that autonomous groups would raise food (esp. collected in Iowa) for specific churches only, which would miss other opportunities. For instance, Warnshuis invited the Christian Reformed Church, that was founded by Dutch immigrants, to join the Inter-church committee to better coordinate the aid to Holland. Even if the denomination decided against this affiliation, he hoped it would keep the committee informed about the needs in Holland so that it could use this information to allocate its funds. Practical considerations informed this initiative, in spite of the accusations by evangelicals of forced cooperation.[20]

The evangelicals had a second reason to suspect ecumenical actions. They feared that the ecumenical project would sacrifice evangelism in Europe. They were correct in their assessment of the priority to seek broad cooperation, but ignored the effort of the ecumenical network to evangelize Europe. It was the FCC's European partners that suggested that the evangelicals make an inventory of what was being done to spread the gospel in Western Europe, explore new methods, and hire one or two experts to coordinate a preaching campaign in designated areas. J. Hutchison Cockburn, the Scottish director of the Department of Reconstruction and Inter-church Aid in Geneva proposed this plan, but soon found out it was a cumbersome process. The committee did not seek a fire-and-brimstone preacher, such as Billy Sunday or Gypsy Smith, but

18 Press release, April 23, 1945, PHS NCC RG 8 Division of Overseas Ministries, 1914-1972, series 8 Church World Service, 1929-1972, box 91 "Europe Files, 1943-1949. Committee on Cooperation with Churches in Europe."

19 "Notes taken by William G. Schram at meeting held in dr. Barstow's office Wednesday, January 29th, 1947," Barstow/Lytle Files (Europe), 1943-1947, PHS NCC 8 box 91.

20 Warnshuis to J.J. Buiten, of the Netherlands War Relief Committee, Grand Rapids, MI, 10 July 1946, PHS NCC RG 8 box 91. More information about American evangelical and fundamentalist relief efforts will follow in chapter 3.

> a vital and courageous evangelical minister of a church, who knows the problem both from the people's side and from the Church's side, who is not so far committed to any one school of evangelical effort, and who is ready to learn from the quite notable evangelical work that is being done in France, Holland, Britain and America. Some of my brethren rather object to the word "Evangelism." Personally, I don't know a better word, but what we have in mind is "The spread of the Gospel and the building up of the Christian Church," and reports from several countries indicate that there are plans for such effort such as have not appeared in many generations.[21]

The author admitted that most ministers lacked the publicity skills that were needed to reach Europeans while the popular evangelism methods of the early twentieth century proved outdated.

Also World Council secretary, Visser 't Hooft supported this idea of outreach. That it did not lead to much action, was not the main point. The ecumenical movement tried to use the revival spirit in the mainline American churches and moreover, was aware that evangelism was a transnational undertaking.

The mainline Protestants invested more in material aid than in preaching. In 1948 Americans donated an estimated 5 million dollars in money and 10 million in kind to Europe, and Baptist minister Wayland Zwayer, secretary for Europe at the Church World Service, expected that this responsibility for Europe would continue, despite the new emergencies in Asia. In March 1949, he explained the need of collecting funds through interchurch channels, next to bilateral national church relations to his colleagues of the World Council Reconstruction Staff. American Protestants were very generous towards Europe, whatever the need, but wanted to see evidence that the European churches took charge of their reconstruction. His advice was cooperation among churches at both sides: "Ecumenical giving must be matched by ecumenical receiving."[22] He pushed an ecumenical program lest "sectarian responsibility cause us to take any backward step... The effect on the average American layman would be tragic."[23] It became clear that interchurch cooperation was as least as important as generosity. The ecumenical goal, however, did not overrule all denominational projects, as long as they did not overlap. Zwayer appreciated the work of the Baptist World Alliance to assist the Comité Inter

21 J. Hutchison Cockburn (former Moderator of the General Assembly of the Church of Scotland) to Barstow, 7 October 1946, Rapids, MI, 10 July 1946, PHS NCC RG 8 box 91 (file Europe committee).

22 "Reconstruction Today: How Giving Countries See it," p. 3, PHS NCC RG 8, box 90.

23 "Reconstruction Today: How Giving Countries See it," p. 2, PHS NCC RG 8, box 90; Merle Curti, *American Philanthropy Abroad: A History* (New Brunswick, NJ: Rutgers University Press, 1988), 504-505. In the fifties donations by ethnic groups declined while giving by religious groups increased.

Mouvement auprès des Évacués (CIMADE) in France in providing housing and care for refugees.[24]

On December 9, 1949 the Inter-Church agency of the NCC discussed a plan to "secure the maximum assistance of the most critical needs and the most promising enterprises of the European Churches."[25] This plan was made to create a flexible response to secure a fair distribution. That was the main reason for ecumenical cooperation. It's budget was close to 4 million dollars with an additional 1.2 million for priority needs. The money was meant for general aid including health programs, scholarships, youth work, refugees and aid to churches in various regions, especially in Eastern Europe, which found itself in similar conditions as Western Europe had seen in 1945.

The document showed that the agency's main concern was the vitality of the church in Eastern Europe, which had to find a creative solution for the ban on religious instruction in schools and for losing all its social services. It especially wanted to support the Protestants in Eastern Germany, fearing that the disappearance of religious instruction would chop away a crucial leg of Protestantism. Dr. Frederick J. Forell, previous director of the Inner Mission in Germany reported "... the church in Berlin is on the verge of collapse. Few people in the United States know how serious the situation of the church is. The collapse of the German church would be the greatest victory for communism and everything possible should be done to support it in this crisis."[26] This assessment encouraged the NCC to invest heavily in Germany and Eastern Europe. They understood the danger for a church to lose its main social function.

Zwayer's agency faced a dilemma of priorities, whether to help resettle the hundreds of thousands displaced persons from Europe in the United States or to provide relief and inter-church aid to rebuild religious institutions in Europe or in Asia. Behind this drive for cooperation was the American Protestant failure to match the provisions that Catholics and Jews made for their share of the quota of resettlement. Only in 1949 did they catch up.[27]

Next to this direct need in Europe, indirect needs elsewhere in the world presented themselves. The Foreign Mission Conference faced two other challenges: the orphaned missions program, which had lost their European sources of income in the war and were considered to be the most important evidence of the ecumenical movement, and aid to Asia. The problem arose when the denominational agencies (not the individual churches) that provided the funds for the Church World Service saw their means decline with 25 per cent

24 "Informal Report – Europe Visit, March 15-April 6, 1949," PHS NCC RG 8, box 90.

25 "Europe Files, 1943-1949. Committee on Cooperation with Churches in Europe, Meetings 1948-1949," "1950 Programme for Europe: An Advance Plan," PHS NCC RG 8, Division of Overseas Ministries, 1914-1972, series 8 Church World Service, 1929-1972, box 90.

26 "1950 Programme for Europe: An Advance Plan," p. 7.

27 "A Memorandum on the Crisis in Church World Service," 16 February 1950, PHS NCC RG 8, box 98.

in 1949. The full amount was allocated to pay the staff. In order to maintain its executive framework it cut back on funds available for Europe and Asia.

Zwayer noticed that whereas Protestants in minority positions had been reaching out, the churches which received assistance from the state and lost these privileges had to adapt. American support was needed for this transition.[28] The three major tasks were aid by an American church of their European counterpart, aid to Protestant minorities in European countries, and support of ecumenical activities. He therefore proposed to change the name from his department to Inter-Church Aid and Service to Refugees. In 1951, Zwayer prepared further plans for cooperation of North American missionary agencies with European churches.[29]

American Protestant observers praised the Europeans for their willingness to forgive each other and rebuild their churches.[30] In 1948 the Board of Foreign Missions of the Protestant churches collected 3.6 million dollars for reconstruction in Europe. These funds were used for rebuilding churches and schools, print literature, support education, and provide temporary staff, for which $ 25,000 was earmarked. At the end of 1947, Presbyterian Charles T. Leber, the secretary for Europe of the Board of Foreign Missions, traveled the continent for six weeks. In his report he emphasized the spiritual needs: "The people of Europe are hungry, cold and mentally and spiritually sick... All eyes turn to America for healing. America cannot do it. But Jesus Christ can. As important and necessary as political and economic programs may be, it is far from sentimentality to insist that the essential issue in Europe today is moral and spiritual."[31]

Reports from France revealed that American financial aid helped the Protestants there to grow.[32] A Presbyterian pastor, Charles Arbuthnot, another former US army chaplain, who was supported by the American Board of Foreign Missions as the United Presbyterian Church representative in Europe, confirmed the need for France to return to Christianity as so few citizens had a living faith and the efforts to evangelize the population of Grenoble as the newly arrived Lutheran refugees from the Baltic who strengthened the French Protestant community.[33] Three years later, the fraternal workers of the Presbyterian Church reported signs of revival, visible in "a return to popular reading of the Bible, a revival of Biblical theology, a larger entry into Christian vocation on the part of young people, a desire to recover lay witness in order to bring the church closer to the alienated groups, and, in general, a willingness

28 "Secretary's Report for Europe Committee of Foreign Missions Conference for N. America," 10 October 1949, PHS NCC RC 8, box 98.
29 Way to Marlin D. Farnum, October 23, 1951, PHS NCC RG 8, box 98, 1949-1951.
30 See Letter nr. 6, Charles T. Leber, 7 January 1948, PHS UPC 161B, box 3.
31 Charles T. Leber, "Report on Europe," 20 January 1948, 5, PHS UPC 161B, box 3.
32 See Letter nr. 6, Charles T. Leber, 7 January 1948, (page 3), PHS UPC 161B, box 3.
33 Charles Arbuthnot to Charles T. Leber, Grenoble, 3 April 1948, PHS UPC 161B, box 3.

Publicity material for one of the 40 church-rebuilding projects sponsored by the Department of Reconstruction and Inter-Church Aid of the World Council of Churches. This picture shows the cornerstone-laying ceremony of the building of a "Notkirche" at Mannheim-Waldhof, in the American zone of Germany, in 1948. The WCC had invested $ 10,000 in this project.
[Religious News Service Photo, RNS-RG1_P-7795 held by the Presbyterian Historical Society, Philadelphia, PA]

to re-examine without prejudice every practical form of organization of the church's life."[34] This result matched the ideals of the Secretariat for Evangelism of the World Council of Churches in Geneva, which published a recommendation for evangelism in France in 1951. The report realized that the parishes had to adapt to an open, urban, individualized culture, if it wanted to be relevant to the modern workers. It sought a solution in a cooperative effort of a team of families that worked towards a communitarian goal, offering social services, and mutual insurance. The program developed from the Protestant church, but that was a small minority: evangelism was 'social evangelism'. It rejected the urge to stimulate personal salvation, as that would separate the personal from the social sphere. It promoted a non-institutionalized living with the workers.[35]

34 Meeting of Presbyterian Fraternal Workers in Europe, Geneva, July 11-15, 1951, PHS UPC 161B, box 3.

35 Secretariat for Evangelism of the World Council of Churches in Geneva, *Evangelism in France* (Geneva, 1951), 30-44. Actually, the instruments that this overview highlighted were similar to those of the evangelical missions: education, films, literature, training, team work, parachurch organizations.

Similarly the board members rejoiced about the Protestant minorities in Southern Europe becoming stronger. They observed a strong desire for unity, but actual slow cooperation. Most funds went to projects by Europeans, not those staffed by American fraternal workers. Their priority was in Portugal and Spain to strengthen the "evangelical cause" but without domination or paternalism. However, the scale of these activities remained miniscule, as it was limited to two couples in Lisbon and one in Madrid.

A second area of Presbyterian support was programmatic: church projects for youth, women, and immigrants, refugees, and to Reformed seminaries in Germany. In Portugal they planned to stage public lectures about Protestantism and Latin Culture, as the Catholic Church claimed those two were oppositional.[36] The presentation given by the President of Princeton Theological Seminary Dr. John A. Mackay in Lisbon received a respectful report in the media, thwarted the fundamentalist efforts to get a following and connected the few Protestants to the larger community.[37] At the sideline the Presbyterians tried to maintain contact with Eastern European churches.

On October 1, 1952, the Presbyterian Advisory Committee on Work in Europe decided unanimously that it would need to stay in Europe, even now the most relief work had been completed, and that it would even needed to expand "international interchange in Christian service as being essential to building the 'ecumenical'."[38] They experienced some of that exchange when they noticed that French Protestants used "Negro spirituals" as means to communicate the gospel, which was not done in the United States by white churches.[39] By the mid-1950s the Presbyterians strongly believed in the combination of evangelism with social work and education. They hoped that the many scholarships to America (1,220 to date in 1954) would help reform the Older Churches by infusing them with experiences from other parts of the world.[40]

The motives and goals for evangelical and mainline churches' concern with Europe were much closer than either of them admitted. They both concluded that Europe was no longer Christian and feared that the Christian character of the nineteenth century with its humanitarian legacy and democracy would be lost in a few generations. However, the added phrase "... to encourage and strengthen the ecumenical fellowship and service of European churches..." raised evangelical and fundamentalist eyebrows. That was exactly what traditional Protestants wanted to prevent.

36 Charles Arbuthnot, Geneva to Dr. Leber, 14 September 1951, PHS UPC 161B, box 3.

37 Letter by Michael P. Testa, 6 September 1951, PHS UPC 161B, box 3.

38 "Advisory Committee on Work in Europe," 1 October 1952, PHS UPC 161B, box 3.

39 E. John Hamlin to Margaret Flory of the Presbyterian Board of Foreign Missions in New York, 7 May 1954, PHS UPC 161B, box 3.

40 "Europe," [1954], p. 5, PHS UPC 161B, box 3. For an overview of Presbyterian staff in Europe, see appendix A to this report.

Even after the emergency ended and Europe had recovered in the early 1950s, aid continued to flow from the United States and churches remained involved.[41] The rationale for this aid was the unequal distribution of the prosperity. This happened within countries as many people didn't benefit from their country's recovery, and between countries as Southeast and Eastern Europe were far from prosperous. Moreover, the American government made enormous surplus of food available and asked the churches to distribute it, which allowed them to reach previously unreached groups. In addition they assisted in helping people help themselves by sending fertilizer, tools, machinery.

The outward gaze to find people in need opened up new areas, such as Argentina and Algeria. Changing arrangements kept the aid offices on edge. While the US government increased its supply of surplus goods for Europe, it stopped paying for transportation. Some countries, Germany and Yugoslavia assumed the transport costs, but most did not. This meant that the costs increased while the revenues decreased. The NCC decided to concentrate shipments to areas of Protestant minorities such as the tiny evangelical church of Greece. CWS helped especially the former church workers in East Germany, refugee centers and Protestant institutions in Italy. In 1955 a million dollars went to Italy and France, more than 80% was for food and vitamins. Increased efficiency made the CWS aware of new needs. So despite the recovery of Europe, the demands for aid increased to provide for those suffering from the severe winter of 1956, to help the refugees in Italy, and to invest in the growing number of self-help projects. The denominational contributions in 1956 were expected to cover only 60 per cent of the $ 125,000 operating budget and in 1955 the deficit had consumed all reserve funds. 80 per cent of the aid to Europe was for refugees coming from the east.[42] A German thank-you letter expressed the impact: "With these gifts you acquired for yourselves in our land thousands of grateful friends who owe to you their lives and the courage to go on living."[43] But by 1960 the German people could take care of their own. Material aid was not necessary.

The reduction in material aid in the late 1950s did not end American mainline churches' interest in Europe. The United Presbyterian Churches expressed their motive for Europe as follows: "Europe is the point of origin of ideologies and secular religions which everywhere today shake the foundations of mankind. No concern for ecumenical mission and deeper relations

41 Report for 1955 (frame 5525): Edward MacSweeney, *Amerikanische Wohlfahrtshilfe für Deutschland 1945-1950* (Freiburg i.Br.: Caritas, 1950), PHS NCC RG 8, box 104.

42 Minutes DCWS Board of Managers Meeting October 25, 1956. (5549): "The needs of the Europe Program may not be so vast as those of the other areas of the world. But the world's greatest needs are all too often inaccessible. Europe has distribution system experienced in making every gift count where it can do most good." PHS NCC RG 8, box 104.

43 Letter from D.F.M. Münchmeyer to Morris E. Wilson, Stuttgart, October 6, 1959, PHS NCC RG 8, box 105.

between the Churches can leave the Christians of Europe out of account. Partnership in sharing spiritual gifts and burdens is essential."[44] The relationship had lasted more than a century. The material support went to small Protestant minority churches and "pioneering efforts in industrial evangelism and Christian social service, theological education, student, youth and children's work, lay centers, and mass communication." The Presbyterian coordinators devoted themselves to meet students and organize lectures in Switzerland, support the American Churches in Paris and Berlin, run a center for evacuees, assist Protestant seminaries in Italy and Spain, Belgium, Portugal and hospitals. Most of it went to institutional support.[45]

Fundamentalist Fears and Rescue Plans for Europe

Also conservative Protestants in the United States became aware of the significant place of Europe, but they observed it from a distance. They were more spectators who were examining their bibles for clues, and in the meantime spent most of their energy in domestic battles. Their priorities outside their own continent was on the non-Western mission fields, and only a few groups made a systematic effort to assess what was happening in Europe. It was an immigrant pastor and editor who collected the scattered information in the monthly *The Prophetic Word* which contributors had intimate direct experience in Europe as missionaries, while he defined Europe's role in the current phase of the world's history within a framework of prophetic thinking.[46]

Editor and publisher of *The Prophetic Word,* Gans P. Raud, was also the founder and president of the American Seminary of the Bible, in Brooklyn, New York. The monthly served as the seminary's mouthpiece to muster support for its mission in Europe. It identified with a small and select subsection of America's Christians, believing that only three to four million people in the United States received sound Christian preaching.[47] The monthly claimed a readership of one hundred thousand.[48] Its authors were often American or British missionaries from Europe, many were affiliated with the European Christian Mission (also known as the Bible Christian Union). In 1939 the mis-

44 BFM COEMAR Records, Work in Europe, June 1959, PHS UPC 161B box 4.

45 NCC could not distribute care packages in Spain and Portugal and sent a few thousand dollars each year to assist the Protestant ministries there.

46 Carpenter, *Revive us Again*, 89-109.

47 "Do You Know America?" *The Prophetic Word* (September 1942), 14.

48 *The Prophetic Word* 115 (October 1946) inside cover.

Gans P. Raud, picture taken from: *A Life Lived for God: The Story of G.P. Raud, Founder of the Bible Christian Union.*
[New York: Bible Christian Union, 1955]

sion counted more than one hundred missionaries working in twelve countries mainly in Eastern Europe.[49] After the war the work moved to Western Europe.

Raud's work offers a unique access to the mindset of the fundamentalist and conservative American evangelicals about Europe. He interpreted the spiritual origin of the World War as a satanic attack on the sources of missionary activity in Protestant Europe. This attack began in Germany: " ... because the German Church neglecting prayer and the Word of God, had listened to higher criticism and nationalistic philosophies which fostered pride of race and made the Church the servant of the state."[50] As a consequence the war broke and threatened to rob Britain and other western countries of their colonies which would halt the spread of the gospel. This line of argument was a common fundamentalist explanation, which linked an alarmist result – the end of missions – to the source of religious liberalism.

49 G.P. Raud, *A Life Lived for God: The Story of G.P. Raud, Founder of the Bible Christian Union* (New York: Bible Christian Union, 1955), 24. After establishing a satellite school in Toronto, Canada, he founded small and short-lived bible schools in Europe: in the United Kingdom, in Marseille (1947), and Rotterdam (1948) and launched magazines in the United Kingdom, Holland, Germany, Switzerland, and France. After Raud died in Paris in 1954, the Bible Christian Union linked up with the Evangelical Alliance Mission with which it merged in 1994.

50 G.P. Raud, "Behind the Scenes in the European War," *The Prophetic Word* (March 1941), 3-6, 33, quote on 5.

The immigrant editor warned his readers that America was not immune to this trend. As the richest nation in the world and most active in missions, the United States was on Satan's list of main targets. At the beginning of the war, he prophesized: "Should Britain fall, America will not enjoy the liberty it has to-day; circumstances will demand closer government regulation of our lives, including, probably, Christian work. A British victory is a victory for America and for foreign missions."[51] A defeat of England would close the door for the gospel in Europe, locking 400 million people out. But the journal was not defeatist. Stories about continued interest in the bible in Europe, encouraged the journal to issue a call to be ready for a sudden peace.[52]

Of course a journal carrying this name had to address the burning question about the Millennium. But Raud wanted his readers to remain active and not conclude that Europe or Russia were lost forever. He warned his readers that the present situation with assaults on Europe and Palestine were not the final battles of Gog in Magog in Ezekiel 38 and 39 and in Revelation 20. The Gog-prophesies in these two books referred to different periods, according to Raud: Ezekiel to the inauguration of the Millennium, and the Revelation text to the end of time.[53]

Raud's concentration on Europe not only reflected his own Estonian background but was also a result of his thinking in terms of racial superiority. Europe was important to God because it was the location of the white race that had dominated the world and had shown a better response to the gospel than colored people and thus had sent more missionaries.[54] Over and over again Raud explained in his magazine that St. Paul, the best preacher among the disciples, was sent to Western Europe because he had the best skills: "The white nations must be evangelized – even though they were civilized!"[55]

Had Britain and America sent more missionaries to Europe, the chances for war would have reduced because Spain could have been an ally instead of an enemy, and France would have resisted Germany.[56] He regretted that the missionary stream had been directed to Africa and Asia and not to Europe. The editor was optimistic, that the war had softened the hearts of the Europeans for the reception of the gospel based on his experience of thousands of

51 G.P. Raud, "Are the Dark Ages Returning to Europe?" *The Prophetic Word* (April 1941), 3.
52 W. Stuart Harris, "News from the European Field," Ibid. (April 1941), 26.
53 G.P. Raud, "Gog and Magog: Will They Arise in this Age?" Ibid. (September 1941), 3-4.
54 G.P. Raud, "Europe Important to God," Ibid. (October 1941), 21. This was an echo of the Anglo-Saxon expectation raised by late nineteenth-century authors such as Josiah Strong. See Paul Boyer, *When Time Shall Be No More: Prophecy Belief in Modern American Culture* (Cambridge: Harvard University Press, 1994), 229.
55 G.P. Raud, "Europe Important to God," *The Prophetic Word* (October 1941), 21-23; "Why Europe Needs the Gospel," Ibid. (September 1945), 357-363, quote on 357.
56 G.P. Raud, "The Role of America and Great Britain in Europe," Ibid. (December 1941), 34-36.

conversions after World War I among soldiers and refugees.[57] The good record of Britain in distant mission fields had gained God's favor.[58] To make up for that neglect before the war more American missionaries had to go to Europe to secure its future. Already in August 1942, the European Christian Mission began to recruit potential missionaries for Europe for after the war, though it also prepared to bring relief.[59] Europe was weak. The Protestant nations had suffered great monetary losses, and lost human lives, especially among the Jews.[60] This news was seen through a spiritual lens. When the horrendous fate of the European Jews became known in early 1943, the monthly feared the extinction of the Jews and called for a daily prayer for the rescue of the Jews from Hitler's plans. Otherwise they were lost without hearing the gospel.[61]

This missionary goal undergirded Raud's interpretation. The purpose of the *Prophetic Word* was not to prove the bible right, but to build support for the church to "call out and bring to maturity the members of the church." The monthly listed some surprising developments, such as the withdrawal of Turkish troops from the Balkans, as probable fulfillments of prophesies in the books of Daniel of Revelation, but usually felt more comfortable with more general prophecies such as "God calls out from the Gentiles a people for his name" as in Acts 15:14 and that a remnant of Israel would be saved (Romans 11:5), which together would create a new Church of Christ.[62]

The editor placed these prophesies in a historical narrative of political success: "Countries which have maintained conditions favoring the dissemination of the gospel at home and abroad enjoy the greatest measure of prosperity, enlightenment, and prestige. Two leading nations, the United States and Great Britain, hold prominent positions in world evangelization."[63] He predicted even larger roles for the British and Americans in international affairs after the war. That was part of the divine plan, which had secured the discovery and peopling of North America after the Reformation, so that it became a Protestant stronghold, secured by the separation of church and state. The arrival of many immigrants from countries closed to Protestant missionaries had exposed them to the gospel. Yet, some undermined America's religious values or felt too comfortable to spread them.[64]

57 G.P. Raud, "The Lamps of God Shining in Europe," *The Prophetic Word* (January 1942) 5-7.
58 "Great Britain and Europe," Ibid. (September 1942), 15.
59 "The Future Europe," Ibid. (August 1942), 6-7.
60 "Attack and Counter Attack in Europe," Ibid. (November 1942), 38-40.
61 "An Urgent Call," Ibid. (January 1943), 3.
62 G.P. Raud, "The Roman Empire, Rising or Falling?" Ibid. (December 1942), 4; "What Prophecy is Being Fulfilled To-day?" Ibid. (February 1943), 56-58. See "The Key to the Scriptures," in Raud, *A Life Lived for God*, 65-72.
63 Ibid., 57.
64 "The Unique Place of America in Divine Plan," *The Prophetic Word* (July 1943), 291-296.

The destruction caused by the war had a spiritual meaning: Europe looked like a great ploughed field, Raud's leading man in Europe W. Harris Stuart explained, and this image promised a harvest.[65] In the midst of the war, Raud mapped out his vision of Europe and promoted it to the top of evangelists' priorities.[66] This spiritual reading of the times blocked a blind faith in political solutions that excluded God. It took the calls for world peace plans as a ploy of Satan to use "the unconscious cooperation of unsaved men in order to bring about, if possible, a world where God is shut out entirely, where all military, economic, educational, political, and religious activities bend to his authority and worship... Not an international police force but the prayers of believers are the most potent means to obtain peace."[67] Later that year, the editor repeated his low expectation for a successor of the League of Nations, but not all political proposals were doomed. Raud emphasized the need for freedom of religion in Europe, as the most important of Franklin Roosevelt's Four Freedoms.[68]

American conservative Christians were pessimistic about the course of human history. Even if the Axis powers were defeated, prospects for a lasting peace looked grim.[69] Thomas MacDonald, the associate editor of *The Prophetic Word*, repeated the need to evangelize Europe at a planning conference in early 1944. European politics would not change, MacDonald believed, as internal rivalries must lead to new wars. The best strategy was to invest in those countries with the chances for mobilization of staff and money. American churches welcomed European students to liberal seminaries and he proposed to beat liberals at their own game by opening bible schools in Europe. The European student "... needs the foreign worker to help him know his Bible, to strengthen him in the life of prayer and faith and in his executive work."[70] Despite the fact that mainline European Protestant thinkers had reached similar conclusions in identifying Nazism as a tribal, pagan religion, MacDonald was part of a growing militant mood against theological modernism, which he defined as "the road to paganism, pantheism, or even atheism." He explained: "A country where modernism dominates the churches becomes sooner or later a mission field."[71] Not surprisingly, Nazi Germany was the key example.

65 "Christ's Return and European Events," *The Prophetic Word* (March 1943), 126-129.

66 G.P. Raud, "Have Russia and Europe Had Their Chance?" Ibid. (October 1943), 465-482.

67 "Postwar Planning in Relation to Prophecy," Ibid. (January 1944), 4-5.

68 "Deciding the Fate of a Continent," Ibid. (November 1944), 482 .

69 Boyer, *When Time*, 111-112. For similar arguments against international politics without God see Markku Ruotsila, *The Origins of Christian Anti-Internationalism: Conservative Evangelicals and the League of Nations* (Washington DC: Georgetown University Press, 2008), 171-185.

70 Thomas MacDonald, "The Potential Values in Europe," *The Prophetic Word* March 1944, 97-104, quote on 103.

71 See for a condemnation of Nazism the work of the Dutch theologian Hendrik Kraemer, *The Christian Message in a Non-Christian World* (New York: Harper, 1938), 17. Quotation by MacDonald in the issue of June 1944, 258.

However, theological modernism was not the only threat. In early 1945, *The Prophetic Word* noticed with concern that the Catholic Church regained its leading position in education in France, which showed a renewed spiritual interest and a lack of alternatives to Catholicism.[72] The editor was moderately hopeful that the San Francisco conference to launch the United Nations Organization would strengthen freedom of religion in the world and urged the readers to pray for this goal. Meanwhile reports from various European nations noticed more openness for Protestants but also warned that this new tolerance might inaugurate a new world religion, which would exclude the claims of Christianity on the truth.[73] The editor used the authoritative *New York Times* to picture Europe as the "New Dark Continent", quoting the leading European correspondent C.L. Sulzberger: "The soul of Europe today represents a Luca Signorelli Day of Judgment fresco: it is warped, twisted, agonized and not yet surfeited with blood-letting."[74] This gloomy portrait strengthened the pessimistic outlook that the editor had on human moral progress, though allowing some ray of hope.[75] Increased cooperation among nations marked the advance of a unified world regime, with uniform rules and no space for individual liberties or faith.[76]

Germany's surrender in May 1945 did not set the fundamentalist mind at rest, as the main causes of the war had not been addressed. The contents of the monthly magazine was not as apocalyptic as its title indicated. Its main prophesy was that God would build his church and the readers could help fulfill this prophesy by prayer and financial contributions.[77] The famine in Europe and the enormously high casualty rates were signs of the horsemen of the Apocalypse (in *Revelation* 6: 7-8) and heralded the approach of an age of tribulation. This interpretation warned the readers to be suspicious of announcement of (false) peace.[78] The editor calculated that half of Europe's population, two hundred million, professed no religion and were easy victims of the Communist promise of salvation.[79] The world had shrunk now that transcontinental bombing was an imminent threat.[80] Advocates of planned internationalism substituting for national sovereignty, such as Harold Laski, paved the road for world dominance.[81]

72 "The World Scene," *The Prophetic Word* (March 1945), 124.
73 "From the Editor's Desk," Ibid. (May 1945), 210-211.
74 C.L. Sulzberger, "Europe: The New Dark Continent," *New York Times*, 18 March 1945, 5, 50-52. Reprinted in abridged form in *The Prophetic Word* (June 1945), 241-247.
75 "Out of Balance," *The Prophetic Word* (June 1945), 257. Reports about the Netherlands confirmed that the austere circumstances did not bring out the best in people, see 248-249.
76 "The Tendency to Uniformity," *The Prophetic Word* (June 1945), 258.
77 "The Prophetic Value of Our Witness," Ibid. (June 1945), 259.
78 *The Prophetic Word* (July-August 1945), 291-302.
79 Ibid. (September 1945), 361.
80 Ibid. (December 1945), 500.
81 Ibid. (February 1946), 83.

Raud saw a renewed interest among educated lay people for reading the bible, which he attributed to his own 25 year preaching career in Europe.[82] Yet, a real break-through did not happen. He blamed the delay to the modernist teaching of the bible in the main churches and the call for reformation instead of regeneration.[83]

In 1946, the effects of the peace became visible and Raud's mission had to put his ideas into practice. The Baltic origin of the editor made him sensitive to the Allies for allowing the Soviet Union to rob the Baltic states of their livestock, food, and possessions. This caused unprecedented starvation in that region. In April 1946 Raud denounced the concessions that the United States and Britain had done to "Russia", which was a godless country with no scruples.[84]

Raud proclaimed "Europe the Center of Present Prophecy" in the October 1946 issue.[85] A poem expressed Europe's need and America's answer: [86]

> Will you listen to the cry of Europe?
> Will you hearken as her children weep?
> They are hungry, but the fields are barren,
> They are thirsty and the well is deep.
> ...
> They are waiting, Europe's millions waiting,
> Only few are freed by Christ as yet,
> Who will go, and who will help the going,
> Hasten then, before the sun is set!

The plan was quite simple: distribute the bible or parts of it and that would take care of its own.[87] Apparently the number of students applying at the American Seminary of the Bible in Brooklyn swelled in the spring of 1947. Simultaneously the monthly declared that most pulpits and seminaries denied Christ's divinity and were filled with the spirit of the anti-Christ.[88] The missionary call functioned as a factor in the struggle for educational survival.

While many prophetic interpreters underscored that the world was living in the shadow of the atomic bomb, which dwarfed all hope of man-made solu-

82 G.P. Raud, "The Bible-reading Movement in Europe," *The Prophetic Word* (March 1946), 98-101. It escaped Raud that these meetings resembled the prewar elitist gatherings of the Moral Rearmament Movement.

83 "Revival Imperative in America," Ibid. (March 1946), 140-144.

84 "Men and Policy in Postwar Europe," Ibid. (April 1946), 190-192; "Mass Starvation in Europe," Ibid. (June 1946), 284.

85 G.P. Raud, "Europe the Center of Present Prophecy," Ibid. (October 1946), 393-400.

86 D. Phelps, "What Light for Europe?" Ibid. (November 1946), 441-446.

87 Della Phelps, "True Tales of European Christians," Ibid. (January 1947), 39.

88 *The Prophetic Word* (April 1947), 224 and 243.

tions, the *Prophetic Word* continued to stress the enduring central political role of European powers:

> Four-fifths of all African believers live in British territories. There are four times as many Protestants as there are Catholics in British territories. That, dear friends, is what it means to have an evangelized European country controlling territory in other parts of the world. We must look to God that He will help us get the gospel into the nations for Europe, especially into those which hold influence over other lands. All that God will do in reaching the white people of Europe will have its reaction throughout the entire world. God's work will prosper everywhere if we will go to Europe first.[89]

The European Christian Mission extended its activities to Western European countries with a dual purpose to reach Catholics, such as in the Netherlands where a Mr Looy did open-air preaching in the Catholic south, and to bolster the number of true Spirit-filled Christians by establishing a bible school and a magazine. Again the seed of destruction was liberal theology, which had cast doubts in many hearts.[90] This cause was also a call for a different curriculum. In the meantime the mission agency distributed clothing and food to its coworkers in Europe. Raud's conclusion was "Truly, Europe is ripe for the sowing of the gospel. Everywhere the hears have been plowed by suffering, starvation, and bereavement: they are prepared soil."[91] The editor positioned Europe ever more forcefully at the divine timetable: "Europe has been and will remain the center of the major activities of God and Satan until the end of this age. After Christ comes for His church, the center will be transferred to Palestine and the Middle East."[92] John Winston, who worked for the Belgian Gospel Mission, confirmed this line of thought. Europeans had a tremendous influence on the world as world travelers, colonizers, governors, owners of trade and commerce, models of culture and society for others, and as people who were the cause of war and possibly sought world domination. However, since very few Europeans knew the bible, they were ignorant about the arrival of a new phase in history.[93] The events in Palestine indicated that the next dispensation was about to begin.[94]

Raud's interpretation echoed in fundamentalist circles. W.O.H. Garman, president of the fundamentalist American Council of Christian Churches (ACCC) made a tour of Europe as a guest of the State Department in late 1947 and reported completely in line with the *Prophetic Word* that Europe harvest-

89 Thomas MacDonald, "A History Lesson for Missionaries," *The Prophetic Word* (May 1947), 277; Boyer, *When Time*, 118-119, 136-137.
90 *The Prophetic Word* (December 1947), 660, 665.
91 Ibid. (December 1947), 672.
92 Ibid. (January 1948), 30.
93 Ibid. (February 1948), 67-68.
94 Ibid. (March 1948), 129.

ed the bitter fruit of modernism. He expressed his hope that bible schools would change the continent.[95] At the end of the year, Arie Kok, a former Dutch diplomat in China and chair of the foreign relations commission of the ACCC, spoke to the students of the Seminary of the Bible that conditions in Europe seemed difficult, but that new opportunities arose as the continent was full of hungry hearts.[96]

In February 1950, Gans Raud warned his readers not about the imminent threat of the Bomb as such, but as an opportunity to preach salvation. He was more concerned about liberal Christians united in the World Council of Churches who might close the mission fields to evangelical missionaries. Similarly the growth of atheistic communism might block the advance of the gospel.[97] In fact, the *Prophetic Word* kept its distance from the identification of specific political events on the world scene. Too much emphasis on the apocalyptic demise of the planet would tempt believers to lose heart and it wanted to activate people.[98] An internal tension between passivity and activism accompanied this kind of prophetic interpretation. Divine scenarios could only be accepted, not changed, but this went against the urgency of the times and the call for action.[99]

The *Prophetic Word* occupied a unique place in the Protestant publishing world with its focus on Europe. Thanks to its European roots, direct information sources, and independent nature, it could develop a comprehensive Eurocentric interpretation of history based on fundamentalist convictions that offered a most explicit and urgent rationale for action. However, within the conservative branch of American Protestantism it was a specialist operation.

Scattered Perspectives

Evangelical magazines with broader horizons that reached conservative audiences with a general contents reported less frequently on Europe than the *Prophetic Word*. These periodicals shared the function of the *Prophetic Word* as pillars for bible schools. *The King's Business*, issued from the Bible Institute of Los Angeles, and *Moody Monthly*, connected to Moody Bible Institute in Chicago, were the most prominent ones.[100] Despite the domestic and nation-

95 *The Prophetic Word* (May 1948), 263-267 and (September 1948), 451.
96 Arie Kok, "In Europe the Wind is Contrary," *The Prophetic Word* (November 1948), 990.
97 G.P. Raud, "Are Fields Closing to Foreign Missionaries?" Ibid. (February 1950), 65; (November 1950), 580.
98 Boyer, *When Time*, 146-147.
99 Ibid., 219, 252.
100 See for similar journals in this period, James Enns, "Sustaining the Faithful and Proclaiming the Gospel in a Time of Crisis: The Voice of Popular Evangelical Periodicals During the Second World War," in L. Guenther, ed., *Historical Papers 2004* (N.p.: Canadian Society of Church History, 2004), 113-132.

al orientation of these magazines was visible in their comments on the news from an American perspective, which included a rejection of any plans to outlaw war by submitting the nations to an international body. This idea sounded "strangely similar to the old formula for getting rid of rats by burning down the barn," the editor of *The King's Business* argued.[101] The same editor blamed Darwinism and the concept of the survival of the fittest for causing the war, thus turning the intellectual struggle against evolutionism as an instrument against the downfall of the United States.[102]

This peculiar religious perspective grew up from the late 1930s, as international affairs became more dangerous. From the outset of World War II, many conservative Christians expected the manifestation of the Antichrist. This lead to highly original interpretations, such as the one by Louis S. Bauman, pastor of the First Brethren Church in Long Beach California. He identified the Antichrist's advance in an accumulation of economic, political, and spiritual power in Europe. In line with anti-Catholic tradition, he saw the papacy as the Antichrist. The Pope used the political power of Mussolini to gain power. Mussolini played with Nazi Germany to threaten the Jews, who called on him as the pseudo-Messiah.[103] This creative reading of current events showed the flexibility of this interpretation. Within half a decade the papal ecclesiastical threat would be replaced by the ecumenical movement as the sign of the Antichrist.[104]

When World War II spread in Europe in May 1940, mainline Christians had to reassess their pacifism and increasingly were concerned with the immediate fate of the European Jews, evangelical Christians considered these events as part of the end times, whatever the specific scenario.[105] The authoritative Moody Church moderated the idea of an imminent apocalypse reminding its audience that wars and rumors of wars were signs of the end, but not the end itself. "The rise of the beast, the anti-Christ, in the day of the great tribulation will be by and through satanic power which is something far different than even the worst that human malevolence can suggest or perpetrate."[106] The events were caused by humans, who could not create a period of global peace. The editor admonished his flock to pray "for all that are in authority that the affairs of the world may be so ordered that we may lead a quiet and peace-

101 Dan Gilbert, "Significance of the News," *The King's Business* (February 1941), 43, 79.

102 Dan Gilbert, "The Forces Behind the War," Ibid. (March 1941), 86.

103 Louis S. Bauman, "The Three Stepping-Stones of the Antichrist to Power," Ibid. (October 1940), 365, 370, 397.

104 John A. Patten, "The Word 'Happens' in Europe," Ibid. (April 1943), 122. This was not yet the case in 1943. Willem Visser 't Hooft, secretary general of the WCC (in process of formation) was quoted positively for his observation about a revival of religious interest in occupied Holland.

105 Andrew Preston, *Sword of the Spirit, Shield of Faith* (New York: Alfred A. Knopf, 2012), 327-341.

106 "Shadows of the Great Tribulation," *The Moody Church News* 25.6 (June 1940).

able life in all godliness."[107] When in the fall of 1941 the conviction grew that America would become involved in the war, Harry A. Ironside, Moody's senior pastor, called for prayer for "an early and righteous peace."[108] Meanwhile the call for salvation never ceased, as the poem "Soldier Boy" expressed:

> Soldier boy, soldier boy, as you are going
> To fight with your might for the Red, White and Blue
> While the distress of the nation is growing
> And country is calling, God too calls for you.[109]

The editors used most war news to serve domestic ends. Kenneth M. Monroe, Dean of the Bible Institute of Los Angeles, BIOLA, explained the intellectual causes of the World War in February 1941: higher criticism, philosophical skepticism, pessimism, and animalism.[110] The question of God's will for this war was personalized as a judgment on pleasure-seeking humankind, "leaving His creatures to their own devices."[111] An army chaplain called for reform, to change "our God-dishonoring educational institutions, about America's pleasure madness, and about demanding that Bible truth be preached from the nation's pulpits."[112] The physical enemy, mostly Nazi Germany, was the instrument of the spiritual enemy, which was feared for its universal power. This feature allowed fundamentalists to pass the torch from fascism during the war to liberalism after the war. But they lost the leading position in this battle to a new formation of evangelicals, who gradually exchanged separation for cooperation.

Evangelicals Prepare for Action

During the war the more cooperative part of conservative Protestants joined hands to set up a new association to challenge the global liberal network. The next chapter will explain this in more detail. At the end of the war evangelicals had only recently organized themselves nationally and were still in the process of choosing their leaders.

Among the most explicit interpreters of this view was James DeForest Murch, the editor of *United Evangelical Action*, house organ of the National

107 "From the Editor's Viewpoint," *The Moody Church News* 25.7 (July 1940).
108 "Wars and Rumors of Wars," Ibid. 26.11 (November 1941).
109 Wilda Schrock Oatly, Ibid. 27.6 (June 1942), 5.
110 Kenneth M. Monroe, "Will America, like Germany, Suffer Defeat?" *The King's Business* (February 1941), 46-48.
111 "Could God Stop the War?" *The Moody Church News* 27.11 (November 1942).
112 James B. McLeroy, "The Civilian's Tremendous Responsibility," *The King's Business* (June 1943), 208.

Association of Evangelicals (NAE). In 1948, he warned American Protestants that the World Council of Churches (WCC) could very likely develop into a super church. His quote "one church for one world" as the goal of the new global organization resembled to fundamentalists the monopoly of the Roman Catholic Church in the Middle Ages. Murch saw too many ominous mechanisms at work in the WCC to be at ease: the potential result of one Super-Church, which allowed all kinds of theological aberrations and leftist social policies, which would disrupt effective evangelism and missions, and its thirst for power would threaten to oust those who brought the traditional evangelical message. The WCC denied these charges and emphasized it was only a council, but the goal of global unity made many evangelicals uncomfortable and alert. Some gave the WCC the benefit of the doubt and hoped that its evangelical contingent still present in the established churches would move the organization into their direction, but most were suspicious. One critic, the German-American industrialist and evangelical philanthropist John Bolten, even applied the biblical parable of the mustard seed as symbol for the power of the Kingdom of God to the WCC as a warning for the threat of the overgrown tree of apostate Christendom in which the nations would take refuge. This interpretation let him to believe that the 'Monster Church' would "drive us soon underground and kill us." He emphasized the need to organize Christians against this threat.[113]

This conclusion was similar to Oswald J. Smith's, who summarized Germany's development to his constituency in the *Peoples Magazine*: "As I see it, it all started with higher criticism. Modernism came from Germany and when the Bible went, morals went. It is always so. Then comes judgment, and that has been the history of Germany."[114] The manifestations of the Antichrist might be different, the source was the same, and world domination the goal.

The reality of the atomic bomb made evangelicals believe that the chance of the formation of a world government accelerated, either because one of the nations dominated the others militarily, or because the other nations had come together to create a body that should prevent this from happening. A fundamentalist commentator predicted a few months after Hiroshima that other nations would gain access to the atomic knowledge in five years' time.[115] In the spring of 1947, a pastor received a prominent platform for his message that Christians should not expect peace to last, because he expected danger for the promulgation of the gospel in his own country, a battle for the soul of

113 James DeForest Murch, "Amsterdam, 1948. An Evangelical View of the World Council of Churches," reprinted form *United Evangelical Action* (hereafter *UEA)* 1 February - 15 May 1949; *UEA*, 1 February 1953, 16; Letter John Bolten to Francis A. Schaeffer, 6 July 1948, WCA SP 113, box 1 file Clarens 1948. Bolten would be treasurer of the WEF from 1951-61.

114 First quarter 1949, 19.

115 Frank E. Lindgren, "The Atomic Bomb," *The King's Business* (January 1946), 9.

America, for the liberties of men. A new wave of antipapism emerged that labeled the Roman Catholic Church as a major threat by infiltrating the world.[116]

With so little confidence in the official ecumenical goals, conservative Protestants believed that only a separate organization would protect their interest against this global threat.[117] Immediately the national network – the National Association of Evangelicals was founded in 1942 – tried to find global partners.

Before the war had ended, local congregations, such as Chicago's Moody Church took on this task and prepared the stage for missionary action, as it saw businessmen, administrators, and educators do the same for postwar opportunities. It campaigned against defeatism as if the doors in Europe and elsewhere would remain closed for ever, and it believed that any peace settlement would be short-lived. As the political road proved unstable, all energy was directed to drafting and executing spiritual plans. The trajectory began with bolstering the teaching about missions by stirring the sense of personal spiritual needs, which would lead to telling others about it. Missionary organizations should accelerate their distribution of stories and opportunities and candidates for the ministry who interrupted their training, to serve in the armed services, should be encouraged to complete their programs to maintain their motivation. Missionaries, seminaries, and student bodies should think strategically about their new tasks, radio broadcasts describing the new challenge should add to the awareness, and prayer groups intensified.[118] A missionary spokesperson at Moody Bible Institute observed that the war had removed two thousand "Teuton missionaries" from Asia and Africa, leaving 700,000 sheep without shepherd. This vacuum needed to be filled with British and American replacements. These missionaries would build bridges between East and West.[119]

At the front of this preparation was the European Youth for Christ campaign and domestic revival meetings, for which special farewell services and mass prayer meetings attended by seventeen thousand people had been organized. The Youth for Christ campaign in Europe qualified perfectly as an innovative tool. "Europe needs three things: 1) Men for leadership. 2) New methods that will appeal to European youth. 3) Equipment with which to do the job,"

116 David W. Ewart, "The Christian's Warfare," *The King's Business* (May 1947), 9-12.

117 See Murch's justification in "The News behind the News from Denver," *UEA*, 1 February 1953, 19 and 31.

118 "Preparation Now for Post War Missionary Advance," *The Moody Church News* 28.3 (March 1943), 3-4.

119 The Committee of Reference and Council, "The Challenge of the War to Foreign Missions," Moody Bible Institute Archives, Chicago, Departmental Missions, box 1, file missions [1945].

Torrey Johnson reported back to his supporters in Chicago.[120] The evangelicals were warming up for an offensive, partly out of fear for marginalization, mostly out of hope that they could fill a spiritual vacuum in Europe.[121]

United Evangelical Action, the periodical that since August 1942 sought to unite Protestants behind the mission of the National Association of Evangelicals, trumpeted these views around the nation. NAE-president J. Elwin Wright reported on his postwar trip to Germany that the country's guilt lay in a lack of true spirituality and respect for the bible. As hope for the future, he added that thousands of its ministers and especially the more conservative churches had resisted the Nazi regime. Wright believed that the war had seriously weakened theological modernism in Germany, but that the new danger was that Germany became the target of "a barrage of American nationalism by way of the Federal Council of Churches in New York and the World Council in Geneva."[122] He found evidence for this trend in the unifying efforts of the Evangelical Church in Germany in Treysa, as an experiment of an inclusive national church for all Protestants. The leaders of the confessing church succumbed to the temptation of the ecumenical movement and aligned with the organization that allowed "doctrinal infidelity."

Wright believed that the German people stood at the crossroads of choices for the future and presented spiritual revival as one of the (preferred) options. American evangelicals could influence this process "[b]y flooding Germany with Bibles, Testaments, spiritual literature and, as rapidly as permission can be obtained from the military government, by sending picked men equipped intellectually and spiritually to assist in the development of the sort of leadership in Germany which will be alert to the dangers of an ecumenical movement which leaves Christ out of its reckoning. I have come back from Germany convinced that the country more than any country on the face of the globe is ripe for spiritual revival."[123] This hope stimulated the NAE to fuel the anti-modernist forces in Europe and elsewhere.[124] And this brought them in direct competition with other American groups fostering plans for Europe.

120 "Five Youth for Christ Leaders Fly to Europe on March 18," *The Moody Church News* 31.3 (March 1946), 4; "Youth for Christ in Britain," Ibid. 31.5 (May 1946), 3; "Youth for Christ News," Ibid. 31.8 (August 1946).

121 European Catholics shared the diagnosis that Germany faced a spiritual vacuum and needed a religious revival to reunite Europeans. See Maarten van de Bos, *Mensen van goede wil. Een geschiedenis van de katholieke vredesbeweging Pax Christi 1948-2013* (Amsterdam: Wereldbibliotheek, 2015), 30-40.

122 J. Elwin Wright, "How Guilty Was the German Church," *UEA* (1 December 1946), 3-4.

123 J. Elwin Wright, "What about the Future of the German Church?" *UEA* (15 December 1946), 5-6.

124 "Wright: World Co-operation," *UEA* (1 January 1947), 12-13.

Still from the film *Battleground Europe* covering Billy Graham's evangelism campaign in Europe in 1955. Created by Great Commission Films Production.
[Used with permission of the Billy Graham Evangelistic Association]

Battleground Europe

In sum, in the course of 1943 American Protestants realized that the allies would win the war in Europe and they envisioned what the postwar situation would bring. The two main wings of Protestantism drafted a vision of future threats and opportunities and both camps created plans that combined aid and evangelism, but in different concoctions. The mainline churches sought to restore the religious infrastructure and use material aid to practice and advance ecclesiastical unity. The conservative Protestants gave priority to a spiritual intervention and were eager to radically reform the religious landscape of Europe.

The mainline churches pursued an institutional agenda, that continued the prewar ecumenical path. Aid was part of the encouragement strategy to help European churches to resume their social responsibilities. Unified action was a means to increase efficiency and a principle to avoid 'colonization' by American denominations. The mainline churches also recognized Europe's spiritual need, but their efforts for a parallel missionary program lacked means and a sense of urgency. Their efforts to strengthen Protestant minorities remained small.

For most conservative Protestants in the United States, Europe was not only defined as a new missionary target, it was also an important battleground in response to the abject ecumenical plans of the mainline churches. Conservatives concluded that theological liberalism had been at the root of the war and thus would liberal plans jeopardize the future stability of the world. Initially they had more fear than hope. But their angst for ecumenical domination was supplanted by an expectation of a global revival that needed a seizing of the moment. Action-driven initiatives assuaged their anxieties, raised their hopes, and broadened their horizons. It offered an alternative route to spiritual restoration that required massive mobilization of resources. And here they encountered an internal obstacle, because the fundamentalist wing of the conservative alliance was wary of cooperation with others who did not share its strict standards. This internal dispute spilled over from America to Europe.

ORGANIZE!
COMPETITION FOR EUROPE IN THE 1940S

Landing in Europe

On 20 March 1946, a commercial aircraft landed at Preswick Airpost near Glasgow with evangelist Billy Graham and five American colleagues bound for a six-week tour of Western Europe. The trip was a bit improvised as bad weather had detoured their London flight first to Ireland and then to Scotland. They eventually reached London by train. They lodged in mansions, held ad hoc revival meetings in hotel lobbies, auditoriums and churches, and met thousands of people, causing a stir among reporters everywhere. They held widely publicized meetings with business leaders, politicians, and ministers. The well-dressed young men who accompanied Graham understood the concerns and discouragement that existed for many young people in Europe, and their empathetic approach proved to be a magnet that drew the youth to express their willingness to commit themselves to Christ. An evangelist expressed his impression of the response in the United Kingdom: "tons of water piled up behind and ready to be broken, pouring a great flood of blessing upon this broken, barren land."[1] In this statement he was referring not only to the physical scars of the recent war. He was also pointing directly at the religious situation. When the group preached in Edinburgh, rites of the traditional Church of Scotland contrasted with the excitement of the Graham

1 Report Sun. March 24 [1946] and report fourth week in BGCA, collection 224, Papers of J. Stratton Shufelt, 1930-1979, N.D. Box 1, folder 17 "Youth for Christ, European Teams: Letter and Reports, March-April 1946, May-June 1947."

mission. During the afternoon prayer service in St. Giles Cathedral, an evangelist was struck by the attendance of only two souls and the "cleric in imposing robes, who had one attendant, carrying a mace, symbol of religious authority. It was a lesson to us from God, showing us how ritual and formalism have failed the world."[2]

The warm response to the Youth for Christ campaign was eagerly contrasted to a cold and uninspired formalism of organized religion. This new organization lead by Graham had staged rallies all over the United States during World War II presenting itself as a morally sound alternative to the forms of entertainment frequented by teenagers and young service men and women when they were off duty. At Graham's American events, fundamentalist ministers gave short talks that sought to assuage the fears and issues of the younger generation with the promise of the gospel. An attractive program underscored the moral message. It consisted of easy-listening gospel songs sprinkled with testimonies by entertainers, athletes, businessmen, and military heroes showing that traditional Christianity could be exciting and timely. This was the kind of action the new evangelicals longed for and that the leaders of Graham's organization were trained to deliver, being well versed in modern media, mainly radio, and popular music. The moral tone of their campaign matched the moral character of the "Good War" underway. On May 30, 1945, two weeks after a "The Greatest Youth Rally in History" attended by 65,000 in Chicago, Torrey Johnson, a second generation Norwegian immigrant, addressed America's youth with a pressing invitation: "It is possible in your generation and in my generation, in our time, to reach the last person on earth with the gospel of Jesus Christ. Will we do it? Will you accept the challenge?"[3]

The news of this outburst of religious enthusiasm in America spread in the American media, and these stories soon reached all corners of the world. Youth for Christ received invitations from believers worldwide to come stir revival in their area. Theologically, a new sense of urgency inspired by the apocalyptic mood of a global war, motivated traditional believers to make haste in taking the gospel to the end of the earth as a way to help usher in the end times. They readily added Europe as a target area, which had suffered from the ill effects from theological modernism.[4] Torrey Johnson expressed this anti-liberal interpretation of World War II in a radio address:

2 Report second week, page 5-6, in BGCA, col. 224, Papers of J. Stratton Shufelt, 1930-1979, N.D. Box 1, folder 17 "Youth for Christ, European Teams: Letter and Reports, March-April 1946, May-June, 1947."

3 William Martin, *A Prophet with Honor: The Billy Graham Story* (New York: Morrow, 1991), 93.

4 Mel Larson, *Youth for Christ* (Grand Rapids: Zondervan, 1947), 79; Mel Larson, *Young Man on Fire: The Story of Torrey Johnson and Youth for Christ* (Chicago: Youth Publications, 1945), 114, reprinted in Joel Carpenter, ed., *The Youth for Christ Movement and Its Pioneers* (New York: Garland Publishing, 1988).

> Germany today is in disgrace – a nation that has rejected the Word of God and has turned its back upon Jesus Christ and cast aside Martin Luther and the message of the Reformation. They have said, "we have a culture that is *beyond* the culture of the Bible... We have education that is *beyond* that which Martin Luther taught us." They have thus brought about Dachau and Buchenwald and the concentration camps of the present day. We don't want any repetition of what is taking place in Germany! If we are going to save our time from a repetition of that same thing, we must go into Germany with the gospel of Jesus Christ.[5]

The team that landed in the United Kingdom had hoped to enter Germany, but failed to get permission. Nonetheless their European tour was a great success. They prepared to access Germany at a later stage and accepted many invitations to return. The Youth for Christ campaign inaugurated an enduring American interest and investment in Europe, a novel approach and quite different from the occasional visits by American revivalists before the war. Thanks to monthly updates in the Youth for Christ magazines and *United Evangelical Action*, news of the international scope of the revival reached numerous evangelicals back in the United States. Their activity was an echo of the Protestant missionary outburst preceding and following World War I, when John R. Mott had asserted that the goal was to evangelize the world in his generation. Depression and the Second World War had stalled this goal, but victory and prosperity had revived it. This religious atlanticism fit within the increasing political, military, and civic cooperation in the Atlantic world, which was visible in the founding of the UN, NATO, the Marshall Plan, and other global networks and associations.

The Youth for Christ revival of the 1940s connected with the experiences of evangelical chaplains and missionary-minded service men who had witnessed the devastation in Europe first hand. They concurred with their religious leaders that the disaster of this war had a spiritual origin, and that Europe needed American assistance.[6] They compared the religious scene in Europe with their own, and concluded that large parts of Europe were unregenerated. One of these missionaries, Samuel Faircloth, an army chaplain serving the 5th US Army in Italy, was a member of the Conservative Baptist Foreign Mission Society, a group of northern churches that considered the American Baptist Convention too liberal. This group could not organize its own mission society within the existing Northern Baptist denomination and therefore decided to

5 Larson, *Young Man on Fire*, 113.

6 Joel A. Carpenter, *Revive Us Again: The Reawakening of American Fundamentalism* (New York: Oxford University Press, 1993), 178-184. See for instance David Johnson, the new director of the Scandinavian Alliance Mission of North America (soon The Evangelical Alliance Mission) and navy chaplain in Europe during World War II and its aftermath. Vernon Mortenson, *God Made it Grow: Historical Sketches of TEAM's Church Planting Work* (Pasadena, CA: William Carey Library, 1994), 214.

separate. Faircloth concluded that the destruction of Europe and the cruelty of its dictators was the result of secular humanism, which had grown "from the inside" in Germany well before the war. He saw Nazi terror as a logical consequence of decades of anti-Christian philosophy and high-level criticism of the bible in German universities. He felt that this tradition had disarmed the countervailing powers of the German ministry and left their flocks unprotected against Nazism. Other American soldiers shared Faircloth's interpretation and felt an obligation to Europe. In general the postwar religious revival was fuelled by the growing religious presence in the military. Religious services encouraged the display of the public function of institutional religion, stimulated ecumenical cooperation beyond church boundaries, and boosted a religious confirmation of the moral high ground during World War II and into the Cold War. After their eventual demobilization, they planned to return to the continent with gospel tracts instead of bombs. Samuel Faircloth became a missionary in Portugal in 1949 and would stay there until 1985.[7]

These two developments – the postwar revival in America and the soldiers' first-hand experience of the religious conditions in Europe – emphasized the contrast between the two continents and triggered new connections. The missionary enterprise in Europe was given structure thanks to the activities of the National Association of Evangelicals (NAE). This organization of traditional Christians in America had little confidence in the growing liberal climate that they perceived in the mainline American Protestant denominations. They sought to launch an alternative to the Federal Council of Churches, and later to the international World Council of Churches. The global ambition of the World Council especially filled evangelicals and fundamentalists with dread.[8]

Another Battle for Europe

Anxieties about the future meant that the battle raging inside Protestant America was exported to Europe. Evangelicals feared being stifled by an ecumenical blanket on one side and tucked into a fundamentalist straightjacket on the other. When both groups turned toward Europe, evangelicals could not stay behind. Signs of alienation between fundamentalists and evangelicals

7 Interview of author with Samuel Faircloth, Carol Stream, IL, USA, 15 June 2011. See for evangelical commitment to the armed forces: Anne C. Loveland, *American Evangelicals and the U.S. Military, 1942-1993* (Baton Rouge: Louisiana State University Press, 1997), 1-33; Michael Snape, *God and Uncle Sam: Religion and America's Armed Forces in World War II* (Woodbridge, UK: Boydell Press, 2015).

8 M. Silk, "The Rise of the 'New Evangelicalism': Shock and Adjustment," in W. R. Hutchison, ed., *Between the Times: The Travail of the Protestant Establishment, 1900-1960* (Cambridge: Cambridge University Press, 1989), 278-299.

had been visible at the time the United States entered World War II, but this process had gone slowly and complete estrangement had been by no means inevitable. The process of group formation had accelerated in the early 1940s, however, when the Presbyterian fundamentalist minister Carl McIntire forced the issue of whom to include and whom to exclude inside a conservative network. He stood at the crossroads of the fundamentalist/evangelical divide and provoked an even greater separation between them.

Carl C. McIntire (1906-2002) was the son of a Presbyterian minister in Michigan who had hoped to go as a missionary to China, but could not because of mental health problems in his family. Due to Carl's father's illness, his mother filed for divorce in 1920 and raised the children alone. Thanks to her job at the Teacher's College in Durant, Oklahoma, Carl was able to attend college there and then to continue his college education in Missouri. His diploma gave him access in 1928 to Princeton Theological Seminary, where he came under the influence of conservative theologian J. Gresham Machen. Machen left the seminary the next year and McIntire followed him to the orthodox Presbyterian Westminster Theological Seminary in Philadelphia. Machen's move was the outcome of the modernist-fundamentalist controversy in Presbyterianism over the inerrancy of Scripture, a debate that had split many denominations. After McIntire graduated from the seminary in 1933, he went to work in the large Collingswood Presbyterian Church in Collingswood, New Jersey. His missionary interest found an outlet in the Independent Board for Presbyterian Foreign Missions, the conservative counterpart to the Presbyterian Board of Foreign Missions.[9]

McIntire's independent behavior resulted in him being ousted from the Presbyterian Church in 1935. He founded a new denomination, the Orthodox Presbyterian Church (OPC), and the Collingswood congregation became one of the main pillars. He soon alienated his allies, however, fighting over total abstinence from alcohol, rational Calvinist theology, and pre-millennialism, and thus went on to found his own denomination, Bible Presbyterian, and his own seminary, Faith, centered in New Jersey. This line of action was the logical result of McIntire's belief that it was impossible to reform a denomination from within. His advocacy of a complete separation from liberal Christians made him rank anti-modernism higher than pro-Presbyterianism. He secured an influential position among the fundamentalists by maintaining a constant

9 Markku Ruotsila, *Fighting Fundamentalist: Carl McIntire and the Politicization of American Fundamentalism* (New York: Oxford University Press, 2016), 31-58. McIntire's admirers Gladys Titzck Rhoads and Nancy Titzck Anderson describe this episode in their biography *McIntire: Defender of Faith and Freedom* (Maitland, FL: Xulon Press, 2012), 227-236.

public profile, broadcasting the disputes with those who disagreed with his strategy even though they shared his concerns.[10]

This process of alienation led McIntire to create a number of institutions that he hoped would further the cause of his anti-modernist movement, including bible schools, mission agencies, periodicals, radio and television shows, conferences, and networking organizations. He based all of them on the same principle: no compromise with liberals and complete organizational separation. McIntire collected his allies in the American Council of Christian Churches (ACCC) launched in September 1941. Simultaneously, ambitious evangelicals sought a new organizational umbrella. The history of these failed efforts and the bitter competition and mutual disappointments that arose, shows that there was a desire for unity, but that it was complicated by the role of personalities and slogans. The effects of these clashes echoed for a long time in America and in Europe.

McIntire's biographer Markku Ruotsila described McIntire's anti-communist role as "at once broader in scope, more systematic, organized, and pervasive" than the role proposed by evangelicals.[11] These qualities gave him a disproportionate influence compared to the size of his enterprises.

McIntire combined anti-collectivist ideas with the reformed tradition that had crafted an offensive strategy demanding total involvement of religion in all areas of life. Few observers noticed the internal tension that existed between his role as libertarian and as advocate of a restrictive state. He was more successful in finding supporters for his libertarianism than for his stricter views. He drummed up support for his campaigns by promising a minimal state. To this purpose he abandoned his separatism and sought cooperation with non-fundamentalists. He even wooed Catholics and non-Christians while simultaneously blaming ecumenists and evangelicals for opening the door to non-fundamentalists.[12] Another internal tension occurred because of his dispensationalist belief in a sudden rapture of the church before a time of great suffering. This belief made him attractive to American fundamentalists, and amillennial Calvinists. His autocratic leadership style drew the masses in America to his pressure politics and anti-Communist agitation, and it was just a matter of time before he went international with his operations. Before his international turn, and even during it, however, there remained a chance for a joint evangelical-fundamentalist alliance. That crucial phase began in the fall of 1941 when McIntire invited churches and organizations to join him in

10 D.G. Hart, *Defending the Faith: J. Gresham Machen and the Crisis of Conservative Protestantism in Modern America* (Baltimore: Johns Hopkins University Press, 1994); Barry Hankins, *Francis Schaeffer and the Shaping of Evangelical America* (Grand Rapids, MI: Eerdmans, 2008), 11-16.

11 Markku Ruotsila, "Carl McIntire and the Fundamentalist Origins of the Christian Right," *Church History* 81.2 (June 2012): 378-407, quotation on 378.

12 Ruotsila, "Carl McIntire," 387.

founding the American Council of Christian Churches. At the same time the evangelicals hoped to launch their own organization. Clearly, they had to talk.

McIntire's main conversation partner was J. Elwin Wright. A former realtor who ran the New England Fellowship to advance regional revivals, Wright eagerly sought ways to convert his regional work into a national evangelical organization. His "Committee for United Action Among Evangelicals" ran on a track parallel to McIntire's. When he heard about McIntire's plan for the ACCC, he wrote him an appreciative letter indicating his agreement with the initiative, but also expressing his regret about the low number of churches responding to the call for an organization. He pointed to the haste with which the project was undertaken, and the lack of consultation initiated with interested groups. He sensed a great deal of dissatisfaction between the 30-40 evangelical bodies and he tried to bring them together. In response to this unsolicited advice, McIntire postponed appointing the executive committee for his organization. At a meeting in Chicago in late October, the evangelical leaders decided that they did not want to create an anti-WCC movement as the ACCC was intended to be, but rather a broad network of evangelical organizations. They hoped to set in motion a cultural shift that would change the course of history. As this ideal needed wide support, they drew their finances and ideas from the corporate world. Entrepreneurial experts convinced them that positive advertising would generate much better results than negative. Here they had a conflict with McIntire who feared that the organization would be too broad, and include "noisy" Pentecostals whom he abhorred. McIntire wanted frontal attacks and thought negative advertising worked best.[13]

After McIntire rejected the idea of negotiating through informal conferences, Wright lost confidence in the potential success of the ACCC. He felt that by stirring up public debate McIntire would thwart Wright's efforts to unite evangelicals for action and kill the positive atmosphere necessary to boost broad evangelical cooperation. The evangelical leadership feared that the ACCC would destroy their entire plan. In February 1942, Wright still hoped that McIntire would comply, but McIntire meanwhile, had already claimed God's blessing on his enterprise and decided to fight on his own.

To avoid further alienation from the separatist fundamentalists, the NAE tried to organize the Christian Business Men's Committee to mediate a settlement. But McIntire's line hardened as, for him, anything less than full separa-

13 J. Elwin Wright to Carl McIntire, 18 September 1941, McIntire to Wright, 22 December, 1941, Box 249 file 43, Wright, J. Elwin 1941-1947, The Carl C. McIntire Manuscript Collection (222), Special Collections, Princeton Theological Seminary, Princeton NJ, USA; Sarah Ruth Hammond, edited by Darren Dochuk, *'God's Business Men': Entrepreneurial Evangelicals in Depression and War* (Chicago: University of Chicago Press, 2017).

tion from liberal associations was non-negotiable.[14] Wright tried to persuade McIntire by justifying his own openness to the Federal Council of Churches:

> I personally believe that eventual separation from certain denominations which have progressively swung toward modernism during the past decades is inevitable unless a revival comes to them. Until evangelical Protestantism began to become vocal in these last years, there has been little to encourage many of these men who are weak in faith. We believe that much may be salvaged and in some cases even whole denominations, if we pray and believe earnestly for an outpouring of the Spirit in this crisis. This seems to us much better than immediate and arbitrary withdrawal.[15]

But this optimism was soon abandoned when it turned out that the fundamentalists would not grant the evangelicals a hearing. Instead the fundamentalists claimed to be the true representatives of traditional Christians in America, and soon made the same claim abroad. In April 1942 evangelical leaders met in St. Louis. A year later in Chicago they constituted the National Association of Evangelicals. One of the lead speeches there announced that the world stood at the crossroads between paganism and Christianity and said that an evangelical revival could tilt the balance for the better. The global horizon of their mission was clear.[16]

In the meantime Dr. Donald G. Barnhouse, a leader from the prestigious Tenth Presbyterian Church in Philadelphia, explicitly discouraged the NAE from linking up with McIntire or others associated with the fundamentalist movement. He felt such an alliance would scare away potential donors and supporters.[17] However, evangelical and fundamentalist paths would continue to cross. Their ambitions and fears came to an international climax in the year 1948 when they shifted attention to Europe.

In the summer of that year the World Council of Churches formally launched its organization in Amsterdam in order to create an instrument to hold the churches together as an institution. Europe had sufficiently recovered from the war to be able to host this and other meetings. The initiatives of the Marshall Plan, the United Nations, and military alliances filled the atmosphere with internationalism. A number of American evangelical organizations decided to cross the Atlantic to find partners in Europe, specifically in

14 Wright to McIntire, 17 February 1942, McIntire to Wright, 27 February 1942, Wright to H.O.W. Garman, 26 April 1943, McIntire to Wright, 16 November 1943, McIntire Collection.

15 J. Elwin Wright to Carl McIntire, 26 November 1943, Box 249 file 43, Wright, J. Elwin 1941-1947, McIntire Collection.

16 Carpenter, *Revive Us Again*, 146-150.

17 D.G. Barnhouse to J. Elwin Wright, 14 July 1942, PHS, Barnhouse Collection, box 7.28 NAE. He considered the ACCC as the result of the internal Presbyterian conflict of a group of ministers whose spirit was characterize by "intransigence, intolerance and contention," Barnhouse to Rev. J. Lynn Pace, 20 July 1942.

the strategic Netherlands and in prosperous Switzerland. NAE representatives met with European partners in the bible school at Beatenberg, and Youth for Christ organized its first international meeting in St. Clarens, both in Switzerland. In these venues they tried to build an international evangelical network. The American Council of Christian Churches had challenged the WCC by organizing their conference on the very doorstep of the WCC's founding assembly in Amsterdam.[18]

The three American Protestant network organizations tried to expand by incorporating Europeans. In all their efforts they had to take each other into account.[19] Most American evangelicals were not after the destruction of the WCC, but they did reject the formal authority of the Council, as well as its binding concepts, concentration of power, and the fact that they excluded groups who were not represented in national church bodies. Evangelicals feared they would be locked out of the official liaisons between national governments and religious organizations. Instead, they offered a federal organizational model, a solution that was not only an alternative to the alleged monopolistic agenda of the World Council, but also one that could offer shelter to para-church organizations that did not easily fit into a denominational structure.

This organizational model corresponded with the goals of the founders, as historian Michael S. Hamilton has noted. A formal body like a denomination, and also a council of denominations such as the (American) National Council of Churches and the World Council, represented centralized power, which granted privileges to its members and excluded non-members. It worked similarly to the operation of the United Nations. The para-church organizations might have entered the World Council as a kind of NGO. The leadership of the World Council entertained their entry at the beginning, but did not honor it, and even if it had, it still would not have made them full members. So para-church groups fell outside the official organization. As a consequence para-churches set up their own umbrella organizations and they included denominations as well as organizations.[20]

A major incentive that brought evangelicals into national associations was their fear of being denied access to the airwaves for their radio programs. They feared the influence the Federal Council of Churches had over the central

18 David M. Thompson, "Ecumenism," in Hugh McLeod, ed., *The Cambridge History of Christianity* Vol. 9, *World Christianities c. 1914-c. 2000* (Cambridge: Cambridge University Press, 2006), 50-70.

19 Jurjen A. Zeilstra, *European Unity in Ecumenical Thinking, 1937-1948* (Zoetermeer, the Netherlands: Boekencentrum, 1995), 207-274.

20 David M. Thompson, "The Ecumenical Network, 1920-48," in Jeremy Gregory and Hugh McLeod, eds., *International Religious Networks* (Woodbridge: The Boydell Press/Ecclesiastical History Society, 2012), 248-249. WCC founding Henry Van Dusen realized in 1938 that building an organization with churches as official members excluded sources of the church's vitality, such as lay people, youth, and women.

authorities.[21] A similar fear of being excluded in the process of centralization drove the NAE to go international. The Interdenominational Foreign Mission Association (IFMA), the 25 year-old association of mission agencies supported by more than one denomination, chose to remain separate from the mainline organizations and welcomed both denominational and other mission organizations. Soon a new organization, the Evangelical Foreign Missions Association (EFMA), founded in 1945 as a satellite of the NAE, followed suit. Without formally delegated power, these associations operated like corporations, but still lacked the power to negotiate with politicians to gain access to the radio waves. So, paradoxically, the theological pluralists of the WCC were organizational centralizers and in that respect exclusive, while the theological traditionalists were exclusivist in doctrine but organizationally pluralist.[22] The difference in organizational structure would come to shape the interaction of American Protestants with Protestants in Europe.

The ecumenists were excited about the postwar prospects for church cooperation, but also noticed the growing tension with the evangelicals. The Foreign Mission Conference reported in April 1947 that the theological debate between the mainline foreign missionaries and the new evangelicals had poisoned the atmosphere. On September 17, 1947, Betty D. Gibson, the Executive Secretary of the International Missionary Council (IMC) in London, reassured C.B. Burgess at the Colonial Office on Downing Street. She pointed to a report on the EFMA:

> All the indication I received from Mr. Clyde Taylor and other missionary secretaries well known and respected in North America, who are in close touch with the Association, went to show a very considerable sense of responsibility in matters which would be of interest to the colonial governments. For example, before admitting any society to membership careful enquiries are made and it is not accepted unless it is shown to have adequately assured financial support with a responsible committee which uses discrimination in the choice of missionaries and maintains supervision over their behavior in the field.[23]

Both the missionary council and the foreign office took the EFMA seriously. The IMC gave a sympathetic report, but also indicated that the IMC could not provide space for a second representative body in North America dealing with

21 Tona Hangen, *Redeeming the Dial: Radio, Religion, and Popular Culture in America* (Chapel Hill: University of North Carolina Press, 2002).

22 Michael S. Hamilton, "More Money, More Ministry: The Financing of American Evangelicalism Since 1945," in Larry Erskine and Mark A. Noll, eds., *More Money, More Ministry: Money and Evangelicals in Recent North American History* (Grand Rapids: Eerdmans, 2000), 104-138.

23 Letter B.D. Gibson to C. B. Burgess Geneva, 17 September 1947, WCC Archives, inv. 26.19.10 Miscellaneous papers, 1933-1961, Box 2, Evangelical foreign missions assoc. 1947-1948.

colonial affairs. It advised the colonial office that some faith missions believed God would provide their funds, but knew that this might not allay their fear of the evangelicals. Gibson recommended "... that the principles of religious liberty would be observed and that a mission would be excluded only if it disturbed the public order."[24] The final phrase was meant to fend off Pentecostal emotionalism.

The Strategic Value of Relief to Europe

In 1948, the Baptist World Alliance abandoned its centralist policy and replaced the geographical division of its work by an open system in which each Baptist church could link up with any other church. This emphasis on individual autonomy greatly advanced the presence of American Baptist churches and agencies in Europe but it also created competition among various American groups. In France, Southern Baptists, Conservative Baptists, and the North American Baptist Association were active.[25] The new policy gave priority to relief efforts.[26]

The Baptists assessed the situation of postwar Europe as more grave than it had been after World War I. A Baptist observer noted: "Europe is a strange paradox, an admixture of good and evil, which it has become through slow-moving historical processes. The Europe of today is the natural, inexplicable fruitage of the Europe of yesterday... Europe today is bankrupt in all realms of her once proud life."[27] American Baptists and Mennonites, who had maintained free-church connections in Germany, strengthened their prestige by supporting their kin, especially by rebuilding bombed out churches and by founding seminaries. This strategy was thought to be an antidote to tyranny.[28]

24 Letter B.D. Gibson to C.B. Burgess, 21 April 1947 and Marston Logan to B.D. Gibson, 6 May 1948, Geneva, WCC Archives, inv. 26.19.10 Miscellaneous papers, 1933-1961, Box 2, Evangelical foreign missions assoc. 1947-1948.

25 The various Baptist assessments of postwar Europe are published in: George W. Sadler a.o., *Europe, Whither Bound? A Symposium Telling of Southern Baptist Missionary Work in Italy, Spain, and the Balkan States – Hungary and Yugoslavia* (Nashville: Broadman Press, 1951); Baker James Cauthen and Frank K. Means, *Advance to Bold Mission Trust, 1945-1980* (Foreign Mission Board of the Southern Baptist Convention, 1981), 196, 227-228; Wm. J. Hopewell, *The Missionary Emphasis of the General Association of Regular Baptist Churches* (Chicago: Regular Baptist Press, 1963), 61. The Baptist-Mid-Missions was the oldest and largest agency of independent Baptists. Its name refers to the original field of Mid-Africa. The independent Baptists preferred a minimum of organization, but realized that they needed coordination to in order to advance continuity and negotiate with governments. As separatist fundamentalists they affiliated with the ICCC till 1969.

26 Sadler, *Europe Whither Bound?*, 32-33.

27 Ibid., 2, 3.

28 Enns, "Saving Germany," 106, 115.

Next to denominational efforts, interdenominational initiatives were taken. In the summer of 1944 Presbyterian Donald G. Barnhouse drafted a plan for relief, encouraging the NAE to concentrate on Europe as relief demands were high and it was thought that other missionary organizations could take care of Asia.[29] First, the NAE had to secure official recognition of the President's Commission on War Relief and the Red Cross. It went on to justify its goal by quoting Paul's Letter to the Galatian 6:10: "As we have therefore opportunity, let us do good unto all men, especially unto them who are of the household of faith." They inserted this reference to Paul in order to raise funds and they used the informal network of evangelical pastors in Europe to distribute the relief. Barnhouse's advise was to concentrate on a select number of places and not spread themselves thin. He used his experience in World War I in Belgium as a model to show how to work efficiently through bible schools and mission stations such as the Belgian Gospel Mission. His network included editor Phil Howard, Jr. of the *Sunday School Times* who served on the board of the Belgian Gospel Mission and could broadcast the plans.[30]

The NAE took Barnhouse's advice to heart. Secretary J. Elwin Wright went to Washington to visit the embassies of several European countries, all of which encouraged him to collect clothing as a major part of the relief effort. The new organization found an open door in Washington and decided to cooperate with the United Nations Relief and Rehabilitation Administration (UNRRA). As no religious organization could be directly involved in the UN's relief work nor could private agencies directly distribute clothes and food in Europe, an official at the UNRRA office suggested an alternative route: have the Catholic Church supply the salaries for staff members and loan the personnel to the UN organization. The evangelicals realized that they could and should do the same. They thought that any workers mobilized in this way would have a great advantage as soon as the UN withdrew. Moreover, the evangelicals in Europe had no other sponsor, or way to gain access. So Wright planned his operation in two phases and in the summer of 1944 began to collect funds to help alleviate the most pressing needs.[31] From the very beginning the evangelicals needed to cooperate with the state in order to ship supplies to the groups they wanted to support.[32]

Once the NAE had negotiated permission from the State Department to distribute clothing in Norway, Belgium, Holland, and France, they slipped a

29 Barnhouse to Phillip Benson, June 28, 1944, PHS 480 Barnhouse Collection, box 7.30.

30 Barnhouse to J. Elwin Wright, August 29, 1944, PHS 480 Barnhouse Collection, box 7.30.

31 J. Elwin Wright to Barnhouse, August 22, 1944 and Clyde W. Taylor, "Memorandum", PHS Barnhouse Collection, box 7.30.

32 Barnhouse to Andre LaMorte, Aix-en-Provence, 26 May 1947, PHS 480 Barnhouse Collection box 6.1. He used his journal *Eternity* to raise funds for this Reformed seminary. For the relationship between American evangelicals and the state see the special issue of the *Journal of American Studies* 51.4 (2017).

gospel message or tract into each box.[33] In November 1946 as more European opportunities opened up *United Evangelical Action* put out a call for money for war relief goods and part of these funds were also used to float the struggling NAE.[34]

Other fundamentalist and evangelical organizations, such as the board of YFC International considered beginning relief work in Europe, or at least thought to unite evangelical forces in order to counter the impression that the Roman Catholic Church had done everything and could take all the credit for humanitarian aid. They did not want to divide the evangelical forces, which were also present in the WCC. The impulse came from Germany; why pray for safety, when many Germans froze to death or starved? In Italy, American evangelicals who saw their relief packages labelled "A gift from the holy father," were in competition to be acknowledged for providing foreign aid.[35] The estimated 25 million dollars of relief sent by American evangelicals did not reach only those for which it was intended, nor did it lead to credit for the NAE. But apart from the sincere motives of the primary donors, it is safe to say that the relief programs also served to enhance the reputation and growth of religious organizations.[36]

The millions of mainline churches, and the growing network of evangelicals seemed to dwarf the fundamentalist contribution. It is true that from the perspective of the recipients in Europe, the volume of aid was minimal, but from the perspective of the sender it served as an important instrument for attracting supporters in the United States. Even a small operation such as that of the Koks can provide us with an example of how private demands from Europe strengthened organizations in America.

Arie and Elsje Kok, a couple who set up an office in Amsterdam to create an international fundamentalist network, believed that distribution of used clothes and food to individual bible-believers would solidify transatlantic bonds.[37] A dedicated American committee collected funds and clothes for the

33 Frank D. Lombar, "Europe's Plight Calls for Christian Compassion," *United Evangelical Action*, December 1, 1945, 4.

34 "Help Europe Now!" *United Evangelical Action*, 1 November 1946, 13; Sarah Ruth Hammond, " 'God's Business Men': Entrepreneurial Evangelicals in Depression and War" (Ph.D. dissertation, Yale University, 2010), 243-44.

35 Oswald Smith, "The Miracle of Youth for Christ in Europe," *People's Magazine* first quarter 1949, 15. Confirmation of American relief goods only to Catholics in Italy in "Confidential News Service," 12 April 1948, BGCA col. 165, box 1 f. 49.

36 Clyde Taylor, "Memorandum on European War Relief". Estimate of relief funds in letter J. Elwin Wright to European representative of the ACCC, Mr. Arie Kok in Hilversum the Netherlands, 16 April 1948. Both in WCA SP 113, box 1 file Clarens 1948.

37 Arie Kok, "Confidential Notes for the Inner Circle of the ACCC" no VI, 4 March 1948, box 19, file 23, The Carl C. McIntire Manuscript Collection (222), Special Collections, Princeton Theological Seminary, Princeton NJ, USA; Hans Krabbendam, "Three-Way Chess: Arie Kok and the Failure to Organize American Fundamentalism in Europe," *Church History and Religious Culture* 94 (2014): 227-258.

Koks through its Sunday School network. These efforts concentrated the attention of donors on Europe, and they came to understand that their relief parcels were instruments for contacting believers in Europe that could save the continent. Their slogan straightforwardly said: "Give food to advance the faith."[38]

A typical food parcel contained 3 lbs of coffee, 2 lbs of sugar, 1.5 lbs of tea, 2 lbs of vegetable fats, 3lbs of lard, 2 lbs of cocoa, 4 large bars of soap, 4 large bars of face soap, and cost $9.95 for each box. The label explained that the ACCC had sent the package, and informed the recipient that it was an "anti-liberal or anti-modernist, anti-socialist and anti-communist" organization, not to be confused with the FCC "whose highest leaders blaspheme the name of Christ by their extreme liberalism, and numbers of whose leaders favor a controlled economy hardly to be distinguished from the rigid controls and enslavement of the people who suffer behind Russia's 'Iron Curtain.'"[39] The recipients were also invited to the first founding ICCC conference in Amsterdam in the summer of 1948, revealing the strategic value of the campaign.

These aid boxes were important instruments in the propaganda war in Europe. In a letter of April 1948 to twenty Christian leaders in Europe, J. Elwin Wright announced that the NAE had already dispensed $25 million dollars in gifts to Europe.[40] This reinforced the argument of the evangelicals that they were effective. Kok realized that NAE groups in Europe were out to get financial support from the United States and that would hurt the ICCC's attraction.[41] The ICCC depended almost completely on American money. Its main periodical, the *Christian Beacon*, had a weekly circulation of 25,000 in 1950, and was sent to 78 countries.[42] On the home front, this activity reached all kinds of people. For instance the European Prayer Group, a weekly missionary student meeting at Wheaton College in Illinois raised $150 for the ACCC by asking all students to donate one penny in a penny bank at each meal.[43]

38 "Christmas Party and Food Committee for European Christians," and letter Ruth Trato to Elmer Meulendyk, Rochester, 4 December 1947, box 327, file 1, McIntire Collection.

39 W.H. Bordeaux to the K & C Export Packing Company, Inc. of Jackson Heights, New York, 8 July 1948, box 312, file 1, McIntire Collection.

40 Elwin Wright to Arie Kok and 19 other Christian leaders in Europe, 16 April 1948, box 19, file 23, McIntire Collection.

41 Kok to McIntire, 14 September 1949, box 19, file 24, McIntire Collection.

42 Kok to McIntire, 1 June 1950, box 19, file 25, McIntire Collection. The Dutch equivalent *Getrouw* had a run of 2,000, but only 200 paid subscribers. "Notulen van de Nederlandse sectie van de ICCC," 5 May 1949.

43 Robert A. Weeber to Food Committee for European Christians, 23 December 1947, box 312, file 1, McIntire Collection.

Solidifying Positions in Europe

In the summer of 1948 the American controversy spilled over to Europe. Whereas the World Council of Churches paid little attention to the two other groups and welcomed leading evangelicals, such as Billy Graham, the conservative Protestants engaged in a fierce competition over who could best represent traditional Christianity. Initially the NAE tried to keep the disagreement with the ACCC out of their European meetings. Wright wrote McIntire: "Europe is in no mood for any evangelical council at present, whether it be sponsored by A.C.C. or N.A.E. [sic] The real need is a fellowship of believers across the world, not a miniature edition of the World Council, even though it be orthodox."[44] Any hope of international fellowship was of course thwarted by the confrontational style of the ACCC.

In the summer of 1948, Clyde Taylor, the NAE representative in Washington, traveled to Britain to secure from the British government EFMA-access for mission work in British colonies in Africa and Asia. He received approval thanks to his contacts within the ecumenical mission board (the International Missionary Council), but strove for direct access. Taylor found the existing British organization of evangelicals (the World's Evangelical Alliance) ineffective. He distrusted their main activity of organizing annual prayer meetings with non-evangelicals thinking that any level of harmony would cause the organization to be overrun by the WCC.[45]

In all these competitions, numbers mattered greatly. The new evangelicals had hoped to find more explicit support in the US, and were therefore sensitive and anxious about the self-aggrandizement of the ACCC. They accused McIntire of inflating the membership statistics of his organization in order to get recognition from the government and access to radio time from the broadcasting networks in America. Wright challenged the veracity of the ICCC's numbers, offering to pay a missionary organization of McIntire's choice $1,000 if he would submit the membership records to an independent audit.[46] McIntire rejected the offer as childish, and turned the tables by publishing the identity of a number of NAE agencies and churches that were also part of the Federal Council of Churches. McIntire warned his opponents that this discussion would distract Christians from battling modernism, which, in his view, was the real issue. But he was not about to change his course.

44 Wright to McIntire, 6 July 1948, box 249, file 45, Wright-Kok-McIntire, McIntire Collection.
45 Clyde Taylor, "Confidential NAE Report," 1, WCA SP 113, box 1, file Clarens 1948.
46 McIntire to Wright, 7 May 1948 and Wright to McIntire, 5 June 1948, McIntire to Wright, 23 June 1948, Wright to McIntire, 6 July 1948, box 249, file 45, Wright-Kok-McIntire, McIntire Collection. The May 7 letter was clearly meant for publication and went through at least two heavily edited drafts.

Carl C. McIntire at the time he launched the ICCC in Amsterdam, 1948.
[Collection Historical Documentation Centre for Dutch Protestantism, VU Amsterdam]

In its offensive turn, the ACCC portrayed the NAE as a weak group, dominated by Pentecostals, and touted itself as the powerful organization.[47] The ACCC hoped to win over European churches by prophesizing that liberals would curb "Bible believing Christians." In the *Christian Beacon*, Francis Schaeffer, McIntire's envoy in Europe, warned against taking up with the wrong partners. "In Holland, many of these men [WCC leaders] support the Labor Party, which is the Socialist Party in Holland, and this party has joined with the Roman Catholics to control the Dutch government."[48] Of course to him, no good could come from that.

The NAE restrained itself from pushing its issues on European national groups. They offered advice, but avoided any moral pressure, as Wright re-

47 Letter J. Elwin Wright to Arie Kok in the Netherlands, 16 April 1948, WCA SP 113, box 1, file Clarens 1948; Letter F.A. Schaeffer to C. Veenhof, Kampen, the Netherlands, 21 November 1947, Arie Kok's memorandum of 31 January 1948 about the differences between ACCC and NAE, Veenhof Collection 296, inv. 98, Historical Documentation Center for Dutch Protestantism, Amsterdam.

48 Francis A. Schaeffer, "Should a Christian Tolerate the World Council? Or is Liberalism Dead?" *Christian Beacon*, 29 July 1948, 4-5.

alized that Europeans were sensitive to American dominance.[49] McIntire responded that he did not want to dominate other nations, but that the purity of the church needed to be guarded. This basic disagreement kept both parties divided despite numerous efforts at mediation and reconciliation.[50]

While both sides tried to sell themselves as a unifying umbrella organization, they suffered from the reciprocal public attacks. Still they knew that neither side would see any profit from being considered too proud to give in. Therefore, they eventually tried to bridge the gap in private conversations. Entrepreneur John Bolten was a major liaison between the NAE and ICCC in 1950. He hoped to present a united front towards foreign authorities. During a car trip, Bolton and McIntire talked for three hours in the company of Stacey Woods, the general secretary of the international student organization, Intervarsity Christian Fellowship. Woods appreciated the ICCC's candid opposition to the WCC and realized that his organization could fit into the churches connected to the ICCC.[51]

McIntire was confident that the NAE would not get very far in Holland, which was the main ICCC bulwark in Europe. He invited Bolten and Woods to become part of the ICCC, which also allowed mission boards and associations as members. Bolton was tempted since he already advocated stronger opposition to the WCC and persuaded NAE president Harold J. Ockenga to put pressure on Wright to abandon his plan for a global tour, for which there was no money anyway. McIntire smelled victory, hoping that the NAE would have to stop its international efforts: "If we can block their establishment of an international organization and if the meeting in Holland does not come off, then I think that NAE or J. Elwin Wright's efforts to start something on the world level are pretty well done."[52] Both organizations stood at the threshold of their international launch. Both had applied for international NGO-status at the UN.

As the chairman of the Interim Committee on the matter of Relationships of the NAE, Bolton hoped to unite NAE and the ACCC into a conservative block, but when he discovered that McIntire was eager to absorb the NAE, he feared that a combined organization would lose any leverage it had to cooperate with others. He preferred to invest his energy externally to support the religious re-

49 Wright to McIntire, 3 July 1950, box 249, file 46, Wright, J. Elwin 1950-51, McIntire Collection.

50 McIntire to Wright, 6 July 1950, and Wright to McIntire, 15 July 19150, box 249, file 46, Wright, J. Elwin 1950-51. See memorandum of meeting on October 9, 1950 at the New York Dorset Hotel, box 170, file 20, Bolton, John 1944-51, McIntire Collection.

51 "A Confidential Report," 11 October 1950, box 170, file 20, Bolton, John 1944-51, McIntire Collection. Bolton had been raised close to Düsseldorf and had met Hitler in 1928, but had broken with him and moved to the US. He accompanied Graham to Germany in 1954 and later. Pollock, *Billy Graham*, 136-137.

52 "A Confidential Report," 11 October 1950, 4, file 20, Bolton, John 1944-51, McIntire Collection.

vival, rather than spending resources on an internal goal to eschew all liberal connections.[53] When Bolton informed McIntire about his priorities, the latter was shocked. He had counted Bolton as his ally. When Bolton failed to block Wright's global trip, which was funded at the last minute by Billy Graham who had collected $4,300 for this purpose, McIntire concluded: "The fight has just begun!"[54] This outcry further alienated Bolton, who replied, "... you are wrong by blasting everybody in your magazine and attempting to whip everybody into line who does not accept your dicta."[55] Bolton believed unity was most necessary; McIntire claimed truth was the higher value. This standoff necessitated separation. McIntire repeated his adagio: "... it is sin to remain in fellowship with the apostasy and to have communion with the modernist and the ungodly."[56]

The result of this final fall-out was that in the years 1950 and 1951 the leaders of ACCC and NAE set up national organizations of conservative Protestants in Asia and South America that warned against each other. Bolten used the term "civil war"[57] to describe the situation, which reached its apex in Europe during a conference in Woudschoten in the Netherlands in the summer of 1951. Representatives of ICCC and NAE met there to discuss the WEF, but could not agree on the explicit need for separation. The ACCC still hoped to persuade the NAE to give up, emphasizing that the ACCC had been the first one to organize internationally.[58] When that argument failed, McIntire used every conceivable tool in his arsenal to promote his case. He published reports on his European trip in a pamphlet, and in his weekly *Christian Beacon* (May 8-26, 1951). And he announced a series of international conferences in the years to come.[59] For his part, McIntire noticed that in Holland there was more publicity for the ICCC than anywhere else, and he used this opportunity to expose the objectionable features of the WCC. He also reported that the NAE had hardly any presence in Holland. He once again pounded on the Biblical command, "Have no fellowship with the unfruitful works of darkness, but rather reprove them," (1 John 1:7), writing in his travel letters, "The only true way to have a witness to the WCC is *outside* in a true Scriptural fellowship of Christians, such as the ICCC."[60]

53 Bolton to McIntire, 13 October 1950, page 4, file 20, Bolton, John 1944-51, McIntire Collection.
54 McIntire to Bolton, 20 October 1950, file 20, Bolton, John 1944-51, McIntire Collection.
55 Bolton to McIntire, 18 October 1950, file 20, Bolton, John 1944-51, McIntire Collection.
56 McIntire to Bolton, 27 October 1950, file 20, Bolton, John 1944-51, McIntire Collection.
57 Bolton to J. Gordon Holdcroft of the Independent Board for Presbyterian Foreign Missions, 23 January 1951, file 20, Bolton, John 1944-51, McIntire Collection.
58 A. Warnaar Jr. to John Bolton, 25 August 1951, file 20, Bolton, John 1944-51, McIntire Collection.
59 Carl McIntire, *A Testimony in Europe: Travel Letters on Mission* (Collingswood, NJ: Christian Beacon Press, 1951).
60 Ibid., 16.

It is tempting to point to the uncompromising character of Carl McIntire as the main source of all conflict, and there is much to support this claim. He was a self-made man from a broken home. Oratorically gifted and an excellent organizer, he pursued a strong and simple agenda: fight liberalism. But that does not provide the entire answer. More complex men advised him, men who had witnessed the effects of liberal Protestantism and felt they understood its role in paving the road to communism. This scenario loomed up from the mission fields of China. It was Arie Kok, the former postman from the Netherlands turned Pentecostal missionary, who set this chain of events in motion.[61]

Kok's experience merged three crucial elements of fundamentalism that help explain its appeal and its limitation abroad, namely its transnational character, its global anti-Communism, and its rejection of Pentecostalism. His experience as a Pentecostal missionary in the 1910s, and a Dutch diplomat in Beijing during the 1920s had turned him into a Calvinist and a militant anti-Communist. His interaction with conservative American missionaries had opened his eyes to how unrestrained theological modernism could undermine the power to resist totalitarianism. His disillusionment with Pentecostalism resulted in a complete rejection of this spontaneous spirituality. Kok's diplomatic status, international network, and willingness to set up an office in the Netherlands for the ICCC enabled McIntire to expand his American organization internationally starting with Europe.

Kok and McIntire were, however, too optimistic about their chances. One of the many missionary agencies they approached for support was the Belgian Gospel Mission. Though the Belgians were sympathetic to the cause, they were reluctant to embrace the ICCC's uncompromising attitude. In 1948 American missionaries in Belgium in the Gospel Mission defined their attitude towards fundamentalists and evangelicals as "benevolent neutrality," a term that captured the hesitant response of many kindred groups.[62]

Though few churches affiliated with the ICCC, its presence and active anti-WCC and anti-NAE barrage caused the evangelicals to operate with caution lest they be seen as affiliated with the liberals and forfeit the confidence of their separatist brethren. The ACCC kept a close watch at home on organizations that were in some way connected to an ecumenical body and exposed them via guilt by association.[63]

61 Ruotsila, *Fighting Fundamentalist*, 85-112; Krabbendam, "Three-Way Chess," 227-258.

62 Annual Report 1948, Evadoc, KADOC, BE/942855/1639, Belgian Gospel Mission, file 874.

63 This almost happened to the conservative TEAM organization, see Vernon Mortenson, *God Made it Grow: Historical Sketches of TEAM's Church Planting Work* (Pasadena, CA: William Carey Library, 1994), 229-230.

European Sensitivies

Sooner or later churches and organizations had to decide whether or not to seek international affiliation and if so, with which organization. The need for atonement and religious rapprochement across borders in Europe spurred churches to invest in international contacts. They used already existing as well as newer interlocking networks of denominational bodies and voluntary agencies. The *Nederlandse Hervormde Kerk,* the largest Protestant church in the Netherlands, had as its contact person for the World Church Service (the international organization for humanitarian aid) the same person who was the liaison with the government. He had the authority to approve construction permits to rebuild war torn churches and other buildings, to transfer money abroad, and to import religious tracts free of charge. This meant that the trump cards were all in official hands. And clearly the NAE felt squeezed between the powerful and truly international WCC and the vocal and clearly American ICCC. The few national networks of evangelical organizations in Europe were cautious and did not immediately jump on the NAE bandwagon. Before that could happen, the American presence needed to be toned down.[64]

The NAE organizers recognized the importance of cultural sensitivity and prepared the sessions that would take place in Clarens, Switzerland in close consultation with their European partners. The Europeans insisted on being treated as equals and remaining autonomous. They emphasized the informal character of the first meeting. Thanks to American travel allowances, more than one hundred delegates from fourteen countries met in the clean and affordable accommodations of St. George's School, a Church of England boarding school at Lake Geneva. The American strategy was to pretend there was no strategy and it worked. The European delegates accepted the American federal format, and the NAE-declaration of faith, and they agreed to open up their own national associations of churches to include societies and individuals. In exchange, the Americans promised financial aid to those countries with organized evangelicals and opened up the pages of the *United Evangelical Action* to spread the news about evangelical progress in Europe. Only some British evangelicals did not support the founding of this new organization because they figured that they already had their own.[65]

The American delegation used the opportunity to add action to organization. Its members traveled to Italy to link up with some Protestant ministers before returning to Switzerland for the European Youth for Christ conference at the bible school in Beatenberg. This school was founded in 1934 and was fa-

64 Clyde Taylor, "Confidential NAE Report," 3, WCA SP 113, box 1 file Clarens 1948. Americans dominated the ICCC, which scared a number of European groups away.

65 J. Elwin Wright, "Minutes of the Clarens Conferences of Evangelicals August 7-10, 1948, St. George's School, Clarens, Switzerland," 1, WCA SC 113.

miliar territory. It had hosted a number of international conferences on world evangelization. Other members of the American delegation spread out to visit other evangelical assemblies in Europe. Overall the delegation discovered that there was a variety of approaches to international organizing. For instance, Youth for Christ had a large American contingent and was adult-led, while the International Fellowship of Evangelical Students (IFES) was more European and was student-led.[66] But more importantly, both groups engaged in action, something the American evangelical leaders liked to see. They called it "storming the gates of the enemy in Europe."[67] Elwin Wright, the NAE secretary for international cooperation, tested the cooperation of German evangelicals before leading his delegation as observers to the founding conference of the World Council of Churches in Amsterdam. They had pitched the first pins for a structural Europe presence.

NAE executive secretary Rutherford L. Decker, pastor of the Baptist Temple in Kansas City and a future (1960) presidential candidate for the Prohibition Party, concluded, "I came away from Europe more profoundly convinced that united evangelical action is the need of the hour all over the world."[68] It was Decker's view, that in pursuit of this evangelical objective the WCC and the ICCC acted as bureaucratic obstacles. He thought that Protestant Europe was divided between the established churches who were unfamiliar with evangelism and the missionary-minded free churches who had local hopes, but limited means. Furthermore, Decker believed that both depended too much on strong personalities and were distrustful of others. The pressure of war, the threat of communism, and other material burdens prodded free and established churches to seek mutual support, he said, even if they lacked a plan and the means. They assumed that Americans could provide both. Decker recommended that the existing activities, mostly the translation and distribution of evangelical literature and tracts, be made more efficient before moving to launch any new initiatives. He also recommended close cooperation with the (British) World's Evangelical Alliance.

After this testing of the waters, it took two years before there were any follow-up meetings due to the political and economic tensions caused by the Berlin Blockade and the formation of NATO. But the times were urgent as J. Elwin Wright concluded, "We are rapidly approaching the time when it may become more difficult for evangelicals to continue their worldwide propagation of the gospel unless they are able to join their hands effectively in defense

66 "Youth for Christ World Conference," BGCA 285, Torrey M. Johnson Papers, box 25 f 1.

67 Wright, "Minutes of the Clarens Conferences of Evangelicals August 7-10, 1948. St. George's School, Clarens, Switzerland," 7.

68 R.L. Decker, "Confidential Report" and "Confidential resume and report of trip to Europe, July 30 - Aug. 30, 1948," 9, WCA SC 113 NAE, box 1 file Clarens 1948.

of their Christian liberties."[69] He reasoned that this freedom was jeopardized by Communist and Catholic threats as well as by the political leverage of the WCC. The Evangelical International's main task, according to him, was to protect the freedom of religion. But, he added, the evangelicals also had to work within their own ranks.

In 1949, an unidentified American evangelical complained in a five-page memo about the lack of American leadership and called for "The World Assembly of evangelicals."[70] Thirty American interdenominational (evangelical) organizations met in the spring and unanimously voted to hold such an assembly, but when an executive committee proposed to meet on August 20-27 many organizations dropped out. The writer blamed them for lack of vision beyond their own horizons and a tendency to leave the initiative to others. The NAE turned down the invitation to be the convener of this assembly because they thought it should come as a result of a joint venture, adding that there were already many national conventions. The author characterized these groups as tribes interested mainly in their own well-being. Their leaders, he wrote, are

> good men, but by and large they are little men, jealous of their place in the sun, sure that nothing matters beyond the program of their particular organization… Perhaps, after all, the liberals do have the statesmanship which we so sadly lack. Or perhaps again, some of those whom we term liberals are simply disillusioned evangelicals who are fed up with the complacency of the little mutual admiration societies which dot the evangelical landscape and have wandered into other pastures to find out for themselves if liberalism has the answer.[71]

The NAE retorted that "broad and unstable heterodoxy" does not help either, saying that evangelicals should be more visionary and self-critical and should use the spiritual union as a base for cohesion. They boasted that the NAE was working out a plan to bring international delegates together, and accused the document of being directed against the separatist forces in the evangelical family. This frustration showed the urge to break away from petty parochialism and the realization of global trends.

Decker's suggestion of linking up with existing evangelical networks did not immediately meet a positive response in England, the keeper of the nineteenth-century legacy. The British leadership of the World's Evangelical Alliance – founded in 1846 – was not persuaded by the current need for cooperation, since it had already been functioning for a century. The British Alliance was more optimistic than the Americans about the World Council of Churches

69 J. Elwin Wright, "The Movement for Evangelical Cooperation part Two: International Developments," [1949], WCA SC 113 NAE, box 1 file Clarens 1948.

70 BGCA 338 WEF box 12 f 17 WCC 1950-54 Cooperation.

71 Ibid., p. 3.

Group portrait of 65 of the 91 delegates, observers, and visitors from 21 countries participating in the convention at Woudschoten, the Netherlands, that decided on August 7, 1951 to found the World Evangelical Fellowship. The convention drafted its constitution and by-laws and chose members of a general committee and four standing committees.
[BGCA Collection 165 WEF photo file]

and advised that the evangelicals should not abandon the WCC and leave it in the hands of the Modernists, which they warned, could result in a pact with Rome. Traditionally this British group had a more inclusive foundation than the NAE. The Americans remained dissatisfied with this slow vehicle, though they tried to accommodate to it as much as possible.[72]

The other European countries with small evangelical minorities responded positively to American wooing. In the Netherlands, as a more pluralistic country than most of its neighbors, most Protestant denominations decided to join the WCC. A few smaller denominations stayed aloof and considered the

72 Ian M. Randall, "American Influence on Evangelicals in Europe: A Comparison of the Founding of the Evangelical Alliance and the World Evangelical Fellowship," in Hans Krabbendam and Derek Rubin, eds., *Religion in America: European and American Perspectives* (Amsterdam: VU University Press, 2004), 263-274. The WEA went through a period of indecisiveness. It clearly had an ecumenical mission, as it had been founded to counter the divisions within Protestantism, but sought spiritual not organizational unity. It's decision to allow individuals as members supported this goal and prevented a head-on competition with the WCC. Its representatives at the founding event of the WCC were optimistic about its chances to avoid being swallowed up by modernists or Roman Catholics or merge into a super church. Later on this optimism evaporated, but the WEA still did not want to undermine the WCC. It fully supported the input by the Billy Graham Campaign in the mid-1950s. J.B.A. Kessler Jr., *A Study of the Evangelical Alliance in Great Britain* (Goes, the Netherlands: Oosterbaan en le Cointre, 1968), 90-94.

NAE-proposal a safe middle ground, both confessionally reliable and action driven, yet open to including associations as well as churches. Twenty-one people from eight different denominations decided to found the Netherlands Evangelical Alliance in 1949. The Dutch Protestant Radio Station NCRV solicited sermons from American evangelical ministers that they intended to broadcast in translation. The NAE believed that the radio station could develop into the nucleus of the evangelical movement, but did not want to alienate existing contacts. Station NCRV's director Gerard Hoek prepared a trip to the United States to learn from Christian Television.[73]

The Dutch were happy to host the next conference leading to the foundation of the World Evangelical Fellowship. It was held in Woudschoten in August 1951, with the intention of tying the movement closer to Europe. But only Spain and Britain made any sincere commitment to the project. The other continental European representatives found the infallibility clause in the WEF-constitution too legalistic and restrictive. Thus they met a year later in Siegen, Germany, where the mood turned away from full cooperation. These continental partners found the Americans too combative, too separated from church communities, and too self-assured. Despite the fact that the Americans had time and again reassured the delegates that they could maintain their independence, in September 1952 this continental contingent founded the European Evangelical Alliance (EEA) in Hamburg, Germany. The British did not like the option of having to choose between their American and European friends and decided to take on membership in both organizations. The Dutch became observers in the EEA. Thus, when the dust settled, it was clear the American evangelicals had only partly succeeded.[74] In the meantime the ICCC had sent free brochures to all 800 congregations of the *Gereformeerde Kerken,* the second largest Dutch Protestant church, all to no avail.[75]

73 F. Dresselhuis and A.H. Oussoren, "De gulden middenweg," brochure of founding meeting of the National Association of Evangelicals in the Netherlands, 12 March 1949; Dr. Ir. R. H. Borkent, foreign secretary of the Netherlands Gospel Center, to J. Elwin Wright, 28 March 1950; Letters James Deforest Murch to G.H. Hoek, 22 June 1950 and J. Elwin Wright to various ministers, 24 March 1950 and to G.H. Hoek, 18 March 1950 and 1 November 1950. All in BGCA col. 338, WEF, box 9 f 2 "Holland" 1948-1951. Interestingly, it was the Evangelical Broadcasting Association, EO, that took on this central role in the late 1960s.

74 Frank Hinkelmann, "Die Glaubensbasis der Europäischen Evangelische Allianz," (unpublished paper Theological University Apeldoorn April 2005), 4-6; Kessler Jr., *A Study of the Evangelical Alliance*, 97.

75 Letter F. Dresselhuis to H. Ockenga, 20 September 1951 and Wright to Dresselhuis, 11 April 1950, BGCA col. 338, WEF, box 9 f 2 "Holland" 1948-1951. The Woudschoten conference center was run by dr. H.C. Rutgers, a former treasurer of the World's Christian Student Movement, see letter Dresselhuis to E.M. Evans, 27 November 1950, BGCA col. 338, WEF, box 9 f 2 "Holland" 1948-1951. In each letter they begged the Americans for some money (a few hundred dollars). D.M. Howard, *The Dream That Would Not Die: The Birth and Growth of the World Evangelical Fellowship 1846-1985* (Exeter, UK: The Paternoster Press, 1986), 34.

A decade later, Clyde Taylor felt that the legacy of the European Evangelical Alliance had slowed down the process of activation. He observed that the affiliated national groups in Europe were weak and were only kept afloat through the efforts of a few strong leaders. Taylor thought that it was the EEA that had prevented incorporation in a larger, more ambitious WEF. The Europeans resisted American attempts to open an attack on the WCC. They voted down a proposal that would have discredited organizations that compromised on the statement of faith. Meanwhile the mainland still hoped for cooperation, while the British fully intended to stay neutral. The result was that the young WEF was left in American hands until 1968 when the need for concerted action overcame all nuances in strategy and left behind any thought of justification.[76]

The fundamentalist ICCC had lost the battle in Europe. Its exclusivism and constant attacks on fellow believers tired supporters and scared potential members. In contrast, American evangelicals showed more restraint in promoting America, gave more money, and especially, had more to show in terms of action. The quick and remarkable spread of Youth for Christ and the many smaller mission initiatives connected Europe to a growing international evangelical subculture. Initially these American evangelicals operated more out of fear than hope, but their initial angst about ecumenical domination was compensated for by the growing expectation of a global revival. Action-driven initiatives assuaged their anxieties, raised their hopes, and broadened their horizons. When all was said and done they had been successful in attaching Europeans to a global evangelical chain.[77]

76 Clyde W. Taylor, "Implementing our Evangelical Unity," *UEA*, December 1963, 27; Kessler Jr., *A Study of the Evangelical Alliance*, 99-100.

77 For a more detailed analysis of this failed fundamentalist effort see Krabbendam, "Three-Way Chess" and the recognition of Francis Schaeffer that the ICCC was too aggressively American see Markku Ruotsila, "Francis Schaeffer in Europe: The Early Missionary Years," in John Corriga, and Frank Hinkelmann, eds., *Return to Sender: American Evangelical Missions in Twentieth Century Europe* (Zürich: LIT-Verlag, 2019), 17-31.

TO WORK!

OUTREACH IN EUROPE, 1940s AND 1950s

Evangelism in Practice

Very few Europeans knew about the internal struggle among American Protestant organizations to find strategic partners in Europe. Newspapers reported widely about the founding of the World Council of Churches, European delegates to evangelical and fundamentalist meetings published their experiences in denominational journals, but outside an occasional church consistory no-one really noticed. That was different with the appearance of Youth for Christ International in Europe. This whirlwind organization reproduced the mass youth rallies in the United States in Europe's urban centers which proved that the format of these evangelical vaudeville shows concluded with a call for conversion, worked abroad as well as at home. As the European response was impressive, it fed the expectation that this was the beginning of a new revival.[1]

Meanwhile evangelicals in the U.S. military and volunteers in Europe linked up with Protestant minorities and kindred groups. Some spread the word about the Youth for Christ successes in the United States and encouraged European contacts to ask for a similar programs in Europe, others became motivated to begin mission work for their denomination. With a revival in mind

1 William Martin, *A Prophet with Honor: The Billy Graham Story* (New York: Morrow, 1991), 93. For a detailed account of Youth for Christ's reception in Europe see Hans Krabbendam, "Billy Graham and American Evangelicals in Europe, 1946-1986: Building Bridges or Separating Continents?" *Trajecta* 26.1 (2017): 195-218.

the young YFC organization didn't hesitate and sent a team to Europe in March 1946. They took care to publicize their warm welcome widely in the American media.[2]

As the name indicated Youth for Christ wanted to win the young generation for a commitment to Jesus. The enormous attention for international events, and the military contacts expanded their horizon to in include Europe. YFC president Torrey Johnson described them as "moral casualties of World War II reaching out for reality."[3] All over Europe, gospel teams secured moral support from leading theologians and practical assistance from youth ministers by creating an umbrella for interdenominational cooperation and providing models for a continuous organization. By encouraging the young generation to share the responsibility for the audience, they democratized religious organizing. The "fun" part of the meetings promised freedom and linked youth with the world, while the emphasis on moral strictness secured Protestant continuity and preserved the church tradition. It was an emotionally satisfying combination.[4]

YFC had effectively mobilized staff and finances for its European campaign among American ethnic groups in, mostly, the Midwest. A Dutch-American baker on Chicago's South Side, Joseph Biegel, canvassed the Dutch-American business men in the Windy City to find the five thousand dollars needed to send a team to the Netherlands. Dutch Reformed ministers in Holland, Michigan, and Chicago took a leave of absence for two months to travel to their ancestral country. Editors of ethnic religious periodicals published positive reports and private correspondence confirmed these stories. This combination fortified the impression that a global revival was erupting, which energized all levels of participation. Missionary work in Europe could be a quick, rewarding experience and was part of a "transnational" higher plan. Acts of resistance by, for instance, Communist protestors, only proved that the campaigns were signs of a spiritual battle, with high stakes.[5] The sense of urgency was particularly strong towards Germany at the crossroads of the Continent: "only a spiritual revival [could] save Germany and Europe."[6]

2 *Youth for Christ Magazine*, September 1946, 31.

3 *Youth for Christ Magazine*, November 1946, 4-5; Spencer C. De Jong, "YFC Holland Report," brochure in J. Stratton Shufelt Papers, box 1, folder 17; Douglas Fisher, "The Holland Story," in The Papers of Torrey Maynard Johnson, Sr. (hereafter TMJ Papers), 1919-2001: box 27, folder 5, Holland (1946-1949), Collection 285 of the Billy Graham Center Archives, Wheaton College, Wheaton, IL (hereafter BGCA).

4 Lesley Hartzell, "Fourth and Fifth Week YFC Itinerary," in J. Stratton Shufelt Papers, 1930-1979, Collection 224, box 1, folder 17, Youth for Christ, European Teams: Letters and Reports, March-April 1946, May-June 1947, BGCA; Thomas E. Bergler, *The Juvenilization of American Christianity* (Grand Rapids, MI: Eerdmans, 2012), 174.

5 De Jong to Torrey, early November 1946; Transcript of telephone conversation, 5 October 1946, TMJ Papers.

6 News Letter no 2, May 31, 1947, Shufelt Papers, BGCA.

But access to Germany was difficult, military zones and travel restrictions hindered communication, there was a lack of basic needs, and the presence of American occupying forces could work against them, especially in the southern Catholic part of Germany. Most pietists in Germany were traditionally disengaged from the world, but the Methodist leadership and the army supported the first Youth for Christ rallies in 1947.[7]

Graham's international reputation began during the Greater London campaign, held in the Harringay Arena in March and April 1954. This event acquainted the citizens of London, Amsterdam, Berlin, Copenhagen, Paris, Geneva, Oslo and a score of other cities with this American-style of outreach. The many spectators from all over Europe became convinced that something similar could be arranged in their own countries. He also gave them the instruments of modern corporate organization. The length of the United Kingdom campaign necessitated copying the corporate structure that the Billy Graham organization had created in Minneapolis. The organization chart of London 1954-55 was a model of efficiency with a central executive committee supported by six subcommittees to collect funds, create publicity, distribute films, train volunteers, recruit prayer partners, and prepare follow up. In some way or another national committees applied these principles of marketing religion in Europe.

These campaigns activated European evangelical Christians to reach out, not only to the unchurched, but also to each other. As an outsider Graham tied them to a common goal that lifted them over their separate church walls.[8] This aspect motivated German Protestants to use Graham to overcome differences and work towards unity. This work was put in motion by the merger of Lutheran and Reformed churches in the Evangelische Kirche in Deutschland.[9] This movement was necessary in order for the church in West Germany to assume leadership to renew the moral basis of the nation, especially with a new enemy of atheistic Communism rattling at the door. In preparation for his West German crusade in 1954, Graham took care to unite established and

7 Uta Balbier, " 'Youth for Christ' in England und Deutschland: Religiöser Transnationalismus und christliche Nachkriegsordnung," *Archiv für Socialgeschichte* 51 (2011): 209-224; Enns, "Saving Germany," 162.

8 Ian Randall, "Conservative Constructionist: The Early Influence of Billy Graham in Britain," *Evangelical Quarterly* 67.4 (1995): 309-333. Already in 1952 Graham had given Mel Larson permission to write his biography. Letter Billy Graham, 12 November 1952, and Prospectus Billy Graham Continental Tour, June 12-30, 1954, 2: "These [visitors] returned to witness to their more skeptical countrymen, opening doors that no foreigner could have otherwise entered." BGCA col. 338, box 29, file 22.

9 Andreas Probst, "Billy Graham in Westdeutschland 1954/55 – Ein amerikanischer Exportschlager auf Missionierungsfeldzug" (MA Thesis, Ruprecht-Karls-Universität Heidelberg, 2012), 20. Liberal theology was not the only source of tension within the Protestant community. Additional differences dwelled on the different strands in the Reformation tradition: Calvinists had a high expectation of a rapid global transformation, while Lutheran expectations of quick results were much lower. Ott, *Beyond Fragmentation*, 58.

Cover of *Moody Monthly* featuring the Billy Graham evangelism campaign in London in 1954. [Used with permission of Moody Bible Institute and the BGEA]

free churches. He shook hands with theologian Martin Niemöller, as was his custom to assuage concerns by the religious establishment, and his interpreter was an evangelical German student at Moody Bible Institute.[10] As in other European countries, the majority of the German audiences were Christians. Despite the official right of freedom of religion, it proved hard in practice to change one's church affiliation.[11]

In Graham's German crusade the military was explicitly visible, soldiers attended either specialized meetings or as part of the general crowd and kept order. This was different in other European countries, with fewer U.S. troops. By putting the blame on theological liberalism as the cause of World War II, Graham served two ends: he avoided blaming the German people directly for the atrocities, and secondly, by drawing explicit attention for Germany he reinstalled its importance in the Western arena.

The established churches in Germany welcomed the Graham campaigns as they hoped these events would help them restore their place in society. However, their approval was conditional. The churches gave priority to social programs and delegated evangelism to other religious organizations and independent evangelists. The authorities were concerned about loose cannons, charlatans, and cultic figures. In the fifties the results of their own evangelistic work proved disappointing, loading evangelism with negative connotations.[12] In an effort to advance an experiment that would turn this downward spiral by the leadership of the official organized evangelists network within the EKD replaced local parochial campaigns by mass meetings in tents and invited Billy Graham in 1954. Though he did not charm everyone by his cold war rhetoric, the church authorities hoped to invite him back in 1955. However, the EKD disengaged when Graham's organization demanded autonomy in dealing with local groups, and one of his partners, Robert P. Evans, opened a new bible school without consulting the organizing committee that was to invite Graham.[13] The combined concern with final authority and the difficulty of finding enough staff to organize events, led to the EKD's disengagement in the campaigns, which in turn cleared the platform for German evangelicals.[14]

As in other European countries local evangelical groups in Germany assisted in the mass meetings. In 1954, Graham spoke to thousands of soldiers at the military base in Frankfurt am Main, for 25,000 at the Eislaufstadion in Düsseldorf, and his tour climaxed in the Olympic Stadium in Berlin which 80,000 Germans attended. More than elsewhere in Europe, Graham's presence

10 Wilfried Zibell, as mentioned by Probst, "Billy Graham in Westdeutschland 1954/55," 41.

11 Probst, "Billy Graham in Westdeutschland," 46.

12 Gisa Bauer, *Evangelikale Bewegung und evangelische Kirche in der Bundesrepublik Deutschland: Geschichte eines Grundsatzkonflikts (1945 bis 1989)* (Göttingen: Vandenhoeck & Ruprecht, 2012), 167-201.

13 Ibid., 202-207.

14 Ibid., 221.

in Germany had political meaning, cementing contested areas with a common Western political identity. The crusades in Europe connected national expectations of rechristianization with the advocacy of the Free World against Communism.[15] The German press praised Graham's program, appreciated the fresh look and a powerful message. Simultaneously, critics questioned the expenses, the entertainment character, and the occasional American culture insensitivities. However, these remarks echoed all over Europe and were heard against all kinds of expressions of American popular culture.[16]

The Janz Quartet, a musical band of brothers-in-law of German heritage, had first accustomed their conservative Mennonite subculture in Canada to the use of popular music for religious purposes, and gladly joined Youth for Christ for a its 1951 tour in Germany in 1951. They brought older American revival hymns in a German translation. Five years later the Janz mission decided to set up a permanent mission in Germany with Canadian support and provided the continuity for the intermittently Graham crusades. They were successful cultural brokers as long as the Southern Gospel songs were not yet cast aside by rock music.[17]

The results of Youth for Christ were promising; team reports quoted thousands of participants and hundreds of conversions in the late 1940s.[18] It was this moment of decision, however, that proved to be a "clash of cultures". The revival practice defined a Christian as a person who had explicitly responded to a religious experience with her/his emotions and her/his will. Most of the audience belonged to a tradition in which a formal educational path led to church membership, by confirmation or a confession of faith. The evangelists presented their "warm" lived religion of the heart in contrast to the "cold" religion of the mind. Their programs in civic buildings summarized the gospel in common speech, opened the flour to a testimonial, and prepared the senses with harmonious music.

This approach to the need for religious experience was part of a larger trend of individual expression of a reflective self that emerged in the 1950s and erupted in the 1960s. The Beat poets are a clear marker of this trend. In religion, individual expression was an alternative to the ritualized collective sense of belonging. This collective style was identified as cold. The rallies

15 Uta Balbier, "Billy Graham in Berlin: German Protestantism between Americanization and Rechristianization," *Zeithistorische Forschungen/Studies in Contemporary History*, Online-Ausgabe 7 (2010) H.3. Url < http://www.zeithistorische-forschungen.de/16126041-Balbier-3-2010 > visited 1 August 2019.

16 Enns, "Saving Germany," 198-202.

17 Ibid., 163-178; Friedemann Walldorf, "A Friendly Space: Popular Music in North American Evangelical Missions to Germany from the 1950s to the 1990s," in John Corrigan and Frank Hinkelmann, eds., *Return to Sender: American Evangelical Missions in Twentieth Century Europe* (Zürich: LIT-Verlag, 2019), 119-137.

18 *Youth for Christ Magazine*, February 1947, 4-5, 54.

taught the teenagers and young adults that they did not need formal permission from a clergyman to enter the fold, but to make their own desire explicit, for instance by simply singing in English or their native tongue: "Jesus Christ is the Way, Jesus Christ is the Truth, Jesus Christ is the Life, and He's mine, mine, mine." Thus they made an individual choice to become part of an exciting movement that involved individuals and crowned their activities with a divine meaning. Some churches adopted these American models and national organizations continued the work of the Americans, recognizing the fact that these foreigners, as liberators, were part of the attraction.[19]

Youth for Christ arrived at the right moment in Europe. It endorsed the contents of traditional Protestantism, extended the wartime moral discourse to juvenile behavior and familiarized European youth with innovative modes of religious expression. Evidence of true conversion was changed behavior and the desire to participate in missions. A slow-down of activities could indicate a weakening of Christianity. The religious infrastructure in Europe was not attuned to this approach. Few established churches could offer the new (or revived) converts the spirituality that they needed including expressive songs, space for spontaneous emotions and shared experiences, and sermons with current relevance. These churches saw their motivated people slip away to Baptist, Pentecostal, and Full Gospel churches.[20]

A Different Approach for Catholic Europe

The religious conditions in Catholic countries were different and similar results could hardly be achieved. They lacked volunteers, organizers, money, and an infrastructure for channeling converts to religious communities. Here the ground needed to be worked individually. Mission projects in Portugal, France, and Italy showed how American evangelicals tried to create a structural presence in Catholic Europe by denominational and by interdenominational missions.

The beginning was more accidental than planned. A number of American missionaries ended up in Catholic Europe because they had to abandon their projects in European colonies. They decided to make the best of the sit-

19 Jan van Capelleveen et al., *De story van Youth for Christ* (Kampen: Kok, 1977), 41. Peter van Rooden worked this idea of the expressive self out in Peter van Rooden, "Long-term Religious Developments in the Netherlands, ca 1750-2000," in Hugh McLeod and W. Ustorf, eds., *The Decline of Christendom in Western Europe, 1750-2000* (Cambridge 2002), 113-129 and "The Strange Death of Dutch Christendom," in Callum G. Brown and Michael Snape, eds., *Secularisation in the Christian World: Essays in Honour of Hugh McLeod* (Farnham: Ashgate, 2010), 175-196.

20 Sipco J. Vellenga, *Een ondernemende beweging. De groei van de evangelische beweging in Nederland* (Amsterdam: VU Uitgeverij, 1991), 106.

uation by relocating to the mother country, after having learned the European colonizers' language. This happened to Magnus and Clara Foreid of the Scandinavian Alliance Mission who could not stay in Mozambique in 1936 and decided to settle in Portugal. They set up small congregations in Alges and Queluz, close to Lisbon, until war conditions forced their return to the United States. During the war, they convinced their board that European countries should be added to the list of target areas. They returned to Portugal in 1946 with a number of new missionaries. Because these missionaries took on most of the responsibilities, the churches remained small. After forty years of input in the mid-1980s, only nine small churches were the result. Since then, TEAM changed its strategy by involving locals more and intensifying the cooperation within the team.[21]

Parallel to TEAM the Conservative Baptist Foreign Mission Society (CBFMS) discovered Portugal as a mission field in 1945.[22] This mission agency was created by conservative Baptist churches that had left the Northern Baptist Convention during World War II because its mission board allowed liberal missionaries who denied cardinal doctrines of the Christian faith to serve. They organized this alternative Mission Society. One of their first missionaries was the previously mentioned Samuel Faircloth, a 1943 graduate from Wheaton College and a class mate of Billy and Ruth Graham. He took a degree from Eastern Baptist Theological Seminary in Philadelphia and enlisted as army chaplain serving the U.S. Fifth Army in Italy. As many other American soldiers, he felt Europe's hunger for a spiritual message. After the war, Faircloth and other U.S. chaplains helped Protestant ministers reunite with their scattered congregations in Southern Europe.

Though CBFMS had affiliated with the EFMA, Faircloth was not exclusive. He approached representatives of the World Council of Churches and the American Council of Christian Churches, but concluded after a meeting with general secretary Willem A. Visser 't Hooft that the unity that the WCC tried to achieve was too organizational, in fact "fabricated" and not "a sovereign work of the Holy Spirit".[23]

In the summer of 1949, the Faircloth family (Sam, his wife Arlie, and baby daughter Becky) left for Portugal with 53 pieces of luggage, including three church organs, three bicycles, and four large boxes of relief clothing.[24] The tiny

21 Vernon Mortenson, *God Made it Grow: Historical Sketches of TEAM's Church Planting Work* (Pasadena, CA: William Carey Library, 1994), 190-192, 723-735.

22 The Evangelical Alliance Mission (TEAM) was the first American mission working in this country since 1936.

23 Interview of author with dr. Samuel Faircloth, June 5, 2011, Carol Stream, Illinois. He was a missionary to Portugal between 1949 and 1985 and then academic dean and vice president for Academic Affairs of Tyndale Theological Seminary in Badhoevedorp, The Netherlands, from 1985 through 1990.

24 Field Letter 1, 1 June 1949, BGCA col. 658 Faircloth field letters.

Portuguese Baptist Convention had asked the Americans to open a seminary to educate national pastors needed in their churches. Portugal was the poorest country in western Europe and ruled by dictator Antonio Salazar. Foreigners were followed constantly by secret police trained by the Nazi Gestapo and had to struggle to obtain and retain their visas.

Faircloth counted five thousand born-again Portuguese in a seven million population. He found willing audiences but few able preachers and therefore founded the Baptist Theological Seminary of Leiria (Seminario Teoloogico Baptista de Leiria) in 1950.[25] This institution graduated over 60 per cent of the Baptist ministry during the years 1950-65, before it was eventually replaced by another seminary supported by the Southern Baptist Foreign Mission Society. Faircloth reported a monthly score of ten to thirty converts in various parts of Portugal, which he travelled by a "mechanical missionary" (a Dodge). The growth in the number of people attending services in early 1950 provoked angry responses by Catholics and Communists and stimulated the missionaries even more. In the summer of 1950 they prepared the ground for a twenty-day Youth for Christ campaign.[26]

Five years later, at the beginning of his second term, the seminary had grown from three to twenty-seven students, and the first Portuguese ministers were ordained to minister to newly planted churches. Support from America was sought to buy a new car, lawn mowers, tool chests, and photographic supplies for publicity purposes. Diplomatic pressure from the US State Department helped Faircloth navigate the visa restrictions. In late 1956, the church body counted 31 churches with 25 missions and 2,215 regulars attendees. It had accomplished more than the colleagues of TEAM, but it was still a long way to meet the target of one hundred churches.[27] In a country that was almost exclusively Roman Catholic, these posts were all but invisible, but in the United States the news spread. The number of American churches that supported Faircloth tripled from 12 in 1948 to 36 a decade later, monthly newsletters and mission presentations during furloughs helped Americans to identify a new trend, seeing Europe as a mission field.

The TEAM-members in Portugal specialized in the printing and distribution of religious tracts, which demanded their presence in the country.[28] In the fall of 1953 Albert and Mary Lee Bobby, who had joined the Portugal-TEAM feared that all Protestant missionaries were ousted as a result of a Portuguese

25 In 1974, Faircloth helped found the Portuguese Bible Institute (Instituto Biblico Portugues) that copied the curriculum of Moody Bible Institute in Chicago and prepared its graduates for Christian service.

26 Field Letter 4, 6, 9, 12, 16.

27 Field Letter, March 1955, April 1955, January 1956, May 1956, December 1956. The mission had 21 ordained pastors, 58 preaching laymen and 12 women workers.

28 BGCA col. 171 file 6 Bobby correspondence 1953-1961, Portugal Conquest for Christ, 1953. Page 11-12 gives titles.

agreement with the Vatican. The missionaries maintained close contacts with the US ambassador to get their visas approved. The ambassador admitted there was no religious freedom in Portugal. The solution was to leave for Spain and return with a 60-day resident visa. They stayed for half a year, partly in the same hotel with other American missionaries as the paper work was processed. When they returned they were forbidden to continue their line of religious work. They found an alternative in preparing radio programs that were broadcasted from Tangiers and followed up with correspondence. Nevertheless, the work suffered from the rule that they had to leave the country for six months before they could resume their activities.[29]

In their response to counter Catholic monopolies, the evangelists found an ally in Walter E. Van Kirk of the (American) National Council of Churches. In 1952, Van Kirk met confidentially with William Dunham of the Spain desk of the State Department to discuss the problems Protestants were facing on the Iberian peninsula. Dunham explained that the free world needed to accept the dictatorship in Spain to keep the Communists out. Van Kirk responded that his Protestant constituency was getting restless about the lack of religious freedom in Spain.[30] The State Department considered the authorities in Spain as far more hostile towards Protestants than in Portugal, as the Spanish constitution indicated that Catholicism was the official religion of the Spanish state and an integral part of the national identity. When organized protesters damaged Protestant churches, this provoked the American consul to request protection of the American missionaries' property. The US Embassy pressed for equal rights to non-protestants, however, the situation for Protestant missionaries really improved only in the late 1960s.[31]

When the visa problem was solved, TEAM returned to spreading religious tracts as its main activity at evangelism campaigns, supported by food programs, radio broadcasts, children's programs, and bible study groups. Albert Bobby was responsible for the distribution of tracts and found support from two other American evangelical agencies, the World Home Bible League and

29 Letters Mr. Bobby to pastor, 3 October 1953, 29 April 1954, February 1955, 8 March 1955, BGCA col. 171 file 6 Bobby correspondence 1953-1961. Other couples had to stay in Spain for a year and two months and were then refused entrance.

30 Report of Conversation between Mr. William Dunham of the Spain desk of the State Department and Walter E. Van Kirk, 13 May 1952, PHS NCC RG 6, Division of Christian Life and Mission, 1945-1973, Series II Department of international Affairs, 1950-1972, box 25.

31 OSS/State Department Intelligence and Research Reports, Europe, 1950-1991 Supplement, Intelligence Report, Portuguese Background Series No 6180.4, 11 March 1953, Role of the Church, 3: "the hierarchy has occasionally expressed distrust of domestic Protestantism"; Spanish Background Series No 6098.10, 18 March 1953, Protestants and Jews, Religious Toleration: "Protestants particularly suffer from numerous deprivations of human rights..." and No 6098.9 17 March 1953, Role of the Catholic Church. See J.D. Hughey, Jr., "Baptists in Spain," in Sadler, ed., *Europe*, 79-90; Dean Acheson to U.S. Ambassador to Spain Stanton Griffis, 10 August 1951, United States Department of State, *Foreign relations of the United States, 1950. Western Europe* (1951) vol. 4: 861-862.

the Every Home Crusade, hoping "... if He tarries, to reach every home in this needy land with a tract and a gospel of John."[32] In addition he helped spread 30,000 tracts through in the Portuguese-speaking world. When the Conservative Baptist Foreign Mission Society established a bible school in Portugal, TEAM sent its Portuguese converts there. This made them part of the network of evangelical bible schools in Europe that served as a cohesive force in the fragmented missionary endeavors.

The anti-liberal agenda of many evangelical mission agencies curtailed the full potential of female missionaries, as Albert's partner Mary Lee experienced. Whereas, in the first decades of TEAM in the 1910s and 1920s, women had occupied leadership positions because the pressure of the end times was felt, women had to submit to male authority in the 1950s, in order to avoid any suggestion of liberalism. Nevertheless, Mary Lee and other women found useful occupations by entering private homes and making female friends, which proved often more effective than the contested public meetings, over which men presided. This solution worked as long as female workers looked favorable about American gender roles. But when the second feminist revolution also knocked on the doors of conservative agencies, these arrangements felt increasingly unfair and unproductive as the stories of female missionaries in the 1960s and 1970s reveal.[33]

The work had moved to a next stage with many Portuguese joining the mission. This caused the problem of unequal pay for the same work, as Americans had higher stipends than the Portuguese. There was nothing that could be done to change it.[34] In 1965, two encyclicals resulting from Vatican II confirmed religious freedom. These improved the situation in Catholic countries.

The process of Protestant church plantings in Italy was similar to Spain, but went more slowly than in Portugal. After the first Conservative Baptist missionaries of Italian descent arrived in 1947, they concentrated their work on Naples, but could not get a congregation started. They concentrated on a book store, organized an evening bible school, and cooperated with agencies specializing in literature and child evangelism. In the period 1960-1990 Conservative Baptist missionaries established 17 congregations, but only five survived. Some of these churches were really only preaching stations, others suffered from competition from Pentecostal and Brethren churches. Half of newly baptized members dropped out. The low success rate discouraged the missionaries and caused a high turnover rate. Lack of vision, disagreement about the

32 Al Bobby to Augie, 3 October 1960, BGCA col. 171, file 6, Bobby correspondence 1953-1961.

33 For a more detailed account of the activities in Portugal see Hans Krabbendam, "Full Members of the TEAM? Evangelical Women in the European Mission, 1945-1980," *Journal of American Studies* 51.4 (2017): 1095-1116.

34 Al Bobby to Stanley, 24 May 1963 from Washington DC, BGCA col. 171 file 7 Bobby correspondence 1962-1978. Part of the problem was that American Christians did not feel the same urge to fund native workers as they did American missionaries.

direction, and the failure to train an indigenous leadership depressed growth. The missionaries were too independent and the members did not identify fully with the mission agency.[35]

The new churches were obliged to transfer ten per cent of their budget to the association while Italians were slow to assume the high costs of supporting their own ministers. As a result an average of only one in ten American missionaries returned to Italy after furlough for a second tour of duty. This cycle of discouragement furthered in a lack of unity. In contrast, TEAM allowed the indigenous churches more freedom, more ownership, and did not expect them to follow an American model.

This example shows that conservative evangelicals took initiatives in Catholic Europe in response to practical situations and personal encounters. Their goal was to found new congregations, but it proved to be hard work that was partly inspired by internal American competition. Fragmentation and the small scale exhausted their resources and necessitated financial life-lines to the United States, if only to create distance between evangelicals and the money-asking ways of the Catholic Church. The result was that it created a new dependency. Considering these challenges evangelicals more easily invested in the distribution of religious literature. Taken individually, these efforts were of little consequence, but together they built an image of concerted action in Europe in America and contributed to a new evangelical network in Europe, with Billy Graham's crusade as a rallying point.

Recognition of Europe as an Official Mission Field for Evangelicals in 1952

The combination of beginning mission posts and the mass campaigns of Graham in Europe converged into one movement in the 1950s. Since 1948 Youth for Christ had been building a string of national boards all over Europe and championed a European evangelical network that had grown around the 1948 meetings in Switzerland and the Netherlands. American missionary organizations created bridgeheads in all European countries. The small and scarce American-supported agencies that were active in Europe before the war saw their numbers grow, so that by 1952 250 American missionaries were counted. They represented one percent of the total number of American missionaries and consisted of a dwindling number of fraternal workers sent by American denominations, mostly Presbyterians and Baptists, to assist sister churches in Europe, and a growing contingent of evangelical missionaries. The largest

35 Marion F. Martin, "The Conservative Baptist Mission in Italy: Past Achievements, Future Opportunities" (Deerfield, IL, D. Miss. Thesis, Trinity Evangelical Divinity School, 1994), 216-259.

concentration of these new missions were in Catholic countries such as Italy, Belgium, France, Portugal, Spain, and Austria, and with smaller ones in Britain, Holland, West-Germany, and Scandinavia.[36] The ministries of American evangelicals in Northern European countries targeted youth and mobilized Christians, while in the South they tried to plant new churches and distribute literature. All regions identified the need for educational programs.[37]

This trend put Europe on the American missionary map. In 1951, the Belgian Gospel Mission – one of the first American mission organizations active in Europe – joined the Interdenominational Foreign Mission Association, strengthening the institutional links with the United States. The *IFMA News Bulletin* of December that year began to list Europe as a separate category. The issue listed a number of initiatives: The Evangelical Alliance Mission (TEAM) sent four missionaries to France, Wycliffe Bible Translators planned to set up a Linguistic Institute in Britain, and Genoa, Italy, hosted a missionary conference for 35 missionaries.[38]

The next issues of the news bulletin reported new initiatives from other parts of Europe, actively engaged readers to pray for the visa troubles in Spain and Portugal, and soon filled an entire page in the newsletter including political news. Among the 31 member associations in the IFMA, five, later six, had workers in Europe.[39] It was clearly a Protestant endeavor, as the editor of the bulletin explained: "One hesitates to even mention France as being a mission field, but we must remember that there are at least 30,000 villages and cities

36 R. Pierce Beaver, "Distribution of the American Protestant Foreign Missionary Force in 1952,"*Missionary Research Library, Occasional Bulletin* 4.10 (13 July 1953), 1 and Beaver, "The Expansion of American Foreign Missionary Activities Since 1945," *Missionary Research Library, Occasional Bulletin* 5.7 (4 June 1954), 5-6.

37 See for the seven main activities, church planting, personal evangelism, mass evangelism, literature distribution, broadcasting, theological education, support of national churches: William L. Wagner, *North American Protestant Missionaries in Western Europe: A Critical Appraisal* (Bonn: Verlag für Kultur und Wissenschaft, 1993), 41-50.

38 *IFMA News Bulletin*, December 1951; Aaldert Prins, "The History of the Belgian Gospel Mission from 1918 to 1962" (Ph.D. Dissertation Evangelische Theologische Faculteit Leuven, 2015).

39 *IFMA News Bulletin*, February and April 1952; American European Fellowship, Belgian Gospel Mission, Gospel Mission Union, Slavic Gospel Association, The Evangelical Alliance Mission, *IFMA News Bulletin*, July and October 1952. European Evangelistic Crusade joined IFMA in 1953 and Greater Europe Mission in 1955, also belonged to the EFMA; the Bible Christian Union in joined in 1957. In 1956 ten organizations were active in Europe. The May 1953 issue hinted at a one thousand circulation of the news bulletin. De Gasperi government was welcomed and its fall deplored (July-August 1953) and rejoiced in the election of Adenauer (September/October 1953) and it drew attention to the presidential elections in France in 1954. It expected changes of policy from the top down (see expectations from the Fanfani cabinet in the January-February 1954 issue. See William L. Wagner, *North American Protestant Missionaries in Western Europe: A Critical Appraisal* (Bonn: Verlag für Kultur und Wissenschaft, 1993), 24-25 for a list of agencies.

without any Protestant testimony."[40] The entry of organized Protestant missionaries increased the number of Protestant-Catholic encounters. When the Vatican pressured European authorities to oust missionaries, close chapels, and prevent worship in private homes, American Protestants and Catholics voiced their protests in the media and American ambassadors took action.

These actions and reactions left American evangelicals with a bleak political and religious picture of Europe. In 1951, students at Moody Bible Institute learned about Europe through a cartoon of a globe featuring Europe surrounded by dark forces of strikes, crime, war, sin, fear, doubt, and political strife, from the student president of the Missionary Union: "They [the Europeans] are sick of the old way of life, unhappy about the present uncertain mode of living and do not know which way to turn. Such a situation presents a great opportunity and challenge to the Christian Church and to us as individuals."[41]

The *IFMA News Bulletin* noticed in the spring of 1953: "It is estimated that 75% of Europe's population is 'pagan'."[42] The editor hoped to compensate for the "lack of intelligence on the part of [American] Christians concerning world affairs" as the "affairs of the nations, politically, economically and socially ought to be of real concern to us."[43] This sense of urgency came from the combined pressure of Communist and Catholic forces and the surprise of the fall of China: "We never really thought China would fall."[44] It praised the restrictions on Catholic domination in Yugoslavia and bewailed the news about the resumption of United States' diplomatic relations with the Vatican in March 1954, because the Roman Catholic hierarchy continued to suppress civil liberties.

The *Bulletin* reported progress, when visas were issued and Communism suffered setbacks. The editor used corporate metaphors to encourage missionary activities in Europe. He linked the electoral losses of the Communist Party in the Netherlands to the American investments of forty million dollars in that country. "If Christians were only as willing to invest funds in Europe in the gospel ministry, it would bring eternal dividends." Later that year he quoted the success of the advertising campaign by the Knights of Columbus for Catholic converts as evidence that money had a real impact on mission projects.[45]

Despite these silver linings, the reputation of Europe in the *Bulletin* grew darker every year: "One cannot help but think of Communism as almost synonymous with Europe, as this Godless religion seems to grip more and more of the peoples of Europe in an ironclad grasp." Stories from Spain confirmed that

40 *IFMA News Bulletin*, December 1952.
41 *Moody Student*, 4 April 1951 and 25 May 1951.
42 *IFMA News Bulletin*, March 1953.
43 Ibid., May 1953.
44 Ibid., September/October 1953.
45 Ibid., May and November/December 1954.

the Catholic hierarchy feared Protestants more than Communists.[46] The mid 1950s appeared to be the darkest hour, because after that the visa regulations relaxed. Especially the Italian decision to grant legal status to the Assemblies of God raised positive expectations for other Protestant groups in the region.[47]

Meanwhile the missionaries expanded their repertoire to find a hearing in Europe. In 1952, the "Jubilaires," Moody's male quartet, made a five-month tour of six European countries on behalf of Youth for Christ and found eager audiences, but few public conversions. The singers explained this reticence from young people's fear of having to give up all worldly amusements and that communism would soon overwhelm them and threaten the lives of Christians. "The people of Europe are open to the Gospel, but very little is being done to meet their great spiritual need."[48]

Methods that had proven their effectivity in the United States were copied in Europe. The TEAM evangelists in France began in early 1952 with organizing children's and youth clubs, distributing tracts, and have public meetings in tents. The work proved hard, as it took three years to report the first baptism. When they found out that a flourishing youth group disbanded as soon as the missionaries left on furlough, they realized that they would have to work more fundamentally. Planting new churches and linking them in an association helped, but even so the results were modest, with twelve converts after six years of work.[49]

The newly designed *IFMA News* continued to point out opportunities and initiatives in Europe, such as the availability of radio stations for programming, the founding of new literature organizations which could profit from election results which might expand civil liberties.[50] By the end of the decade, optimism ruled. In April 1959 *IFMA News* rejoiced: "The Summit Meeting in May, the solidarity of NATO, and other political issues, and the increasing economic stability all add up to important and strategic days that could mean much for the future of Europe. It is a day of opportunity for the gospel."[51]

The countries that were culturally farthest removed from the United States – Catholic-dominated, dictator-led, Communist-threatened, and often

46 *IFMA News Bulletin*, July 1954.

47 Ibid., November/December 1954 and *IFMA News*, September 1955.

48 *Moody Student*, 22 February 1952. Yet, American evangelical agencies in Europe complained about the lack of visibility of the European mission field in American colleges: Letter J.C. Winston of the Belgian Gospel Mission to Harold R. Cook, head of the mission program at Moody Bible Institute, 5 January 1953 and response, 17 February 1953, which confirmed the lack of visibility (there were more Moody graduates working in Europe than listed; they needed special intellectual qualifications for work in Europe.) KADOC, Leuven, Archief Belgische Evangelische Zending (1900 (c)-2009), inv. 527 Moody Bible Institute, 1953-1955.

49 Mortenson, *God Made it Grow*, 738-744.

50 *IFMA News*, March 1957.

51 Ibid., October 1960.

poor – darkened the image of Europe among American Protestants. On top of that evangelicals noticed that the north-western part of Europe lacked religious zeal and, even worse, prevented the penetration of the gospel worldwide. This perspective attracted attention to the training centers for missionary candidates, first in the United States, but soon also in Europe.

Training, Recruitment, and Funding

The main providers for evangelical missionary agencies were students and bible-school graduates, as were the aforementioned families. The bible schools in America were actually modeled after European examples, but had become distinct centers of education in the 1920s to train home and foreign missionaries. Their number grew quickly so that throughout the century they made up the backbone of a new kind of evangelicalism. In response to the challenges of the corporate and communication revolution, labor unrest, the growth of free churches, and wide-spread reform aspirations in the United States, they created a new subculture.[52]

At the beginning of the Depression close to fifty institutions were in business and this growth rate continued without decline. Twenty-five new bible schools opened their doors in the 1930s and an equal number during World War II. Enrollment at these one hundred training centers varied from a handful to hundreds of students, who were taught bible study, missions, music, and practical training in communicating the gospel. The goal was to equip mostly adult students for practical service as the instructors considered a lengthy scholarly training a killer of enthusiasm. Through the early decades of the twentieth century the curriculum expanded to include Christian education, languages, and pastoral care. The institutions weathered the economic crisis because they were low-cost and flexible. The older ones supported their activities by adding publishing houses, conference centers venues, and radio stations. Evangelicals redesigned the old time religion as a symbol of orthodoxy. Without a fixed creed its contents became malleable, which proved a useful instrument for positioning nondenominational organizations against the stagnation of traditional institutions and the threats of modern theological methods. Doctrinal innovations such as dispensationalism served as evidence of the value of plain reading of the bible, which generated almost scientific certainty.

52 Virginia Lieson Brereton, *Training God's Army: The American Bible School, 1880-1940* (Bloomington: Indiana University Press, 1990), 57-58; Timothy Gloege, *Guaranteed Pure: The Moody Bible Institute, Business, and the Making of Modern Evangelicalism* (Chapel Hill: The University of North Carolina Press, 2015).

Moody Bible Institute (MBI) was the leading light among American bible schools. It became the model and hub of the new evangelical identity. The institution was founded by famous evangelist Dwight D. Moody in 1886 and classes began three years later. Originally it planned to host 200 men and 50 women, but in practice, Moody attracted a majority of women. In the 1910s MBI had invited scholars to contribute to a body of documents, the fundamentals project, to codify true orthodoxy in an effort to disentangle it from radical faith healers and revolutionary workers for justice who used religion for populist ends. However, the fundamentals turned into a straightjacket against liberalism that had only a limited appeal to the masses. MBI set out to restore respectability to avoid association with the extreme expressions and secure broad appeal. As conservative Protestants distanced themselves from fundamentalists, they embraced middle class values and adopted the metaphor of productivity for their religious plans: true Christians were productive. The new training centers had to help them to spread the Protestant message quickly and professionally.[53]

The practical purpose of these bible schools was to mobilize students for the end of times. The most efficient way to prepare them was to use a deductive method: the grand scheme of the bible was clear and the students needed to appropriate and apply the supporting texts. The questions for bible study pointed at a dispensationalist outcome and avoided scholarly commentaries, which more often than not caused confusion, created dependence on others, or slowed down application. This approach forged a spiritual bond with the one source and created a synthesis. This empirical method created a preference for dwelling on biblical facts, and looking for missionary principles and spiritual mechanism and laws. The curriculum gave the impression of objectivity and strengthened the conviction of the students. Moody Bible Institute provided the standard. It promoted memorizing as an important tool and emulation of moral examples of biblical protagonists. Both practices built an arsenal for commitment to the task and for persuading others to admit their sinfulness and need for change. Lapsed Christians especially appeared to be open to this approach of quoting pivotal bible verses. Other courses prepared the students to approach a variety of audiences. After World War II the social sciences entered the curriculum as part of the increasing sophistication in methodology and variation of fields.[54]

The structure of the program at MBI did not single out Europe as a destination that needed special skills or preparation. It needed more efforts to

53 Gloege, *Guaranteed Pure*, 117-192; Gene A. Getz, *MBI: The Story of Moody Bible Institute* (Chicago: Moody Press, 1969), 100-104. See for similarities in the curriculum at Prairie Bible Institute: Timothy Wray Callaway, "Training Disciplined Soldiers for Christ: the influence of American Fundamentalism at Prairie Bible Institute during the L.E. Maxwell Era (1922-1980)" (Th.D. Dissertation, Pretoria: University of South Africa, 2010), 378-383.

54 Brereton, *Training*, 90-97.

recruit missionaries for Europe. One of them was to invite foreign students. The internationals fluctuated between 70 and 80 students out of one thousand students, with the great majority coming from Commonwealth nations (Canada), and only a handful from Europe.[55]

Originally bible college students had targeted the domestic field, the working class, and immigrants. The urban setting was important initially, but gradually many schools moved to the suburbs where they could more easily expand or chose the countryside, such as Prairie Bible Institute in Three Hills, Alberta, Canada. Moody, however, stayed in the inner city. As president William Culbertson explained in 1951: "... so that the various opportunities for Christian ministry are near at hand... these and many more are the places where our students learn first-hand that the gospel is the power of God unto salvation to him that believeth."[56]

The spiritual atmosphere at these schools was demanding and often steeped in perfectionist expectations, including a strong emphasis on self-sacrifice. The program kept students continuously busy with applying principles, planning occasions to share the gospel, seeking confrontation, training discipline, worrying about financial means and the right destination.[57]

The bible schools followed the trend in North American education that promoted practical training. This objective stimulated the founding of high schools and vocational schools. Together these schools offered an alternative for higher education for those who failed to meet college standards. These secondary schools presented themselves as really democratic institutions. Also the bible school prided itself in welcoming all classes of people. Their goal was to train students to become mostly teachers, and this was a relatively easy job. Optimistically the schools believed that people would change when the reasons were convincingly presented to them. After the pioneer phase, in which women held positions of prominence, the female presence had been pushed back in search of respectability and accreditation. The schools functioned as a unifying force in American fundamentalism.[58]

In 1948, MBI chose a corporate structure, which prepared the access for Moody students to a BA degree at other liberal arts colleges. This was a sign of the increasing importance of academic standards among the schools' leadership. Many bible schools developed into colleges which granted degrees and sought accreditation. They abandoned excursions in other fields (media, cor-

55 MBI Archives Box annual reports educational department 1953-1955. An average of four European countries were represented.

56 W. Culbertson, "The Spiritual Contribution of the Bible Institute and Bible College in World Crisis," [18 October 1951], 8, MBI Culbertson collection, box 6.

57 Brereton, *Training*, 114-126.

58 Ibid., 159.

respondence courses) as these activities proved a burden for further academic development.[59]

In the 1940s the curriculums of the bible colleges were streamlined by the American Association of Bible Colleges, upgrading their degrees to the level of colleges. The founding of the Accrediting Association of Bible Institutes and Bible Colleges in 1947 (which went through various name changes) marked the aspiration to reach a level of respectability and provided the model for other accrediting organizations, including those in Europe.[60]

The bible schools offered missionaries what the seminaries lacked: practical training. In the mid-1950s, the mainline-evangelical researcher Kenyon E. Moyer investigated the quality of the missionary education at established seminaries and found it "far from satisfactory."[61] This study among 915 missionaries who served between 1932 and 1952, revealed that a third of them left after five years of service and only 21 per cent stayed longer than 20 years on their posts. This meant the replacement need was high. Of course the times were exceptional with a political crisis following an economic one, but the level of early withdrawals seemed to increase. The researcher wondered whether a better orientation and preparation might have caused a relocation and not abandonment of the field. At least 14 per cent of the dropouts could have been prevented had there been a more careful selection. The great majority of missionaries, four out of five, lacked training in principles and methods of missions, cultural orientation, and language. Evangelical schools like Moody had developed training programs with many practical components. The older seminaries had to adapt as well. The report suggested a number of practical improvements, such as radio workshops, summer schools, social sciences, practice in shoe repairing and soap-making, and a special program for missionary aviation.

The desire of candidates for missions was the key criterion for selection. Ruth Eileen Witmer's experience was a good example of how candidates grew into missions. She had been raised in a committed evangelical family. Her fa-

59 Brereton, *Training*, 71-86.

60 The Accrediting Association of Bible Colleges (1957), the American Association of Bible Colleges (1973), the Accrediting Association of Bible Colleges (1994), the Association for Biblical Higher Education (2004), the Association for Biblical Higher Education in Canada and the United States (2009). See <http://www.abhe.org/pages/NAV-OurHistory.html>. It claims an affiliation of 200 of the 1200 institutions in North America. Other accrediting organizations are regional, most are not officially recognized by the American Department of Education. The EEAA does not have the legal authority to accredit academic degrees within the single states of the EU. It only provides standards for peer institutions.

61 Kenyon E. Moyer, *A Study of Missionary Motivation, Training, and Withdrawal (1932-1952): Based on Questionnaires Answered by 915 Missionaries Who Represent 16 North American Mission Boards* (New York: Missionary Research Library, 1957). See Kenyon E. Moyer, "The Selection and Training of the Overseas Personnel of the Christian Church," *Occasional Bulletin* 8.8 (15 August 1957), 5; Robert T. Coote, "Finger on the Pulse: Fifty Years of Missionary Research," *The Free Library* 24.3 (1 July 2000), 98-105.

ther taught at Fort Wayne Bible College and pastored a Missionary Church (a branch of the Mennonite Church in Indiana). Her environment breathed missions that was so strong that she believed, "I should go to the mission field unless I have a good excuse to stay home." From an early age on she attended the weekly Friday night mission presentations at the college and the missionary summer camps. She went to nursing school as preparation for missions and enrolled at Wheaton College, Illinois, where she found her future husband before graduating in 1955.

Wheaton helped her, and many other students, to expand her horizon and discover the many options among missionary agencies. In the early sixties she linked up with TEAM. She remembered the tiring procedure: "... the applications were quite long and involved and complete, and then there was quite a long wait because they had a lot of references to ask. And not only did they get references from the people we gave them, but they asked each of those to give a couple of references. So... there was a lot of investigation which was very good. ... I felt that TEAM was very thorough in their applying ... not only in their academics but in their checking of the emotional stability of the missionaries. I thought that the tests that we had were very good. And I don't feel that the period was too long, because it... it gave you, you know, that much longer to really evaluate what you were doing and to become acquainted with the country that you're going to. ... And then climaxing with candidate school, which was great. By the time we left I felt we were very prepared. ... I cannot say that I was really apprehensive about going at all. I was very confident." At candidate school "we had good corporate sessions when everybody was together, then we broke up into smaller groups according to countries or to continents." Witmer went on to South Africa, but the procedure was similar for other continents, including Europe.[62] While she had been thinking about missions since her childhood years, most missionaries decided their destination during their final year in college or after graduation.[63]

Mission preparation was much more than taking mission classes. The entire program breathed missions, and many bible classes emphasized God's mission to the earth.[64] The students responded by keeping the missionary fires burning through weekly program to study and pray for missions, and most importantly, to organize annually an intense three-day conference offering a wide menu of missionary options. It was from this student initiative that the school offered formal missionary courses in 1915.[65] By 1950 the course schedule added missionary technique to train students in aviation, radio, and

62 BGCA Collection 317- Ruth (Witmer) Cook, T3 Transcript, interview by Paul Ericksen in Fort Wayne Indiana on 1 October 1985.

63 See Moyer, *Study of Missionary Motivation*, 29.

64 Interview by author of Dr. Robert J. Vajko, a graduate of Columbia Bible College in South Carolina, on 24 September 2012, Carol Stream, IL.

65 Getz, *MBI*, 167.

photography. The missionary course familiarized the students with the life of missionaries, comparative religions, the history and science of missions, phonetics and languages, tropical hygiene, and later first aid, bookkeeping, manual training, and cooking. These courses revealed the main destinations of the graduates: missions in less developed areas. In 1945 Harold R. Cook, former missionary in Venezuela, took on the responsibility for the missions track and wrote mission manuals.[66] He outlined his expectation for his school in an interview at the end of World War II: "When the war is ended the opportunity for the gospel message will be greater than ever before. When hearts are bleeding, the gospel is received most readily. If the church takes advantage of the opportunity, multitudes in the war-torn countries will turn to God."[67]

Cook attributed a crucial civic role to foreign missionaries. They were in a unique position to "render a genuine patriotic and national service, both to the country from which they come and the country in which they serve... It is clear that foreign missionaries are true soldiers of the better order which is to bind the world together after the war." They could break down the barriers between east and west.[68]

Cook took (married) men as the norm (with proper warnings for the risks of families competing with the purpose of missions), yet the majority of missionaries were women. The gender distribution among Moody's students was identical to that of foreign missionaries, four men to six women. In 1953 for example 45 men and 61 women went abroad, out of 94 male and 125 female graduates. This proportion would only change in the mid-1960s.[69] The track of missionary preparation continued to appeal to women.

The overrepresentation of women was no reason for jubilation. In 1948 the annual report announced that enrollment of women should be capped at 40 per cent and in 1950 the review of the missionary report exclaimed: "Note the increase in the number of men!"[70] This concern for female overrepresentation was inspired by the drop in male attendance in the war and limited capac-

66 Getz, *MBI*, 160-162; Harold R. Cook, *An Introduction to the Study of Christian Missions* (Chicago: Moody Press, 1954).

67 MBI archives, Departmental missions box 1, Memorandum of interview with Dr. Cook [1945].

68 Ibid.

69 MBI Foreign Missionary report 1970: 77 of the 130 students in the missionary department were women. The year 1965 was the first in which men outnumbered women. After 1974 (till 1990) men slightly outnumbered women (600 against 580). In the total number of students over the years men and women reached parity. MBI Foreign Missionary Report, 1953. Box Annual Reports Educational Department 1953, 7. In 1965 there were more men than women from Moody going abroad (49 against 40). Between 1976 and 1980 men outnumbered women, and after 1980 the gender balance was restored. In total for the period 1948-1990 women outnumbered men with 53%. Different reports, such as the annual educational report give different figures of departed missionaries since they left during the year, and not always notified the Institute.

70 MBI Annual report Educational Department 1948, Foreign Missionary Report 1948.

Class of students at Moody Bible Institute in the 1940s-1950s. Dr. Harold R. Cook teaches a mission course to mostly female students.
[Used with permission from the Moody Bible Institute Archives.]

ity in dorms and class rooms. The measures were not perpetuated. Moreover, the most popular track at Moody was foreign missions: 73 of the 162 graduates in 1952 were enrolled in the mission track in addition to 20 who specialized in children's work.[71] The cause of this female overrepresentation was easy to trace: men with missionary ambitions could attend seminaries, where evangelical women were not welcome. Bible schools were the best alternatives for women.

As the Missionary Union was the crucial factor in the candidate's choice of destination of the missionaries, in which half of the students was actively involved, a closer look at this voluntary student body helps to trace the discovery of Europe as a mission field.[72] Under supervision of the Director of the Missionary Course and the business manager of the Institute, an executive board of students inculcated the student body with the missionary spirit by daily devotionals, informative meetings, weekly Saturday evening inspirational meetings, Sunday outreach to raise awareness and funds in neighboring churches, climaxing in a three-day mission conference each fall. Students themselves contributed thousands of dollars from their own meagre budgets to missionary causes, mostly in non-Western countries. Each semester the stu-

71 MBI Annual report Educational Department 1953, 9.

72 "What is the Missionary Union?" MBI Archives, Departmental Missions, box 1 File Missionary Union [1952 history]; MBI, Report of Survey, The Moody Bible Institute of Chicago, 1961, 61.

dents elected the executive board membership and introduced new means to raise mission awareness, such as mission displays in showcases, special money drives to buy missionary books, and weekly news updates in the *Moody Student* newspaper. Missions were a daily presence for Moody students, as the Moody Yearbook in 1947 explained:

> With the strains of "To the Ends of the Earth" dying in our ears many have answered God's call to service in another land. Over half a century of continuous existence has given Missionary Union a prominent place in student life. Nearly every morning and noon, as we leave the dining hall, we are called to turn aside to Massey Chapel for a half-hour of prayer for some mission field. Saturday evening devotions, conducted by Missionary Union, give us the opportunity to hear missionaries and glimpse scenes of their work with now and then a challenge from those who are graduating and setting out for their own fields of service. The need of the foreign field is again called to mind in our own rooms when the Missionary Union collector makes his monthly visit to receive what we may have to offer for the seventy missionary works which the organization helps to support. On Sunday comes the privilege, through deputation meetings, to present to churches throughout this area the missionary need. These and various other related activities are all carried on under student leadership of eleven executive and fifty prayer band officers.[73]

An indication of the students' strong inner motivation was the fact that despite numerous restrictions, female missionaries continued to flock to the mission field. They had better chances in non-denominational agencies than with church organizations. When church planting became the main purpose, women in fundamentalist and evangelical organizations could only work in assisting functions, but when the sharing of the gospel was the main task, they were part of the core activity. Their schooling set them already on a course for future tasks. The requirements for the candidates expected by the agency of the Conservative Baptist Foreign Missions Society showed how this process worked. All male candidates needed a completed seminary or bible school education. For female candidates it sufficed to have had two years of higher education with a minimum of 30 hours bible classes. Missionary wives could join the team without academic credentials. These requirements revealed that biblical instruction was not a standard part of the female preparation. Women in evangelical missions knew that. They were even more theologically conservative than men.[74] However, this did not prevent them from initiating their "own" ministries.

73 *The Arch* (Moody's yearbook) (1947), 41.

74 Glenn F. Arnold, "A Comparative Study of the Present Doctrinal Positions and Christian Conduct Codes of Selected Alumni of Moody Bible Institute: 1945-1971" (Ph.D. dissertation, New York University, 1977), 95.

The shift towards Europe was visible in the MBI statistics. The 1949 annual survey of Moody graduates serving abroad as missionaries showed little more than 2 per cent of the almost two thousand missionaries served in Europe. The turn came in 1951 when ten out of 120 missionaries (or 8 per cent) with Moody credentials sailed out and this trend continued steadily, with a record of 16 out of 106 graduates in 1966 (almost 15 per cent). The board adapted the curriculum in 1969 by introducing third-year seminars concentrating on specific areas, though amidst the many other courses this two, later three hours, per week were electives and seemed not fundamental. By the end of the 1970s, MBI had dispatched 298 missionaries to Europe, of whom 154 were still on active duty. This figure was close to the 10 per cent share that Europe had among the American missionaries worldwide.[75]

As Moody provided ten percent of American missionaries the presentations and the prayer bands for various regions were an important indicator for the popularity and the sense of urgency of each field. Information about foreign destinations also came through international students who shared first-hand experiences and opportunities. Jan van Capelleveen from the Netherlands explained in 1949 European conditions after the war. He had been a volunteer at the early Youth for Christ campaigns and the organization had sent him to Moody with a colleague to take courses in the Christian Education track for five semesters to learn how to organize a bible school in Holland. At Moody he chaired the European prayer band.[76]

The advantage of Europe was its proximity and the cultural overlap. Students were kept informed about staff that went to Europe during the summer to show Christian films and assist in setting up a colportage program. They reported back that distributing literature really worked and that the printer in Spain had converted.[77] The main obstacle was the Roman Catholic Church, which was listed as demanding freedom of religion only for itself, harming Protestant minorities and preventing evangelism. Many Protestants failed to see this.[78]

The Missionary Union encouraged students to dedicate themselves to a mission field. Though most Missionary Union programs hosted missionaries from Latin America and Asia, European visitors shared their experiences.[79] In turn each continent was presented as being neglected, in great darkness, wide

75 MBI Foreign Missionary Reports, 1951, 1966, 1979; *Catalogue MBI*, 1969, 1975-76.

76 *Moody Student*, 22 July 1949, 22 September 1950 and 15 February 1957. An American sponsor paid his expenses. Two of his classmates served with the Baptist Mid-Missions in München. Letter J.C. Maris to C.T. McIntire, 23 February 1956, box 11, file 7, McIntire Collection.

77 *Moody Student*, 10 June and 25 November 1949.

78 Ibid., 3 March 1950.

79 Ibid., N.d. [February] 1951 MU speakers on Bolivia and Hope Bible mission in Europe.

open and eagerly waiting: "Europe, divided and without leadership, gropes blindly for the light. Overlooked by many mission societies, it presents one of the greatest mission fields in the world today."[80] It was not so much the original qualification of Europe's importance – each continent was labeled as a great opportunity – but that Europe took its place as a mission field among the other destinations. Students began to follow the political events in European countries such as Italy and Germany and rejoiced in pro-American electoral victories.[81] Billy Graham drew attention of Moody students to Europe, when he urged them to pray for his London Campaign in 1954.[82] When four years later the Moody Chorale went on a European tour, it explicitly used the cultural kinship with Europe as the cradle of great art where the crowds loved good music. Increasingly Moody students could go on European trips.[83]

Students at Moody constantly felt the pressure to declare a destination of their work. An example of this pressure was the conclusion of the mission conference in the fall of 1961. After three days of intensive presentations about a great variety of mission fields, president William Culbertson was reported to ask

> those who had sensed the leading of God to the mission field during this conference to stand. Then he requested that those who had previously been called to the field join them, and finally those who were willing to go if the Lord led the[m] some future time. After these invitations were given and accepted, it was evident that the students of Moody Bible Institute were united by one compelling force, realizing in an ever-changing world they have an unchanging command: 'Ye are my witnesses… go ye into all the world and preach the gospel to every creature'.[84]

Educational Institutions in Europe

Evangelicals, fundamentalists, and mainliners were all very much aware that the effect of individual organizers, missionaries, or fraternal workers in Europe was limited. The best way to transfer and consolidate skills proved to organize training sessions. These sessions usually began at conferences that often led to educational exchanges. Representatives of American mainline churches felt close to the European churches and abstained from founding new schools as they had done in non-Western countries, but evangelicals and fundamentalists emphasized the differences with Europe and felt the need to

80 *Moody Student*, 25 May 1951 and 8 February 1952.
81 Ibid., 8 October 1954.
82 Ibid., 13 February 1954.
83 Ibid., 9 May 1958. Latin America and Europe were the easiest destinations for summer trips. See Ibid., 27 September 1963.
84 Ibid., 26 October 1961.

train a new European cadre outside the established universities and seminaries. Most denominational and non-denominational agencies of some size set up educational institutions in the early phase. Moody Bible Institute was the model in Europe, as it was in the United States.

Historians have noted the crucial importance of personal bonds as the basis for interdenominational cooperation. The founding fathers of the World Council of Churches in Europe had learned to trust each other during their student years and shared the resistance experience during the war. They used these contacts as vehicles for peace and reconciliation.[85] A similar pattern of shared experiences connected American evangelical pioneers who took to Europe. The central figure was Robert P. Evans (1918-2011) son of Baptist missionaries in French-speaking Africa, a close friend of Billy Graham, a graduate of Wheaton College and of Eastern Baptist Theological Seminary in Philadelphia, and a Chaplain in the United States Navy and Marine Corps in Europe between 1943-46. These characteristics made him the perfect executive secretary for Youth for Christ which hired him to set up activities all over Europe. Evans used his European contacts to found the European Bible Institute in Paris in 1949. Out of his initiative grew a new organization in 1952, the Greater Europe Mission (GEM), which he served as coordinator. Four years later the GEM had grown to 51 workers, mostly in France and Germany, whose main mission was teach evangelical theology and train evangelists.[86]

The bible school as such was not a new phenomenon in Europe. Pietists in England (Spurgeon) and Switzerland (Chrischona) had established the first bible school in the 1840s and 1850s to train staff for new faith missions. Chrischona had a strong transatlantic connection thanks to the 360 students that had gone to the United States in its first century. A few more opened in mid twentieth century and though these institutions enrolled only scores of students, they played a crucial role as bridge heads for American landings, as the 1948 conference in the bible school at Beatenberg showed.[87]

German pietists tried to keep a presence at the theological institutions, but found out that those could not be reformed from within. The growing tension between liberal theological education and the mission schools moved the bible schools to embrace the models of their American evangelical brethren. These were non-denominational and increased the distance between orthodox and liberal. The training of many German instructors at American schools, the models of operation, and the adoption of themes that defined American fundamentalists (inerrancy, dispensationalism, creationism) tied

85 Ryman, "Bureaucratic or Personal Networks? Formation of the Ecumenical Movement During the Second World War," in Gregory and McCleod, *Networks*, 272-273.

86 Robert P. Evans, Newsletter, 28 October 1947, BGCA col. 20 box 72 folder 4; Letter Robert P. Evans to J.O. Percy of the IFMA, 22 November 1956, BGCA col. 352, IFMA, box 7, file 2.

87 Witmer, *Bible College story*, 1962, 15, 34-38.

"Greater Europe Mission staff with Carl Armerding ca. 195," Bensheim, close to Heidelberg. Carl Armerding taught bible at Moody Bible Institute, was Professor of Bible at Wheaton College (future Wheaton college president Hudson T. Armerding was his son). He served on various mission boards, among others as foreign secretary of GEM. In 1955 he took a leave of absence for a mission trip to Europe.
[Courtesy of the Billy Graham Center Archives, Wheaton College, Wheaton, IL]

the schools in German-speaking countries to America.[88] The GEM founded the Bibelschule Bergstrasse in 1955, which went through various names and locations.[89] Most importantly, it challenged the monopoly of state education, by their independence. In every stage of postwar bible school presence, American models guided European processes.

The drive for independent bible schools was also a response to the expected integration of the mainline missionary network in the World Council of Churches. This merger was logical as the World Council wanted to be truly global and on basis of equality. The older established missionary organizations, cooperating in the International Missionary Council (IMC), held their first postwar meeting in Willingen, West-Germany, in July 1952. The result of this conference ended the separation of sending and receiving countries. The leadership agreed that the west and "heathen lands" were all part of the same process and it was not the responsibility of churches to found new churches, but to jointly participate in God's plan for the world, the Missio Dei. The meeting identified the presence of missionary work in Europe (by European churches and agencies!) and called for cooperation among agencies and with humanitarian assistance, and exchange of expertise with younger churches, but not for an outside infusion of the European religious landscape.

88 Bernhard Ott, *Beyond Fragmentation: Integrating Mission and Theological Education. A critical Assessment of some Recent Developments in Evangelical Theological Education* (Oxford: Regnum Books, 2001), 52.
89 The school split in 1959, but continued and inspired the Freie Theologische Akademie in Seeheim in 1974, which moved to Giessen seven years later.

This conclusion made it hard to uphold the separation of church and missionary work and encouraged a merger of the IMC and the WCC. Critics of this merger, such as the American missiologist Ralph Winter, concluded that this new integrative concept confused the various goals of the church rather than spurred missionary activity. As all church activity became missions, hardly anything was done to evangelize Europe. One of the causes of this inactivity was that the proposed WCC-IMC merger excluded the independent mission societies. Agencies were overshadowed by churches in the ecumenical movement. And in the face of unchurching of Europe the WCC organization had no plan to strengthen the church with voluntary associations.[90]

The American branch of the WCC endorsed the choice for direct representation in an international body instead of creating regional councils. This made it harder for lay persons and women to reach the leadership level. And the shift from informal network of friends to formal bureaucratic relations, harmed the penetration of enthusiasm among other groups and the transfer of this enthusiasm to the next generation. The American subsidiary of the WCC accepted its leadership position of the world with a moral earnestness.[91]

While most work for transatlantic reform by American Protestants came from the bottom-up, others tried to strengthen this process from the top down. On 7 November 1953 the Committee on the Christian Responsibility for European Cooperation passed a statement on “The Future of Europe and the Responsibility of the Churches.”[92] This group of 21 Protestant individuals were recruited from the six core countries of the European community. Under the chairmanship of the Dutch Labor Party MP Connie L. Patijn, the committee hoped to advance real political unity in Europe, including a European Defense Community, as a basis for continued negotiations with the USSR. It felt that economic distress, political anarchy, and social unrest might lead Europe into despair which could be prevented by a just redistribution of Europe’s surplus wealth and cooperation among the classes. The churches should emphasize this responsibility. The British representatives begged to differ and wanted to maintain their own special position. The committee accepted the political dis-

90 International Missionary Council, *Minutes of the enlarged meeting and the committee of the International missionary council, Willingen, Germany, July 5th to 21st, 1952* (London: International Council, 1952), 83; Norman Goodall, *Missions under the cross: addresses delivered at the enlarged Meeting of the Committee of the International missionary council at Willingen, in Germany, 1952; with statements issued by the Meeting* (London: Edinburgh House Press, 1953), 178-181, 224; Ralph D. Winter, *The Twenty-Five Unbelievable Years 1945-1969* (South Pasadena: William Carey Library, 1970), 62-65.

91 Thompson, “Ecumenical Network,” 257-8; Ernest W. Lefever, “American Churches and International Affairs. Official Statements of the Federal and National Councils of Churches 1948-1953” [1953], PHS NCC RG 6 box 33.1.

92 “The Future of Europe and the Responsibility of the Churches. A statement passed by the Committee on the Christian Responsibility for European Cooperation, London 7 November 1953,” esp. p. 4, PHS NCC RG 6 box 18.12, Christian Study Group for European Unity.

tance of Britain, but feared for a minority position of Protestants in Europe, especially since the large Protestant contingent in East Germany was cut off from the rest. The committee hoped to advance religious liberty and diversity by fighting any religious monopoly. Cooperation was essential for European survival.[93]

The group strongly believed in a positive role for the United States in the responsibility for Europe's well-being. American Protestants should not turn their back to Europe by embracing isolationism, nor treat it arrogantly. In explanation to the second threat, the group warned Americans that Europe was more than a bastion against Communism, it was a positive idea. McCarthy's hysteria against Communism was as unfruitful as the support for the Franco regime. In contrast with this popular stream, the committee took on the task of seeking contact with Eastern Europe.

Walter W. Van Kirk, the Executive Director of the (American) National Council of Churches, had met the members of this group in Willingen in 1952 and reassured the Europeans that his body supported the efforts for US international commitment and maintained close contacts with the U.S. authorities, supported the United Nations, and expressed approval of negotiations with Communists as instead of a crusade.[94] Time and again he underwrote the necessity of internationalism. Despite the strong opposition from American evangelicals against the ecumenical project, the WCC headquarters kept a file with observations on the Billy Graham campaigns 1954-1955 in England and Germany. The collected clippings praised Graham's organization for its excellent contacts with the press, it's model use of secular venues, and of positive cooperation among churches, and of team work with lay people.[95]

Parallel to the evangelism and the formation of national evangelical associations everywhere in the world, the WEF tried to set up regional exchanges to spread Christian literature and a mission organizational network in the late 1950s as the pressure of the merger of IMC and WCC mounted. The British organization Evangelical Missionary Fellowship tried to prepare a similar European organization. The fear was that evangelical students in Europe would be rejected by missionary candidates in the IMC.[96]

93 H.H. Walz, "The Political Task of Protestantism in Europe," *European Issues* 4 (25 May 1954), 7-17, PHS NCC RG 6 box 19. "The specifically Protestant task in politics will always be a contribution to the political ethos."

94 Letter Van Kirk to the Committee, 29 January 1954, PHS NCC RG 6 box 18.12, Christian Study Group for European Unity. This confirmation by the American churches to support American commitment to European cooperation was published in the Committee's bulletin called *European Issues* 4 (25 May 1954), 4-6, PHS NCC RG 6 box 19.

95 Evangelism consultation, Bossey, July 6-11, 1960, Papers on Billy Graham crusades in Europe 1954 Comments, Geneva, World Council of Churches Archives, inv. 26.19.10 Miscellaneous papers, 1933-1961, Box 10.

96 Jack A. Dain to Clyde W. Taylor at the EFMA, June 2 and 19, 1958 and letter Clyde W. Taylor to Jack A. Dain in London, July 29, 1958, BGCA col. 338 WEF box 24 f 15.

In December 1958, Graham decided to organize an evangelism conference to readjust the goal of world evangelization in this generation to the changing conditions. His friend Harry Denman suggested that the conference be held in Canada or Finland to prevent "the [liberal] European Theology to control the situation."[97] The timing would mark the goal of the next decade(s). At an early stage the Graham organization informed the WCC, which in turn expected growing confidence if different Christians worked together for which it planned the assembly in late 1961. The WCC representatives were more interested in the aim of the conference, particularly whether it would assert the relevance of the gospel and whether the contents of the term evangelism was restricted to mass evangelism by preaching or also include a comprehensive goal of reaching people where they are.[98]

Graham held his consultation in 1960, but also attended the World Council of Churches general assembly in New Delhi in July 1961. Yet, he was very critical of (German) theology, which caused much confusion. Robert S. Bilheimer of the WCC contacted Graham to harmonize the various plans, and WCC chief Visser 't Hooft invited him to express his views at the New Delhi assembly. Despite the fact that on a local level both camps clashed, as was the case in Manchester where the local Council of Churches disapproved of Graham's campaign in 1961. But the WCC leadership regretted this local unwillingness and counted on earlier consultations with Graham which had been cordial and planned the meeting despite the Manchester tensions.[99] The Lutheran Bishops in Germany considered inviting Graham for a campaign in 1963-1964. So the top of WCC was open to the idea of being informed about Graham and realized that unifying ecumenists and evangelicals would not easy, but should be tried nevertheless.

Solid Landing

In the late 1940s evangelicals in America laid out an action plan to advance the spread of the traditional gospel globally and began to collect building blocks for this effort in Europe. The activities of Youth for Christ helped to establish connections with like-minded European. The NAE faced two internal and two

97 Billy Graham to Harry Denman (general secretary of the board of evangelism of the American Methodist Church), 9 December 1958, and Denham to Graham, 16 December 1958. Geneva, World Council of Churches Archives, inv. 26.19.10 Miscellaneous papers, 1933-1961, Box 11 Billy Graham correspondence 1958-1961 (letter of Visser 't Hooft).

98 BGEA to WCC, January 28, 1959.

99 Religious News Service (7 October 1961). Letter Visser 't Hooft to Billy Graham, 5 May 1961; Letter Robert S. Bilheimer to Billy Graham, 19 July 1961; Letter Robert S. Bilheimer to Tom Allen, 27 March 1961; Hans Jochen Margull to Tom Allen, 28 April 1961. Geneva, World Council of Churches Archives, inv. 26.19.10 Miscellaneous papers, 1933-1961, Box 11 Billy Graham correspondence 1958-1961.

external challenges or dilemma's. First it wanted to cooperate with European partners, encouraging them to be much more active than they were used to being, without stirring anti-American feelings. Secondly, the evangelical leadership sought to create a recognizable profile but steer away from both the mainline and the fundamentalists. They envisioned the creation of a network of national evangelical associations in Europe to support American missions as alternatives for failing local churches.[100] Thirdly, it presented Europeans with a working American model, which they could emulate. In October 1949, J. Elwin Wright wrote home triumphantly about the Dutch efforts for coordination: "They are proceeding with care and great expectations to develop a very worthwhile organization here. In every respect they are following our pattern."[101] Fourth, the NAE operated in between two competitors and succeeded to combine the doctrinal cohesion that the fundamentalists promised (but applied too narrowly) with the organizational force of the ecumenical movement. Because they felt the urgency of the moment, they pooled as many forces as they could and maintained a flexible structure. In the next phase issues about alliances and actions needed to be sorted out.

Most European sympathizers with American evangelicals resisted American attempts at an open attack on the WCC by voting down a proposal that discredited organizations which could compromise the statement of faith – the continent still hoped for cooperation, with the British remaining neutral. This left the young WEF strongly in American hands until 1968 when the need for concerted action overcame these nuances in strategy and justification.[102] This combination led to a recognition of Europe as a separate mission field in 1952. The main structural export was the bible school that brought the American evangelical educational style to Europe's mainland. Despite the oppositional style among the three groups, they all had a clear American origin. The results for Europe were that these initiatives created new Europe-wide networks, triggered transatlantic discussions, advanced legal freedom of religion in the Catholic South, and built a critical mass for evangelicals, that rejected fundamentalist alternatives. American evangelicals pressed for a global organization, which few Europeans initially fully embraced. They were afraid to be pulled in an anti-ecumenical movement that exported American controversies about the authority of the bible in Europe. They sought unity and positive goals to pursue. Hence the formation of a European Evangelical Alliance in 1952 next to the World Evangelical Fellowship.

100 Interview Lois Ferm with Peter Schneider, German organizer for the Billy Graham campaigns, 1993, BGEA col. 141 Oral History Project, box 62 file 13.
101 Letter J. Elwin Wright to home, Utrecht, October 7, 1949, BGCA col. 338, Folder 8-1 Correspondence J. Elwin Wright.
102 Clyde W. Taylor, "Implementing our Evangelical Unity," *UEA*, December 1963, 27; Kessler Jr., *A Study of the Evangelical Alliance*, 99-100.

The oppositional rhetoric and offensive organization by the American evangelicals should not obscure the fact that they ran on a number of parallel tracks with ecumenists. Not only did both groups embark on campaigns to bring the baby boomers into the church; their international policies were also often similar.[103] Both sent relief to Europe, assisted refugees, protested against discrimination of Protestants in Southern Europe, engaged women, and were united in their principled rejection of the state church as an organizing structure. Yet, their relative power was very uneven. The ecumenical organization had been in the making for decades, and could boast of numerous official and personal connections with the major European denominations. The liberals had easy access to the civic authorities, a friendly press, and a multi-million budget. In contrast, the evangelicals had just begun to create a modest bureaucratic support system for their global organization including the Europeans, and had collected only a few contacts with individual pastors and evangelists. The evangelicals received recognition from mostly marginal free-church denominations and parachurch organizations. They had yet to break in into the halls of power, and faced a critical press and an imminent bankruptcy. However, all these liabilities were compensated by the asset of Billy Graham.

This chapter corrects the idea that religion was only a vehicle for culture or politics, at least in Graham's intentions. First of all, he did not come alone: there were many evangelists and agencies that supported him and complemented his mission of mass evangelism. Together they changed the menu of Protestantism in Europe, added a new spiritual proposition that defined a (Protestant) believer as someone who made a conscious individual choice that contrasted to those who identified with institutions of religious authority. Thus they paved new roads for transnational religious contacts that confronted Europeans with the American debate about religious liberalism.

103 Thomas C. Berg, "'Proclaiming Together?' Convergence and Divergence in Mainline and Evangelical Evangelism 1945-1967," *Religion and American Culture* 5.1 (1995): 49-76.

MEET THE EUROPEANS!

COOPERATION AND RECONSIDERATION IN THE 1960s

On the threshold of the 1960s, Billy Graham reflected on his personal development in an article published in the mainline periodical *Christian Century*. He identified himself as the public expositor of the basic tenets of traditional Christianity, but did not claim he was the cure-all for the church. He said his experiences had solidified his basic convictions, which included a strong believe in the authority of the bible, the centrality of the cross, the resurrection of Christ, and in his Second Coming. Yet, he had come to accept a wider circle of believers from all kinds of churches and had discovered the social implications of the gospel, even though he still maintained that social change followed individual change. He wrote that he was confident about the coming of God's Kingdom, and that he recognized the mixing of wheat and tares until Judgment Day. Furthermore, he anticipated a decade of upheaval, to which Christianity would bring order, "for it fits the heart and needs of man like a glove." He ended his midterm assessment with the expectation of wonder amidst what he called, "blighting disillusionment."[1]

Developments in the Christian world in this decade would cause plenty of upheaval.[2] A rapid decline in the number of clergy, especially in the Catho-

1 Billy Graham, "What Ten Years Have Taught Me," *Christian Century* (17 February 1960), 186-189, quotations on p. 189.

2 Michael Walsh, "The Religious Ferment of the Sixties," in Hugh McLeod, ed., *The Cambridge History of Christianity* Vol. 9, *World Christianities c. 1914-c. 2000* (Cambridge: Cambridge University Press, 2006), 304-322 and Hugh McLeod, "The Crisis of Christianity in the West: entering a Post-Christian Era?" 323-347; Axel Schaefer, ed., *American Evangelicals and the 1960s* (Madison: University of Wisconsin Press, 2013).

lic Church, dwindling membership in Western European churches, rebellious youth and student unrest, frontal attacks on traditional images of God and God-talk; but also the opening up to the world of the Catholic Church and its embrace of freedom of religion, which caused confusion amidst high expectations and serious anxieties; fierce political debates pro and contra America's intervention in Vietnam and the legitimacy of South Africa's apartheids regime, and about life-style and social issues, such as abortion, birth control, homosexuality, feminism, amidst rapid growth of media and entertainment channels. The rise of new religious movements, both outside and within the Christian tradition further stirred debate. As the world witnessed rapid decolonization, global Protestantism began to integrate mission agencies into the World Council of Churches as the best way to advance equality and include new churches. Many evangelicals working in mainline organizations were concerned about the future of the missionary enterprise and evangelicals outside those organizations were even more troubled. They feared that this merger would curtail the growth of evangelical missions in the global South and discredit their activities in Europe which were in their infant phase and needed continued care. During this decade these diverging concerns deeply polarized progressive and conservative Protestants, even as they spurred leaders to seek religious détente.

Europe's Sad Reputation

The number of evangelical missionaries active in Europe would quadruple in the 1960s to more than one thousand. They were spread over 120 agencies though, fragmenting their force.[3] Still, their experiences added up to a comprehensive view of the religious state of Europe from an evangelical perspective. An overview of the situation was crystallized by missionary Bob Evans, one of the most successful recruiters of missionaries for Europe. Evans was a college friend of Graham, a U.S. Navy veteran, and the founder of the Greater Europe Mission. His influential 1962 book *Let Europe Hear* challenged Americans to correct their perception that Europe was a Christian continent. Evans' assessment was that Europe was in fact de-Christianized, over-civilized, and pagan. Each country had its specific cultural problem that explained its resistance to traditional Christianity. France was materialistic and therefore indulgent. Germany sought its salvation in cults and seemed bewitched. Denmark and most of Scandinavia had lost hope in the future, and nations with strong Christian traditions such as Holland, had become ossified. Hope for improve-

3 *North American Protestant Foreign Mission Agencies* (New York: Missionary Research Library, 1964), 66.

ment was lacking as the next generation seemed to have lost all interest in traditional Christianity and the existing churches seemed paralyzed.

Evans explained the sad condition of the European churches as a result of a long historical process: The Protestant Reformation had failed to bring the full gospel because it had tied churches to territories. The churches had lost authority through internal quarrels, were corrupted by nationalism, had limited their scope, and most of all, had become too rational. The legacy of the Reformation had led to intellectual transformation, but had left the heart unchanged. Evans proclaimed that Americans would redress the problem.[4]

Evans was in line with earlier assessments of the sorry state of Europe which prevented the continent to fulfil its strategic role. He projected Europe as a future power base, a demographically growing area, and a crucial arena in the end of times. In his view Europe's churches suffered from intellectualism and the resulting liberalism or dogmatism disabled their vitality. In a word, Europe was "cold," and time was running out. In light of many national conflicts and two global wars, the present peace could only be perceived as a lull in dangerous times. Evans was sure that it was not only Communism that endangered Europe's freedom. Echoing the fearful opposition that the twelve spies encountered during their exploration of Canaan, Evans identified five "Giants in the land" which threatened the penetration of true (evangelical) Christianity in Europe: Romanism, Communism, Traditional Protestantism, Secular Existentialism, and Militant Cults. The first three threats were matters

4 Robert P. Evans, *Let Europe Hear: The Spiritual Plight of Europe* (Chicago: Moody Press, 1963), 47-89. For a secular view of Europe at that time see David Calleo, *Europe's Future: The Grand Alternatives* (New York: Horizon Press, 1965). Also from within Europe there were critical sounds. Karol Wojtyla observed in the summer of 1947 that Dutch Catholics had created an impressive institutional framework in competition with the Protestants. They kept their distance from other religious traditions and put more energy in loyalty to Catholic unity and strength rather than internalizing the contents of their faith. Tad Szulc, *Pope John Paul II: The Biography* (New York: Pockets Books, 1995), 156-159. Yet, self-criticism of the level of spirituality by the churches themselves was difficult. Also the Neo-Calvinist Protestant Churches (Gereformeerde Kerken in Nederland) were much more concerned about their quantitative and organizational shape than the quality of their spiritual life. See the Dutch sociologist Gerard Dekker, *Een moeizaam gevecht. Mijn geschiedenis met de kerk* (Hilversum: Verloren, 2005), 30-31. A report about the social changes and its consequences for the Reformed churches indicated that the local congregation should resist to allow categorical churches, even though it was hard to involve intellectuals, workers, and young people or young believers did not feel at home. Territorial organization remained the organizing principle. Roelof van Dijk, *"Veranderend getij": Structuurveranderingen in Nederland en hun consequenties voor het kerkelijk leven*, 3 vols. (Amsterdam: Stichting Gereformeerd Sociologisch Instituut, 1961-1962) 3: 55-60. These churches expected an enormous shortage of ministers (revealing that they were still expecting much (natural) growth). The sociologists believed that many congregations were in transition from a homogeneous rural to a differentiated urban setting, where mobility caused social erosion. See E.D. Kraan, *Rapport stand geestelijk leven: Generale Synode Utrecht* (Utrecht, 1959), 86 and 96.

of monopoly, the last two were direct inspirational competitors for the minds and hearts of the Europeans.[5]

Evans believed that the contrast with the United States was enormous. Even potential allies like the established churches stood on an equal footing with Communism as obstacles to Christianity in Europe, he said. Evans chose his metaphors carefully. Next to the Communist "Iron Curtain," he opined that Europe was cut off from real freedom by the Catholic "Purple Curtain," and the traditional "Stained Glass Curtain."[6]

Other, similar books from the early 1960s identified Europe as mission field Number One.[7] Scholars have shown that this startling picture, that contrasted to the rosy scene depicted for the United States, was necessary to emphasize the otherness of the target area. A scheme was conceived in which countries or peoples received a place on a symbolic map of religions, showing dark and light areas.[8]

Evans and other spokespersons for the evangelical missions had success in attracting a growing number of Americans for missionary work in Europe. His Greater Europe Mission was the largest missionary enterprise in Europe. It had one hundred workers, largely thanks to its three bible schools in France, Italy, and Germany. In 1964 its home office in Wheaton, Illinois circulated more than one hundred thousand missionary prayer letters and 30,000 mailings of its quarterly newsletter. In the same year an aggregate of 120 evangelical organizations offered a variety of programs in Europe spreading bibles and literature, reaching out to children and youth, trying to establish evangelical churches, and educating evangelists.[9] Evans was hopeful.

5 Evans repeated the same type of arguments in a special issue of *Christianity Today* of 20 July 1962 and in numerous contributions in other evangelical publications. See his article "Can Europeans Evangelize the Continent?" *United Evangelical Action* (April 1963), 17, 26-27. From BGCA, Collection 506 "Decision Magazine," Box 22, Folder 13, autobiographical file Evans.

6 Walter Frank, General Director's Report 1964, BGCA col. 352 IFMA box 21 f10 (GEM 1964-65). In 1964 the Greater Europe Mission had 114 missionaries working in Europe and operated three bible schools in France, Belgium, and Italy.

7 See also a special issue of *Christianity Today* (Christianity in Free Europe) 20 July 1962. W. Stuart Harris, *Eyes on Europe* (Chicago: Moody Press, 1965), on behalf of the European Christian Mission, a Commonwealth mission project, whose American affiliate was called Mission to Europe's Millions. The World Literature Crusade fostered high expectations of distributing tracts and literature in Europe: Jack McAlister, *Evangelizing Europe: Heart of the World* (Studio City, CA: World Literature Crusade, 1961).

8 Claudia Währisch-Oblau, *The Missionary Self-Perception of Pentecostal/Charismatic Church Leaders from the Global South in Europe: Bringing Back the Gospel* (Leiden: Brill, 2009), 254-272.

9 Walter Frank, "General Director's Report, 1964," BGCA col. 352, box 21, file 10, Greater Europe Mission, 1964-65, 7; *North American Protestant Foreign Mission Agencies* (New York: Missionary Research Library, 1964), 66. Budgets were modest. Only fragments of financial documentation is available. The Greater Europe Mission's budget developed from $ 134,444.84 in 1954 to $ 1,964,003.69 in 1973. (BGCA, Col. 352, IFMA box 38 file 8 "Auditor's

One of Evans' colleagues at the Greater Europe Mission, Walter Frank, justified missionary activities in traditionally "Christian countries." He said that when churches were weak and in an "apostatized [sic] anemic condition," they needed American reinforcements. The growth in missionary staff to 1,600 missionaries in the quarter century after World War II, looked impressive, he added, but these men and women faced the almost impossible task of reaching a quarter of a million towns and cities without an evangelical church.[10]

After the mouthpiece of many independent evangelical mission organizations, *IFMA News*, had identified Europe as a new mission field in 1952, the bulletin felt the need to repeat this observation in 1961 and draw attention to Europe, using the label: "(the) Ignored Continent."[11] A spokesperson for evangelicals in Europe called for ten thousand missionaries in the next decade. Successive issues of the newsletter compared the Christian church in Europe to its religious competitors and found it wanting. Bob Evans pointed out that evangelicals lagged behind cults, Eastern religions, and philosophies. The publicity of the Moral Rearmament movement, the strength of the Mormons, which had 3,500 missionaries in Europe, and the investment of millions of dollars in Europe by competing belief systems gave pause to the evangelicals.[12] Meanwhile the *IFMA News* noted that the European church was weak, with less than three per cent attending public worship service.[13]

At the same time recruiting brochures published by the Assemblies of God explained the threats and opportunities in Europe to American believers. For example, they noted that Fascist Italy had pushed Pentecostals underground, where they had nonetheless multiplied, and emerged from the war as the largest Protestant group. And they pointed to Germany, which they described as suffering from "the ineffectiveness of the State-supported churches…." Greece, in their view, used to be a stronghold against Islam, but still needed complete religious freedom, which would attract thousands to "a saving knowledge of Christ." And they wrote that many Spaniards had spiritual

Reports Greater Europe Mission, 1954-1968, 1973"). The EEC had a 1969 budget of $ 220,047.52 (Col. 352, box 37 f 16, "Auditor's Reports European Evangelical Crusade, 1955-1970"). The Evangelical Alliance Mission spent in 1964 about $ 120,000 of its $3 million budget on Europe, and in 1973 $ 500,000 from its $ 6 million budget (Col. 352, box 39, file 19, "The Evangelical Alliance Mission Finances, 1964-1973"). The Worldwide European Fellowship, Inc. $ 67,535.56 on missionaries in the fiscal year 1963-964, and $ 98,275.35 in 1966 (Col. 352, box 40 file 6, "Worldwide European Fellowship Finances, 1964-1966").

10 Walter Frank, "IFMA Missions and Church Planting in Areas Where Old Churches are Established," BGCA col. 352 IFMA box 27 file 4 GEM 1970-71, p. 1.

11 *IFMA News*, February 1961.

12 Ibid., December 1961.

13 Ibid., December 1961 and May 1962.

hunger, but feared the risk of being rejected as unpatriotic when they sympathized with Protestant believers.[14]

Social and political pressures pushed many mission organizations to use anonymous instruments such as radio broadcasts and the distribution of tracts so as to keep a low profile. The structural confines were formidable. The *IFMA* assessed Spain saying, "Romanism holds the chords of government in Spain and pulls them whichever way she desires at the moment."[15]

Ideas about Europe as the fountain of evil accumulated in evangelical circles in the 1960s. The continent was the source of "Communism, modernism, liberalism, and other false philosophies that have been the scourge of the earth," concluded *IFMA News*.[16] James H. Kane, mission instructor at Barrington College, Rhode Island, and Lancaster Bible College, Pennsylvania, reported in 1963 that all Christian visitors to Europe after World War II came home shaking their heads. "Europe is the neediest of all mission fields today" he decided.[17] TEAM general director Vernon Mortenson had reached the same conclusion during his field trip earlier that year, "In proportion to the need the Christian church is doing less to evangelize Europe than any other area in the world."[18]

It was one thing to reject the monopoly of the World Council of Churches and to enter new territories and flood them with gospel literature. It was quite another to reconstruct the religious infrastructure in Europe. An effort was made toward this end in the 1960s, when the evangelical movement began to gain strength. By the end of this decade the goal to incorporate Europe in the mission scene and into the evangelical family was well underway. Europe hosted 1,500 missionaries, which was about 5 per cent of all missionaries active for American agencies worldwide. The aim was to convert Europeans and to accomplish this the agencies needed to recruit more staff, raise more funds, and create greater synergy among the many small and fragmented initiatives. Despite growth in evangelism, the goal of Europe's Re-Christianization must have been overwhelming, since most of the agencies worked in isolation and

14 Brochures in BGCA in collection 352 Records of the IFMA, box 73, file 2. See also collection 165 EFMA, box 104, file 7.

15 *IFMA News*, January and April 1963.

16 Ibid., December 1962.

17 James H. Kane, "Where are we in Foreign Missions?" BGCA col. 182, Kane, box 1, file 32 lectures [1963]. A few years later he lamented the decline in mission interest, which was noticeable in the drop of students in Missions in American Christian Colleges and bible schools, due to increased competition by the Peace Corps and the increasing popularity of short-term missionary positions. Kane, "Major Concerns of Modern Missions," [end of 1965], BGCA col. 182, box 1 file 20.

18 Mortenson, *God Made it Grow*, 796 (quoted from his report "European Trip," February 15 - March 3, 1963.

world population growth was accelerating.[19] In 1968, for instance, 31 missionary organizations and churches financed 139 workers in Italy and 267 workers were placed in the field by 39 different agencies in France. The scale of each operation remained small. In Italy only 6 organizations had more than ten employees and in France only 9 had that number. Even the largest agencies had annual budgets of no more than $200,000. The average cost for one missionary was $10,000, which meant that American evangelicals spent ten million dollars annually in Europe. Sixty per cent of the resources went to Catholic countries.[20] One solution was to invest heavily in spreading the printed word. Not surprisingly Jack McAlister, the president of World Literature Crusade in North Hollywood, California, advocated this approach. Communists and Cults did the same without "the active assistance of the Holy Spirit," he told the delegates of the Berlin Conference in 1966. "No other agency can penetrate so deeply, abide so persistently, witness so daringly and influence so irresistibly as the printed page."[21]

Experiences at Europe's Core: France

If any one country represented Europe for Americans, it was France. Symbolically secular France served as the opposite pole to religious America, even though both countries shared a republican outlook and claimed universal values. France also served as a transition zone between the Protestant North and the Catholic South. While the United Kingdom and Germany saw much more of Billy Graham than France, the country was an important magnet for evangelical missions. Successes came in the 1960s, after American evangelicals had helped mobilize scattered Protestants in the 1950s.[22]

Robert J. Vajko, a son of Hungarian-American immigrants, heard Bob Evans speak about Europe's need at Columbia Bible College in South Carolina,

19 A similar complaint was heard in the United Kingdom, where more than 180 evangelical societies were active and emphasized their own missions which fed into a split in the British Evangelical Alliance between those who advocated separation or independence from ecumenicals (under leadership of David Martyn Lloyd Jones) and those who regretted the internal fragmentation and promoted more organizational unity: John Stott and the author of the WEF-history, J.B.A. Kessler Jr., *A Study of the Evangelical Alliance in Great Britain* (Goes, the Netherlands: Oosterbaan en le Cointre, 1968), 102-112.

20 "Reports of the 19th Annual Mission Executive Retreat, September 28 - October 1, 1970, Winona Lake, Indiana," 56, EFMA, BGC Library.

21 Jack McAlister, "Literature Evangelism," in Henry, *One Race*, vol. 1, 514 and 515. The delegates were concerned with the cultural context of the printed materials.

22 Sébastien Fath, "La reception de Billy Graham en France (1954-1986)," in Sébastien Fath, ed., *Le protestantisme évangélique, un christianisme de conversion: entre rupture et filiations. Actes du colloque international organisé à Paris (Iresco, EPHE Sorbonne) par le Group de Sociologie des Religions et de la Laïcité (EPHE/CNRS) du 14 au 16 mars 2002* (Turnhout: Brepols, 2004), 81-106.

where he had enrolled in 1958 after a tour of duty in the US military in North Africa and the United Kingdom. He had become a Christian at a Youth for Christ rally in the United States and while in the United Kingdom, married a British citizen who herself had a missionary zeal. The bible classes he attended were permeated with a missionary élan about God's redemptive work all over the world. Vajko joined The Evangelical Alliance Mission (TEAM) and moved to a Paris suburb in January 1965 where he believed he could best implement the strategy of church planting. TEAM staff assisted the French evangelical churches by starting new churches while building a local leadership. Vajko concluded that this method worked better than other groups where outsiders approached the French directly, made converts, and then lost their recruits in the course of time.[23]

TEAM prepared its missionaries in France by enrolling them for a year and a half in courses at the Sorbonne where they studied French language and culture. They trained for their missionary role while they continued their education. They were motivated to create viable evangelical communities, considered a long-term approach at the time, and a change from the urgency of the millennialism that dominated in the 1950s. TEAM realized it must stay close to its goal of church planting and had a realistic fear of bringing down greater restrictions upon itself should it add to its institutional frameworks. Therefore they granted new congregations the choice whether or not to affiliate with them. They knew that fusion or joint action with other denominations could lead their churches astray, restrict their freedom, and stall growth. This strategy worked because TEAM clustered its churches in suburban areas, and church plants in one region reinforced each other and gradually grew into a national network.[24]

The first church building in France sponsored by TEAM went up in 1964. Two years later TEAM boasted five organized congregations with in total one hundred members, served by 15 missionaries. This growth did not result from mass outreach campaigns but from the gradual adding of French families. The families supported the French staff and helped the churches become viable in the early 1970s. TEAM's official chronicler attributed the good results to the cooperation between missionaries and natives, and to the decision to keep the organization of churches separate from missionary projects.[25]

23 Robert J. Vajko, "A History and Analysis of the Church-Planting Ministry of The Evangelical Alliance Mission in France 1952-1975," (MA Thesis Trinity Evangelical Divinity School, Deerfield IL, June 1975), 114; Interview by author of Dr. Robert J. Vajko on 24 September 2012, Carol Stream, IL, and e-mail interviews by author with Sarah Page, 25 February, 20 March and 2 April 2013.

24 Jacques Blocher, trained at Spurgeon's College, and TEAM-leader Art Johnson agreed to closely integrate in a French way and acted independent from the Wheaton headquarters.

25 Mortenson, *God Made it Grow*, 749-759, 776-777, 781-783. TEAM attributed the slow growth rate in Catholic countries to the lack of lay involvement in the churches and the unfamiliarity of belonging to a small minority church.

Thirty years after Evans announced that American evangelicals could change the stagnant condition of the European church, his colleague, William Wagner concluded that they had not been successful. No American mission agency had had a lasting impact on a national culture. All had merely reproduced American pluralism in Europe. At best, some independent churches had gathered the marginal, the eccentrics, and the drop-outs. The basic problem was seen as the lack of contact with the existing churches.[26] What one missionary concluded about France was perhaps true for all of Western Europe, "developed a reputation as a missionary graveyard."[27] This sobering characterization was meant to restore realistic expectations of missionary work in Europe, but indirectly this verdict showed the limited role of Christian Europe in the world.[28]

Renegotiation of the Evangelical Position towards the Mainline Churches

The greatest difference between ecumenists and evangelicals was their relationship to the older European churches. To ecumenists they were partners; to evangelicals they were stumbling blocks. The 1960s were a period of evangelical repositioning, in both Europe and the US. Youth for Christ for their part were able to maneuver between established churches and independent groups. Its European staff discussed the relationship with the churches and concluded self-assuredly, "Brethren with whom we find it difficult to agree may be longing for what we have to give them – namely, our testimony to the saving and keeping power of the Lord Jesus Christ. But we must have a hum-

26 William L. Wagner, *North American Protestant Missionaries in Western Europe: A Critical Appraisal* (Bonn: Verlag für Kultur und Wissenschaft, 1993), 134.

27 Allen V. Koop, *American Evangelical Missionaries in France, 1945-1975* (Lanham, MD: University Press of America, 1986), 94; David E. Bjork, *Unfamiliar Paths: The Challenge of Recognizing the Work of Christ in Strange Clothing: A Case Study from France* (Pasadena: William Carey Library, 1997).

28 There are more reasons for the lack of massive response to American outreach. Both Protestant and Catholic established churches did not appreciate a new church in town and discouraged cooperation. The free churches had a low prestige and new converts could only mature when they broke fully with the old church. They had difficulty to grow spiritually and had not learned to give money to support their own cause. Another obstacle for the expansion of evangelicalism was its primitivist, Biblicist, and restorationist impulses. For instance, Murch was a restorationist whose main desire was to reform the churches in Europe. This was an explicit attack on church authority (see articles in Richard T. Hughes, ed., *The Primitive Church in the Modern World* (Urbana: University of Illinois Press, 1995)). Jacques Blocher reported at the Berlin Conference in 1966 that evangelistic meetings in French-speaking countries hardly found an audience, and that only a Graham mass campaign would make an impression on the larger public (Henry, *One Race*, vol. 1, 250), but the real hope was on individual testimonies in cities.

ble spirit in our approaches to them."[29] Moreover, Youth for Christ thought that they could complement a reception in a "cold" church on Sunday with "warm" fellowship during the week. In the meantime they tried to involve as many ministers from (mostly evangelical) churches in their follow-up training of new converts.[30]

The processes of indigenization and decolonization meant that all over the world Western missionary movements had to fit in existing religious infrastructures. Missionary developments in the global South created new tensions for all partners. Ecumenists feared that mission organizations operating outside of church structures would weaken the church, and in 1960 the World Council of Churches decided to consolidate its authority by tying the International Missionary Council closer to its own organization. Evangelicals feared that tying missions to (liberal) churches would kill missions. They believed that when the ecumenical community identified human progress as the work of God, they had taken a wrong turn towards universalism. According to the evangelicals, the idea that all humans would be saved made the presentation of the Christian gospel redundant.[31] While ecumenists had no great desire to convert Europeans and looked for new missionary ideas lay outside Europe, evangelicals made the fate of religion in Europe their rallying point: if Christians abandoned the public proclamation of the gospel there, the global church would wither.

The main arena of evangelical-ecumenist contention was Latin America. There, significant evangelical missionary activity took place amidst long-term projects of the WCC member churches. A conference organized by the WCC in Lima pressed for rapid social change and urged absorption and integration of missionary organizations into the main ecumenical body.[32] Some missionaries connected with the IMC met separately to fend off a merger with the WCC, and all evangelical mission organizations shared this concern. EFMA feared that the movement to transfer activities to indigenous churches (which they supported) would mean that the WCC would subsidize these churches, causing unhealthy dependency and in turn robbing the American churches of their missionary programs and breaking up the world vision.[33]

Meanwhile, efforts at rapprochement between ecumenists and evangelicals continued. Between 1957 and 1961 the British Council of Churches organized private meetings with conservative evangelicals hoping to find common

29 "Report of European Youth for Christ conference, October 3-6, 1961," BGCA col. 48, box 6, folder 23.

30 The European YFC had not yet been incorporated in 1967, but needed to support national groups in difficulties.

31 Interview Bob Shuster with Arthur F. Glasser, BGCA col. CN 421, tape T8.

32 Baker to Tom Fountain, 30 December 1960, BGCA col. 165 EFMA, box 4 file 14.

33 Clyde W. Taylor, *Ecumenical Strategy in Foreign Missions* (Washington, DC: Evangelical Foreign Missions Association, 1961), 4-5.

ground.[34] Hans Jochen Margull, head of the Department of Studies on Evangelism at the WCC, prepared to speak on Revival and Renewal at the Ecumenical Institute at Bossey outside Geneva, Switzerland in June 1962. The conference was planned at Bossey to discuss what congregations should do in the missions and to consider the key objectives for mission work.[35] Billy Graham was added to the list of participants, but he postponed his decision till the WCC would clarify its course at its assembly in New Delhi.

Both evangelicals and ecumenists were convinced that they needed to find a way to solve the growing tension between them. Since the evangelicals were more apprehensive, they met in secret annually beginning in 1961 at Lake Forest Academy, north of Chicago, and after 1963, at Malone College, in Ohio. A group of about 16 men, leaders of mission organizations and educational institutions, met to present papers on theological concepts, worship, and fellowship. Malone College president, evangelical Quaker, and former missionary, Everett L. Cattell, hosted the meetings. As the treasurer of the World Evangelical Fellowship from 1962 on, he was a person of standing. One of the main concerns of those present was the division caused by the different missionary activities of the American mainline vs. the evangelical churches around the world. A rotating group of evangelical and ecumenist leaders presented position papers and held discussions of them in the sheltered surrounding of the college and without publicity. British pastor Gilbert Kirby, since 1956 the General Secretary of the old and more Europe-oriented Evangelical Alliance, and International Secretary of the WEF after 1962, secured the evangelical connection to Europe. The American Clyde Taylor looked with some concern on the rapprochement between the Evangelical Alliance and the World Council, and feared that the Alliance would de-facto discourage establishing WEF affiliates in other countries. The 1963 meeting clarified the mutual roadblocks to rapprochement. For the ecumenists a dispensationalist or prophetic reading of the bible meant they would be identified as enemies, as many evangelicals called the World Council the Whore of Babylon.[36] Evangelicals felt frustrated by WCC staff that too easily annulled reassuring official WCC statements. Moreover, the evangelicals were concerned that WCC programs would drive the mission organizations and younger churches into one centralized organization.

34 Stanley, *Global Diffusion*, 551; Ian H. Murray, *David Martyn Lloyd-Jones: The Fight of Faith, 1939-1981*, vol. 2 (Edinburgh: The Banner of Truth Trust, 2004), 314-320.

35 Letter Hans Jochen Margull to Tom Allen, Glasgow, 19 September 1961; letter Roswell P. Barnes to Margull, 9 November 1961; letter Tom Allen to Margull, 28 September 1961, Geneva, World Council of Churches Archives, inv. 26.19.10 Miscellaneous papers, 1933-1961, Box 12, Billy Graham correspondence 1961.

36 Joseph F. Pfeiffer, "John H. Yoder and the Secretive Malone College Consultations on Mission 1961-1967," unpublished research paper, Associated Mennonite Biblical Seminary 2008 at www.academia.edu <retrieved 1 August 2019>.

The awakening of Latin American independence – and the growing nationalism in other colonized nations – encouraged Christian bodies in these countries to resist affiliation with an outside organization lest they undermine the cordial relations already established within their nations. WCC representative Eugene Smith felt that his organization should refrain from trying to secure these countries' support. His plea struck a responsive chord among evangelicals, who recognized the sensitivities. College president Cattell admitted that even the slightest effort by the WEF to link up with these countries could be interpreted by both IMFA affiliated groups and WCC-members as an EFMA recruiting effort (since EFMA was related to NAE, which had sponsored the WEF).

Success at these meetings was in the interests of the evangelicals who were gaining ground and self-confidence. In 1964 they had shown initiative by launching their own scholarly missions journal as the evangelical alternative to the *International Review of Missions*.[37] More and more the WEF presented itself as the only alternative to the WCC.[38] This was a low point in the relationship, and WCC observers at the 1966 Wheaton Missions conference were shocked by the hostility against liberals that they encountered there, believing that much of it was ill informed. Some of the evangelical leaders took up the challenge, however, and as a result of these cautious meetings the channels for finding common ground remained open.[39]

The evangelicals had become a force to be reckoned with and they looked for recognition of the WEF's value to the WCC.[40] Simultaneously both WEF and WCC made efforts to transcend their own positions by recognizing the risk (usually considered as caused by the other party) of bringing division in the Christian world, especially in Africa. There the IMFA contingent of faith-based agencies demanded that WEF members cut all ties to the WCC. Cattell proposed to send a Christian education consultant to Latin America, not only to offer assistance, but also to gauge whether they wanted to take the initiative in approaching WEF instead of the other way round. Cattell used the experience in India as an example of how WCC and WEF could complement one another with WCC giving material support, and WEF spiritual support. It was a cau-

37 Taylor to Kirby, 25 March 1964, BGCA col. 165 box 6 file 10.

38 Clyde Taylor to Charles Pitts, 20 March 1964, BGCA col. 165 box 6 file 10.

39 Interview Bob Shuster with Arthur F. Glasser, BGCA col. CN 421, tape T8. The partners included Horace Fenton, John Howard Yoder, Lesslie Newbigin, and Eugene Smith. Taylor appreciated Eugene Smith, even though he found him and not critical enough towards the ecumenical movement, Taylor to Kirby, 24 June 1964, BGCA col. 165 box 6 f 10. Kirby had drafted an article about evangelical cooperation but Taylor kept it under his wing in order not to give its enemies an argument. Taylor to Kirby, 5 August 1962, BGCA col. 165 box 6 file 10. But the evangelicals gave up when the WCC assembly in Uppsala 1968 approved violence for liberation purposes.

40 Everett L. Cattell to Gilbert W. Kirby, 21 July 1964, BGCA col. 338, box 6, file 5.

tious move aimed at mutual recognition. The leading mouthpiece of global evangelicalism, *Christianity Today* became a forum for rapprochement.

Still there were plenty of pitfalls. Clyde Taylor, the NAE General Director after 1963 feared that the idea that all humans would be saved – universalism – would undermine all mission work. He thought that the ecumenists were trying to charm and hoodwink the evangelicals and render them unable to oppose the WCC. A first crisis occurred when the list of attendees at the 1964 conference included outspoken liberals, thus damaging the evangelicals' trust in the project.[41] A second incident in 1966 almost destroyed the confidential nature of the conferences. Their existence and program were publicly announced, provoking Carl McIntire's strong condemnation. Nonetheless, the conversations continued to bridge the gap and gradually the circle of participants grew. It was the general secretary of the National Council of Churches in America, Edwin Espy, who made the suggestion to invite a conservative evangelical from Latin America and one from the United States to the next consultation.[42] His action restored mutual confidence and kept the dialogue going.

As a result of the consultations, all sides were reassured that the World Council was not officially aiming at a super church, even if many of the practices they carried out to financially support cooperative projects seemed to work in that direction.[43] Practical issues became more important than theological ones, and a third crisis soon surfaced. When the General Assembly of the World Council of Churches in Uppsala Sweden in 1968 approved the use of violence in the liberation struggles of the former colonies, the planned consultation was cancelled for the year. This acute sense of crisis killed this project, that was officially abandoned in 1971.

A second, even more significant conclusion from the Uppsala meeting was that the World Council appeared to stop missions altogether. Missionary strategist Donald McGavran, the advocate of the Church Growth Movement, accused them of abandoning the two billion people in the world who had never heard the gospel.[44]

While this happened far from Europe, it had a number of consequences for the American Protestant presence in Europe. First, the exploratory talks

41 Clyde W. Taylor to Horace Fenton, Arthur Glasser and Louis King, 11 June 1964, Louis King to Clyde Taylor, 12 June 1964 and Clyde W. Taylor to Louis L. King, 18 June 1964, BGCA col. 165 box 6, file 8; Letters 10 and 14 and 17 June 1963, BGCA col. 165 box 6 file 10. Billy Graham informed Taylor that the German Evangelical Alliance moved towards merger with the WEF (22 July 1963).

42 Letter Edwin Espy to Robert S. Bilheimer, 20 July 1966, PHS NCC 6, box 25.

43 John Coventry Smith, "Exclusivism and Inclusivism in Ecumenism," Paper at the Malone Consultation, 21-23 July 1967, PHS RG 138 UPCUSA, box 12. Smith was the General Secretary of the Commission on Ecumenical Mission and Relations of the UPC USA and his paper showed that the National Council of Churches set its boundaries.

44 Donald McGavran, "Uppsala's 'Program for Mission' and Church Growth," *Church Growth Bulletin* 5, no. 2 (November 1968): 12.

between evangelicals and ecumenists in the United States hesitantly moved towards a modus vivendi, creating space for missionary cooperation elsewhere. Since evangelicals in Europe were the weaker party, activities in the heartland provided a guide to the chances and limits of mainline cooperation. Secondly, the international evangelical network together with the missionary realignment increased the role of the WEF, which was gaining in maturity as an instrument to connect European evangelicals with an international network. Thirdly, the international scope of the rapprochement helped Europeans formulate their own model of interdependence, which eventually resulted in a merger of the "old" European Evangelical Alliance with the new evangelicals.

All these developments were part of an expectation of change that touched the evangelical subculture deeply. Organized evangelicals faced issues of race, feminism, economic transformation, the expanding welfare state, and foreign policy. The positions they adopted were never taken simply to be oppositional, though they liked to think in contrasts. They made an effort to go beyond stereotyping the other, and consistently engaged in negotiation.[45]

Moody Bible Institute (MBI) stood at the core of the missionary endeavor and there these changes were highly visible. The school accepted a more diverse range of students and opinions, and struggled with older concepts that needed renewal. The new spirit and its accompanying tensions could be found in reflections on the 1960 presidential election. The official mood at the bible college was one of anxiety about the course of the country. John F. Kennedy's rise to power was seen at MBI as the result of a Catholic strategy to train new leaders. His election gave them the incentive to do likewise in training up a core of leadership of their own.[46] But change didn't come solely from outside pressure.

The student-led Missionary Union at MBI struggled with what it thought was waning missionary zeal and it set out to redefine its purpose and program. Rank-and-file Moody students criticized the Union leaders' lack of dedication and serious programming. They demanded that the leaders put a greater focus on results, and engage in a more serious debate on missions' strategy as well as other issues. They wished to see Christianity act as a vital force in the present world crisis. A number of students felt uncomfortable with fundamentalism, saying that it seemed to define a separatist mentality rather than an orthodox theology.[47]

Students began to publicly evaluate and criticize the annual missionary conferences, which some found stressful with long days, large groups, and

45 Axel Schaefer, ed., *American Evangelicals and the 1960s* (Madison: University of Wisconsin Press, 2013), 3-16.

46 *Moody Student*, 18 November 1960.

47 Ibid., 30 November 1962, 15 February 1963.

lack of personal contact with real missionaries. The student newspaper *Moody Student* reported that the student body was poorly informed about the war in Vietnam and featured articles announcing shifts in society and provoking students to think for themselves and not to conform in advance. In 1966 students participated for the first time in a workshop on church unity organized by Catholic students at Loyola University. The MBI students reported that they appreciated hearing pleas for ecumenical contacts from real persons and not only indirectly from texts. All this was far from revolutionary, but it shows that the school had awakened to the need to encourage more diversity and personal choice.[48] A *Moody Student* editorial of November 1966 gave a positive response to the question, "Do Christians belong in social work?" While confirming evangelism as the students' key task, it opened the door to social engagement, "Our primary purpose as Christians, to be sure, is witnessing for Christ, but we have defined this term too narrowly. ...This responsibility we have to others involves the total man... . Is lack of involvement such a serious problem? We think it is."[49]

One result of this changing mood was a drop in attendance at the traditional prayer meetings. The number of weekly participants fell from 400 in 1959, to 250 in 1966, to less than 100 by 1967. Students pointed to a lack of time and study pressures as excuses, but others worried about apathy. Dr. Harold Cook, the director of the missions program, proposed a change in perspective. He proposed looking at the purpose of the mission conferences not as pressure on students to go abroad, but as encouragement to serve God. Staff member Dr. Arthur Mercer addressed confusion about the missionary call. He said the focus should not be on a particular field or ministry. Instead the focus had to be on the gifts of the student who should seek confirmation of his commitment directly from God. The student, not the destination became the decisive factor, and this shift increased the potential for a new view of mission work.[50] The Spring 1969 newsletter of the WEF confirmed this broadening horizon, when it stated explicitly, "As members of the World Evangelical Fellowship we must stand for objective truth and justice in contrast to political manipulation."[51]

Mainline churches discovered these new chances for cooperation, and in tandem with this they displayed a new interest in European developments. In 1966 the United Presbyterian Church (UPC) reported ecumenical dialogues in Europe with Roman Catholics, Marxists, and various other youth. The Presbyterian report rejoiced over this diversity, recognizing its risks, but also seeing

48 *Moody Student*, 8 November 1963, 28 January 1966, 16 December 1966.

49 Ibid., November 1966.

50 Arthur Mercer, "The missionary call," Ibid., 23 October 1964; Dr. Robert Sabath, "MU out of focus," Ibid., 2 February 1968; Harold Cook, *Ibid.*, 6 October 1967.

51 "Editoral Comment," *World News* 3.2 (April-June 1969), 1.

chances for reconciliation: "Contact with Europe brings us this hope – that possibilities for creativity and growth are great."[52] In 1967 the UPC sent a researcher to investigate the shift in values among European youth. He crossed the continent by train and interviewed a small sample of people.[53] Language barriers and accustoming himself to interviewing limited his scope to England, France, Germany, Scandinavia, and Spain. His assumption was that "value systems built on authority are in the process of undergoing a critical challenge... . Hierarchies in these areas are crumbling." And the Europeans, also the older generation, did not seem concerned about this loss of authority.[54] The UPC researcher concluded that the main reason to go to Europe was to get a perspective on the American scene, not to change Europe, as many evangelicals had hoped to do.[55]

Mainline involvement in the political arena of European cooperation came next. The transatlantic Committee on the Christian Responsibility for European Cooperation was still functioning in 1966, but it was undergoing an overhaul after 15 years of struggling existence. The members decided to continue it since it was the "only ecumenical group which can discuss the problems of European and Atlantic co-operation at an expert level,"[56] but they were not really satisfied with the results. The Committee wrote two annual reports about the European Community but the publications failed to attract much attention. They had hoped to reach the Western European churches,

52 "Europe. Annual Report for 1966," and 5927, PHS UPC, 161B box 4 BFM/COEMAR Records.

53 Letter Harold E. Taus-sig to Frederick C. Maier, 12 September 1967. Taussig was a Colorado rancher, public school teacher and college professor in history and political science at Kentucky Southern College and Spaulding College. His sabbatical leave allowed him to explore Europe in 1967-68. His wife volunteered for the president of the Faculté Libre de Theologie Evangelique, a new evangelical seminary in Paris. He published a collection of essays called *Shoestring Sabbatical*, PHS UPC RG 301.2, box 5, Board of National Missions, Institute of Strategic Studies, Everett Perry/Frederick C. Maier files, Study on European Youth, 1967-1969.

54 Letter Harold E. Taussig to Everett Perry, 25 March 1968, PHS UPC RG 301.2, box 5, Board of National Missions, Institute of Strategic Studies, Everett Perry/Frederick C. Maier files, Study on European Youth, 1967-1969.

55 Letter Everett Perry to Harold E. Taussig, 17 April 1968, "A Preliminary Study of Student Protest Values Based on Interviews with Swedish Students." He emphasized the international unity among students and (or because of the unity in) the connections between sexual freedom and political protest/liberation. He believed the search was more for moral values than the place of the church. He believed there were strong connections between student protests in Europe and the United States and that the debate with students should be held on their terms, expressing a new kind of (humanist) morality. They fear the dehumanizing effects of materialism and labor laws and nationalism. PHS UPC RG 301.2, box 5, Board of National Missions, Institute of Strategic Studies, Everett Perry/Frederick C. Maier files, Study on European Youth, 1967-1969.

56 Christian Study Group for European Unity, "Resume of Decisions Taken during Last Meeting of CCREC, Frankfurt, May 21-22, 1966". See for more details Hans Krabbendam, "A Transatlantic Religious Alliance? American and European Protestant Encounters, 1945-1965," *Journal of Transatlantic Studies* 15.3 (2017): 1-17. PHS NCC RG 6 box 18.12.

but had refrained from officially representing them, as they felt that would harm free discussion. Instead the members tried to enlarge their group while accepting its lack of official authority. The Committee on the Christian Responsibility for European Cooperation was not succeeding in stimulating a transatlantic dialogue about the relationship between the Atlantic partners and other parts of the world with regard to economic and political matters (e.g., the pressing issue of Vietnam), but it still hoped to reach out to Americans and Roman Catholics. Its chairman was the Dutch Labor MP, Connie L. Patijn. who indicated that public opinion ignored or misinterpreted spiritual problems. However, the committee's future was uncertain, as the initiative depended on loans from the World Council of Churches. Patijn hoped that the WCC would channel private money in the sum of $25,000 per year to support his group.[57] Yet, the group, according to Monnet's right hand man, Max Kohnstamm, was pessimistic about the future of Europe, which seemed to lack a common goal in 1966. They doubted that the churches in Europe would develop a deep interest in the European project and gave up hope altogether that American churches would.[58]

In the end the transatlantic effort to create a structural framework for engaging Protestant churches in Europe failed to materialize. This was a disappointing result caused by the distance between the member churches and Christian big shots engaged in European politics. These politicians had failed to define the alleged Christian interests in Europe in religious terms.[59] Ironically, the crisis in Europe caused by the French withdrawal from NATO, paralyzed the group so that it again had to organize a meeting to reconsider its mission.[60] They planned to examine the European-American relationship in a global context, matching a theme of the Uppsala conference of the World Council. The group met in May 1968, and concluded that Europe and the United States were diverging in all policy areas. They pointed to divergent views on China, and the Middle East, and noted that Europe's critical attitude annoyed Amer-

57 Christian Study Group for European Unity, Letter of the secretary Paul Abrecht to A.W. Schmidt in Pittsburgh, 30 May 1966 and C.L. Patijn to A.W. Schmidt, 1 August 1966, PHS NCC RG 6 box 18.12.

58 Christian Study Group for European Unity, Minutes of the meeting of "Christian Study Group for European Unity"(formerly CCGEC) 19-20 November 1966, Paris, PHS NCC RG 6 box 18.12.

59 See for other Christian groups (but with an exclusive Catholic European membership) Johannes Grossman, "Ein Europa der 'Hintergründigen': Antikommunistische christliche Organisationen, konservatieve Elitenzirkel and private Aussenpolitik in Westeuropa nach dem Zweiten Weltkrieg," in Johannes Wienand and Christiane Wienand, eds., *Die kulturelle Integration Europas* (Wiesbaden: Springer, 2010), 303-340.

60 Christian Study Group for European Unity, letter Paul Abrecht to Robert Bilheimer, 19 December 1967, PHS NCC RG 6 box 18.12.

icans, especially once the French broke up European unity by leaving NATO.[61] By 1969 the group was prepared to include Roman Catholics and youth. Their specific Christian perspective remained implicit and vague rather than clearly defined. But they tried to change public opinion in the direction of appreciating stability even as they raised awareness of the danger of French and German nationalism. The group aimed to raise consciousness that a stronger Europe would not necessarily reclaim its privileges and go forward to harm the Third World. Indeed they thought the task of the church was to help the Third World to develop. The concluding remarks of the May 1969 meeting expressed the desire of the group to help the churches "read the handwriting on the wall, the signs of danger involved in resistance to common institutions, and the consequent rise of despairing reach for autocracy, etc. If the churches can be awakened to see the moral and spiritual depth of these issues they can help to influence the climate in significant ways."[62]

American observers, however, had little hope that the churches could play this role as they were still being organized by nation. The Americans suggested that the churches had a common need to fix their hopes on the younger generation, those less attached to the old institutions. Meanwhile Americans remained suspicious of the old technocratic elite who made up the membership of the group, and charged them with working to change things from above in direct conflict with young people's desire for change from below.[63] Student participants in the group organized a prayer session, but these efforts paled in comparison with the available evangelical attractions. Youth for Christ had much better success in reaching the young generation in Europe through their use of music, festivals, and drama, and by their specialized magazines that addressed the day-to-day concerns of the youth.[64]

Europe was a hard sell for the mainline churches. The World Council's "Commission of the Churches on International Affairs" ignored the old continent and discouraged building regional institutions except for temporary crisis management.[65] American mainline churches did not feel responsible for Europe and if they weren't otherwise occupied solving domestic problems in the United States, their energy looked beyond Europe to the Third World and international peace issues.

61 Christian Study Group for European Unity, Robert Bilheimer, "Report of Consultation on U.S.A.-Europe Relations, London, May 24-26, 1968," PHS NCC RG 6 box 18.12.

62 Christian Study Group for European Unity, May 16-18, 1969, "Session IV", P. 4 (remarks by Rollier), Session II (remarks Booth, Patijn), PHS NCC RG 6 box 18.12.

63 Christian Study Group for European Unity, Letter C.W. Williams to Robert S. Bilheimer, 22 May 1969, PHS NCC RG 6 box 18.12.

64 December 1967-October 1972: Ron and Carole Wilson (Holland) Newsletter, April 1968 and March 1969, BGCA col. 48 YFC box 16 file 51 Prayer Letters.

65 Memo by C.L. Patijn, "The Future of the Christian Study Group for European Unity," 16-18 May 1969, PHS NCC RG 6 box 18.12.

It was non-Americans inside the World Council who acknowledged Europe's religious challenges. In early 1964 the WCC publication *International Review of Missions*, ran Lesslie Newbigin's survey of the religious condition in Western Europe. This article reported hopeful signs amidst depressing trends.[66] Newbigin had served as a Church of Scotland missionary in Southern India, and held the position of Associate Secretary of missions at the WCC between 1959-1965. From his post in Geneva he noted both the low level of church attendance in the United Kingdom, the abandonment of compulsory chapel attendance in schools, and also a strong interest in spiritual matters, evidenced by high sales of books such as A.T. Robinson's *Honest to God*. Newbigin reported that despite the availability of modern media and art, most churches did not know how to use them for their cause. He noted that the churches spent most of their energy engaging in society. Scotland had maintained some zeal for missions, he said, but the situation in Germany looked bleak. Germans were hardly committed to their congregations, and what seekers there were fell into the hands of American sects, "which tend to draw off the pious," while others were attracted by non-Christian religions.[67] Newbigin was certain that the Protestant churches suffered from internal tensions over the relationship to modern culture, even if they were willing to try new organizational methods, such as the "concept of stewardship, developed in America."[68] The report noted that the recent Billy Graham campaign in Nuremberg and Stuttgart had been "effective in re-activating congregations and helping them to work together."[69]

Newbigin characterized the situation in Scandinavia as troublesome, "The initial difficulty faced by this Church in its missionary task at home is the fact that almost the entire population is already baptized and confirmed. The home mission is therefore understood as a sort of *diakonia* to help the members realize what membership means."[70] In writing about Sweden, Newbigin mentioned that it had witnessed urban growth and also growth in urban churches. But in this scenario, country churches had lost out, especially their contacts with the young generation. Despite the new developments in the Catholic Church there was not much to report about Southern Europe. Newbigin stressed that Protestants had a hard time in these regions, but that some of them were mildly positive about Vatican II, even if they weren't sure whether it signaled a real change.

66 "Europe," *International Review of Missions* 53 (January 1964): 50-66. He was not the first European theologian to identify Europe as a mission field, several theologians had preceded him in the 1940s, see Paas, "The Making of a Mission Field," 63-66.

67 Ibid., 54.

68 Ibid.

69 Ibid., 55.

70 Ibid., 62.

The survey of the religious situation in the next year, was more hopeful. It was written by Philip Potter, a Methodist missionary born on the West Indian island of Dominica and the chairman of the World Christian Student Federation, a rising star in the WCC. He noticed a growing intellectual polarization in Europe, mostly in Northwestern Europe, as well as an increase in Protestant-Catholic dialogue, along with modest expectations for more religious liberty in Catholic countries. He observed studies on applications of faith in society, more effort to raise money for international projects, some evangelism campaigns, and attempts to engage evangelicals in the movement for greater Christian unity.[71] Very similar conclusions came out of the 1969 survey.[72] Most ecumenical consultations were based on the agreement of WCC members "to do everything together which they do not feel obliged to do separately" and to concentrate on urban areas, even though this met with resistance from traditional groups.[73]

The ecumenical movement shared the evangelicals' concern that Protestant minorities in Southern Europe had no access to the media. But established churches such as the Swedish Lutheran Church doubted whether it should even be doing mission work in Europe.[74] This stood in striking contrast to the evangelical missions. When all was said and done, the numerous reports did not trigger American mainline churches to become actively involved in Europe. Nor did European churches show much interest in the European project.

Mainline churches in the United States increasingly expressed concern about the motives behind their country's military policy as well as its effect on the world. Instead of seeing that America was strengthening international justice, they believed the United States undermined it. To them the Vietnam War contradicted the liberal principles of the American nation.[75] In a subculture of the mainline churches, the transatlantic religious relationship united European and American protesters against the agenda of the American state. The growing anti-war movement turned against President Lyndon B. Johnson and triggered a response on the right as well, which expressed loyalty to the White House and stirred up patriotism in the silent majority.[76] For Wheaton College president Hudson T. Armerding nationalism could be seen positively

71 Philip Potter, "Europe," *International Review of Missions* 55 (January 1966): 7-23.

72 *International Review of Missions* 58 (January 1969): 48-71.

73 "Europe," *International Review of Missions* 53 (January 1964): 50.

74 Ibid. 58.

75 Andrew Preston, *Sword of the Spirit, Shield of Faith: Religion in American War and Diplomacy* (New York: Alfred A. Knopf, 2012), 520-538.

76 Grzegorz Kosc, Clara Juncker, Sharon Monteith, Britta Waldschmidt-Nelson, eds., *The Transatlantic Sixties: Europe and the United States in the Counterculture Decade* (Bielefeld: Transcript, 2013); Martin Klimke, *The Other Alliance: Student Protest in West Germany and the United States in the Global Sixties* (Princeton: Princeton University Press, 2010).

as "western nations were cordial to the ministry of the Church at home and generally sympathetic to its outreach abroad."[77]

Traditional Protestants were not shy about rallying to defend the honor of the American nation and resist Communism, which the US government insisted was the enemy in Vietnam. But the intense bombing of civilians and non-combatants, and an elusive peace undermined confidence among evangelicals as well. American missionaries encountered people everywhere who made negative associations between them and US government policy.[78] Meanwhile, American evangelicals continued to expand their activities in Europe and realized at that moment that they had gained a landing. But sooner than expected they too were linked with mainline American culture and their job became to reassess their missionary strategy.

Rethinking Evangelical Missions

Despite their critique of the established churches, American evangelicals realized they could not live without them, especially in Europe. In Wheaton, Illinois, evangelicals could not suppress their sense of self-importance when they drafted a declaration concluding the 1966 Congress on the Church's Worldwide Mission. It proudly stated that evangelicals were responsible for two-thirds of the Protestant missionaries in North America and Europe. In the same statement they also self-consciously rejected isolation, inefficiency, over-organization, and neglect of social evils.[79] The statement expressed an awareness of the renewal taking place within the Catholic Church (without abandoning caution, it said the changes could be cosmetic), cults and non-Christian religions. The Wheaton statement warned most sternly against liberal Protestantism, which "has created an ecclesiastical organization aimed at achieving a religious monopoly." In its original draft it went so far as to label ecumenism hostile to the Christian missionary.

77 Armerding, "Nationalism and Evangelism," in Henry, *One Race*, vol. 2, 303, "Imperialism can quite possibly provide conditions under which the preaching of the Gospel may prosper." But it all depended on the leadership, 304. Representatives from India and South Africa were more critical of the nation when the government was not Protestant, 311, 316-317.

78 Andrew Preston, "Tempered by the Fires of War: Vietnam and the Transformation of the Evangelical Worldview," in Axel Schaefer, ed., *American Evangelicals and the 1960s* (Madison: University of Wisconsin Press, 2013), 189-208.

79 "Tentative Preliminary Draft of propositional statements which might be included in an anticipated 'Declaration' eventuating from the Congress," BGCA col. 165 box 6 file 23; "The Wheaton Declaration," *Evangelical Mission Quarterly* 2 (Summer 1966): 231-244. The approved text said "that create ecclesiastical organizations moving in the direction of a worldwide religious monopoly." Example of visa problems in India caused by the agency not belonging to the NCC in India. Taylor to Kirby, 5 May 1964, BGCA col. 165 box 6 file 10.

The 1966 Wheaton Conference on global missions had been a dream of Billy Graham from the early 1960s, but it had taken the evangelical leadership some time to agree on who should be invited.[80] Graham was in the process of changing his course by adding the training of evangelists to his activities at major international conferences. In Berlin in 1966 two decades after Graham's first arrival in Europe, the European counterpart to the Wheaton Conference took place. The event was organized under the auspices of *Christianity Today*, which was celebrating its tenth anniversary and meant to be a model for an evangelism campaign in Europe.[81] The organizers designed the conference along lines of the famous 1910 World Mission Conference at Edinburgh. Billy Graham reminded the 1,100 delegates and guests that the purpose of the conference was to call "the world Church to return to the dynamic zeal for world evangelization that characterized Edinburgh 56 years ago."[82] The 1966 Berlin conference's significance for Europe was driven home by the march of 1,200 delegates and guests from Wittenberg Square to the Kaiser Wilhelm Memorial Church at Kurfürstendamm, and an open door service for a 18,000 audience on Reformation Sunday, 30 October, which served to reclaim the basic tenets of the Reformation.

Organizers had at first considered Rome as a venue for the conference, but decided not to provoke Catholics who at that moment were in the midst of the Vatican II Council.[83] Reports on the Protestant minority in Italy and other Catholic countries confirmed a new openness. Generally the congress speakers appealed to ecumenical Christians to take evangelism seriously and called for cooperation between missions and established churches to overcome divisions. Representatives of ecumenical institutions were less pessimistic than they had been at Wheaton and praised the opportunity the conference provided for an exchange of views, clearly the result of earlier evangelical-ecumenist consultations.[84]

From every corner of Europe, evangelical representatives called for better education and training of lay people. The situation in the United States

80 Billy Graham informed Taylor about his plans for a mission conference in the summer of 1963, see letter Clyde Taylor to Gilbert Kirby, 22 July 1963, BGCA col. 165 box 6 file 10.

81 "Protokoll der Herbstsitzung des HV der Deutschen Evangelischen Allianz, vom 24. bis 26. November 1964," 6-8, Archives Allianzhaus Bad Blankenburg, Germany.

82 Billy Graham, "Why the Berlin Congress?" in Carl F.H. Henry and W. Stanley Mooneyham, eds., *One Race One Gospel One Task vol. 1 World Congress on Evangelism Berlin 1966. Official Reference volumes: Papers and Reports* (Minneapolis: World Wide Publications, 1967), 22.

83 Enns, "Saving Germany," 232; Graham, *Just As I am*, 561-562.

84 *One Race*, 240-47 and Winterhager, 254-55; Uta A. Balbier, "The World Congress on Evangelism 1966 in Berlin: US Evangelicalism, Cultural Dominance, and Global Challenges," *Journal of American Studies* 51.4 (2017): 1171-1196.

Crowd of 18,000 gathers in front of Kaiser-Wilhelm-Gedächtniskirche in downtown Berlin on October 30, 1966 to hear greetings from Bishops Kurt Scharf and Otto Dibelius of Berlin and a message by Billy Graham.
[©1966 BGEA]

and Canada was presented as offering many opportunities.[85] The conference embraced Pentecostals and granted Thomas Zimmerman, general superintendent of the Assemblies of God in Springfield, Missouri, and faith healer Oral Roberts, timeslots to speak in workshops. It was put forward that the evangelicals needed Roberts' "spiritual energy," and their acceptance of him created an opening for a more holistic approach to mission projects.[86]

One may identify the year 1966 as the moment when the European secular media discovered the "evangelicals" as a coherent religious group with a unique selling point. Thanks to direct contacts, educational projects, and soon mass media events, Europeans would get to know the American evangelicals better than they knew the American mainstream churches. But the evangelicals had even higher ambitions.[87] But in the board room of the German leadership, efforts were made to separate the evangelism campaign in Berlin from the conference that followed, as it resisted the suggestion that Graham's method must be a universal one (which he denied as well). The presence of Graham at the congress increased the interest in the evangelism campaign and the program advocated a wide spectrum of means of communication and technology.[88] The conference concluded with a statement published by German participants committing themselves to evangelism and calling church leaders to collectively support this cause.[89]

The newest technological innovations, such as direct TV connections between European cities, tested during Billy Graham's Earls Court Crusade in London, 1967, seemed to multiply Graham's presence everywhere and offer an alternative to addressing ever larger audiences in ever larger venues. The sense of urgency among American evangelicals gave rise to an efficient organization, which strategically targeted audiences in Europe.

85 Henry, *One Race*, vol. 1, 250, 259, 266, 268-276. See report by Jim Newton, on waning anti-ecumenical rhetoric at the Berlin conference "Ecumenical Evangelism Underscored by Congress," in the *BP Features* (Baptist Press), 14 November 1966, 1.

86 Mark Hutchinson and John Wolffe, *A Short History of Global Evangelicalism* (Cambridge: Cambridge University Press, 2012), 189; Henry, *One Race*, vol. 2, 65, 475 on Christ's return and on the gifts of the Spirit.

87 *Rotterdammer*, 18 February 1967.

88 "Protokoll der Herbstsitzung des HV der Deutschen Evangelischen Allianz, vom 24. bis 26. November 1964," 6-9, and Paul Schmidt, "Allianzumschau," DEA Hauptvorstandssitzung am 28.-31 März 1966, 8, Archives Allianzhaus Bad Blankenburg, Germany. The campaign was held from 12-23 October, the conference from 26 October – 5 November 1966. Peter Schneider, "Weltkongress für Evangelisation in Berlin," *Evangelisches Allianzblatt* 69 (July 1966), 130-131; Peter Schneider, "Zum Evangelisationsdienst von Dr. Billy Graham in Berlin," *Evangelisches Allianzblatt* 69 (October 1966), 186-187; Paul Schmidt, "Billy Graham in Berlin," *Evangelisches Allianzblatt* 69 (November 1966), 213-215; Richard Kriese, " 'Eine Menschheit, ein Evangelium, ein Auftrag,' Weltkongress für Evangelisation vom 26.10. bis 4. 11 .1966," *Evangelisches Allianzblatt* 69 (December 1966), 225-230.

89 "Erklärung der deutschen Teilnehmer am Weltkongress für Evangelisation," *Evangelisches Allianzblatt* 69 (December 1966), 241.

Two indicators of the growing influence of American evangelicals were the large international group of contributors to *Christianity Today* and its strong international distribution. With a circulation of 200,000, it easily beat the 40,000 copies of its liberal counterpart the *Christian Century*. Each new issue of *Christianity Today* reached Amsterdam by special arrangement with KLM and was redistributed throughout Europe within days. It usually took weeks before the *Christian Century* reached its foreign destination.[90] One of the secrets of this success was the evangelicals' access to private American funds. For instance, PanAm Airlines helped transport hundreds of delegates to these conferences. It was exactly this type of close corporate association that led some leftist journalists to be critical of the connections between religion and American consumerism.

Amidst the cultural tensions, the political situation allowed for a more relaxed atmosphere. "Détente afforded the churches the luxury of self-absorption in domestic issues," historian Robert F. Goeckel has asserted.[91] German churches embarked on a conciliatory tour in Eastern Europe, but the building of the Berlin Wall in 1969 inaugurated a period of formal division of the Eastern and Western churches. For various reasons the political distance from America grew. The return of prosperity in Germany stopped American funding. American (mostly Lutheran) churches completed their projects and the German population became critical towards America's engagement in Vietnam. The German authorities were preoccupied with domestic issues especially terrorism, and presented themselves internationally as mediators or reformers in defense of the rule of law.

The Evangelical Movement on the European Continent and the German Evangelicals

With Germany recovered economically and returned to the political center of Europe in the 1970s, it also occupied center stage in religious developments. The Anglo-American holiness and mass evangelism movements had inspired the Germans since the 1870s. The pietist revival movement of the early nineteenth century had resulted in a community of born-again believers who were committed to prayer and evangelism, the *Gemeinschaftsbewegung*. Together with the members of *Freikirchen* they shaped the evangelical movement in Germany. Modern evangelicalism there was a mixture of German and British influences spread in the free churches and in the official state churches, in-

90 *Nieuwe Leidsche Courant*, 1 June 1966.

91 Robert F. Goeckel, "German and American Churches: Changes in Actors, Priorities, and Power Relations," in Detlef Junker, Philipp Gassert, Wilfried Mausbach, eds., *The United States and Germany in the Era of the Cold War, 1945-1990: A Handbook. Volume 2, 1968-1990* (New York: Cambridge University Press, 2004), 466-473, quote on 469.

fused with a dose of traditional confessionalism, and energized by the Pentecostal revival both inside and outside the established churches.[92]

Only a small minority among German Protestants had eagerly embraced the nineteenth-century Evangelical Alliance. In general, religious minorities were suppressed, especially in Lutheran Prussia, and the ecumenical message was rejected as too English, offering not enough doctrinal recognition for Lutherans. Though some church leaders feared that new religious movements would create even more division between churches and believers, the Evangelical Alliance succeeded in using regional conferences to build a national network. This book is not the place to analyze the role of German churches in the war. Nevertheless one should note that the churches' initial high expectation from a strong leader against the decadence of the early twentieth century served to obscure the antichristian character of the Nazi Reich. After the war the German churches were aware of their guilt and their lost authority.[93] In this context efforts to re-Christianize Germany led to inviting Billy Graham, who visited Germany several times.

German evangelicals restyled Graham from an American into a transnational figure. Peter Schneider, who had been converted as a prisoner of war in Wisconsin, so closely mimicked Graham's staccato style, that the audience hardly noticed the difference.[94] During the 1960s the American movement became Germanized. In 1963 *Decision* magazine was published in German and in the following decade original German articles took the place of ones written in translation. In the same period, specifically in 1959, the Germans founded the Evangeliums-Rundfunk, the German branch of Trans World Radio. Evangeliums-Rundfunk was independent, but followed the constitution of the Deutsche Evangelische Allianz and was supported by a broad constituency, showing that German evangelicals were able to cooperate. In 1965 three thousand local alliances of evangelicals were active in support of the larger mass evangelism movement.[95]

92 Friedhelm Jung, *Die Deutsche Evangelikale Bewegung: Grundlinien ihrer Geschichte und Theologie* (Frankfurt: Lang, 1992), 26-34.

93 Frank Lüdke, "Von Bonifatius bis Willow Creek – eine kurze Geschichte der englisch-amerikanischen Einflüsse auf das Christentum in Deutschland," in Frank Lüdke and Norbert Schmidt, eds., *Die neue Welt und der neue Pietismus. Angloamerikanische Einflüsse* (Berlin: LIT-Verlag, 2012), 5-33; Jung, *Die Deutsche*, 39; Jan Bank with Lieve Gevers, *Churches and Religion in the Second World War,* translated by Brian Doyle (London: Bloomsbury Academic, 2016); Jung, *Die Deutsche*, 41; JonDavid K. Wyneken, "The Western Allies, German Churches and the Emerging Cold War in Germany, 1948-1952," in Philip Muehlenbeck, ed., *Religion and the Cold War: A Global Perspective* (Nashville: Vanderbilt University Press, 2012), 18-43.

94 Interview Lois Ferm with Peter Schneider, German organizer for the Billy Graham campaigns, 1993, Col. 141 BGEA Oral History Project, box 62 file 13.

95 Jung, *Die Deutsche*, 43.

A similar trend towards indigenization was visible elsewhere in Europe. In 1963 the Belgium Gospel Mission's leadership decided not to advertise for American missionaries, but to recruit Europeans, as they knew they would be cheaper to support, and more effective.[96] Three years later, in 1966, the board reported that eligible Belgians didn't want to work for an American organization, "Men in this nationalistic day are not made this way." The mission leadership anticipated that the work in Belgium would be completed by 1975 and they could then move on to France.[97]

The 1966 conference on Evangelism held in Berlin between October 26 and November 4 had a big impact on the Deutsche Evangelische Allianz. The new thing coming out of the conference was the idea to concentrate evangelism on already Christian peoples, and not to work on reaching new areas. The atmosphere was critical of ecumenism, but not entirely against it. Representatives of the WCC churches were also present in Berlin. Urgent concerns about world population growth and secularization were the key motivators in organizing this event. The German *Evangelikaler* identified the established church as the main obstacle to evangelism, and committed themselves to more action.[98]

A number of tensions crisscrossed the liberal-conservatism spectrum. One was the bureaucratic and real split between the WCC and the IMC. The other was the high expectation among Calvinists for global transformation, a process for which the Lutherans had only low expectations.[99] While the purpose of integration was to make the churches more missionary, many former colonies were in the process of becoming independent and so had less need for missionaries. Indeed, development workers came to occupy the former place usually taken by missionaries. The agencies feared stagnation and inflexible bureaucratic constraints. They were also alarmed by the prospect of a drain on resources caused by many competing concerns in the churches. In the new anti-colonial world some missionaries identified with the new nationalist movements, others stayed aloof or they sided with the European regimes and white settlers. The times were full of tension and confusion and many of

96 Homer Payne to Lillian Elliott, 26 November 1963, KADOC, Archief Belgische Evangelische Zending (1900 (c)-2009) inv. 1240 Elliott, Lillian: correspondentie met Payne (1963).

97 "Report by Homer Payne to American Comité, May 1966," inv. 850 Stukken Board of Trustees: notulen, correspondentie, ledenlijst (1918-1971), 3. An average of 10 per cent of BGM staff came from the US, but most of the leadership was American. KADOC, Archief Belgische Evangelische Zending (1900 (c)-2009).

98 Jung, *Die Deutsche*, 47-49.

99 Bernhard Ott, *Beyond Fragmentation: Integrating Mission and Theological Education: A Critical Assessment of Some Recent Developments in Evangelical Theological Education* (Oxford: Regnum, 2001), 58.

the support groups at home that got entangled in internal debate saw their finances dwindle.[100]

In 1965 the term "evangelical" appeared for the first time in the *Evangelische Allianzblatt* of the German Evangelical Alliance (DEA). A number of these mission organizations operated alongside the Lutheran church, others were affiliated with the free-church movement, or were interdenominational. In 1968 these groups met to eventually found the Arbeitsgemeinschaft Evangelikaler Missionen (AEM) as a contact group for evangelical mission organizations. Meanwhile American evangelical organizations offered an alternative network. Further evidence of the maturity of European evangelicals can be found in the 1969 national conference of German evangelicals who explicitly explored the question of what it meant to be evangelical. The shift in orientation from Britain to North America in terms of voluntarism and interdenominational cooperation increased the distance between church and parachurch.

The official church leadership in Germany did not recognize the evangelical response as a part of the pluralization process that it actively sought. And according to historian Gisa Bauer, neither did the evangelical contingent in the *landeskirchen* see this pattern.[101] Evangelicals emphasized the intellectual core that had energized traditional believers and ministers in the late 1940s and 1950s. They stressed that those believers had felt that the demythologization project of Rudolf Bultmann's theology undermined the core of Christianity and caused much uncertainty. They rejected the monopoly of academic theology and thought there were other ways of making Christianity relevant for modern times. In 1966 the evangelicals issued an explicit protest, rejecting pluralism in theology and church, and rebuffing ecumenical goals and the politicizing of the church. They deplored the decline of missions, and lack of leadership in social and ethical issues. Graham's Berlin Conference connected them to a larger cause and gave them a podium for confronting their opponents.

The European evangelicals did not seek intellectual solutions, but mobilized a constituency with a strong moral presence with regard to God's judgment on the approaching end-times. Action was needed rather than reflection, and bible schools provided alternative training centers for academic theology and the shaping of religious identity. Thanks to international connections the bible schools could access curriculum and organizational support and achieve accreditation.

The evangelical responses to the quickening pace of modernization, revealed their discomfort with fragmentation and individualization and oper-

100 John Stuart, *British Missionaries and the End of Empire: East, Central and Southern Africa, 1939–64* (Grand Rapids, MI: Eerdmans, 2011), 172-173, 178-184.

101 Gisa Bauer, *Evangelikale Bewegung und evangelische Kirche in der Bundesrepublik Deutschland: Geschichte eines Grundsatzkonflikts (1945 bis 1989)* (Göttingen: Vandenhoeck & Ruprecht, 2012).

ating in the international spotlight, they chose Bultmann's demythologizing theology as a symbol and target. Since the German Church was inextricably linked with society and the state, evangelicals wanted to strengthen the role of the church in society. The unique situation of the *landeskirchen* as the main reference system for evangelicals was unique in Europe.[102]

This shift removed the last reason why the European Evangelical Alliance would maintain an existence apart from the World Evangelical Fellowship. They merged in 1968 and this was a significant move towards global evangelical coherence. An ambitious European mission campaign in the spring of 1970, called "Euro 70", marked this growth. The Germans carried the financial risks of this campaign centered in Dortmund. An evangelical press agency in Germany (Idea) helped to consolidate the gains in organization and worked to establish avenues of communication among the various traditions within and outside the evangelical tradition. One of the key instruments used to solidify the emerging European evangelical network was educational institutions.

Bible Schools Spread

Bible schools occupied a strategic position as a transatlantic linchpin and a source of new identity. The postwar American missionaries linked up with the oldest evangelical bible school in France. Founded in 1921 in Nogent-sur-Marne it had served French evangelicals for decades. It was more French and more practical than the other bible schools in France.[103] When the number of these schools increased in Europe, the new schools adopted the American model for accreditation. The Accrediting Association of Bible Institutes and Bible Colleges in 1947 in America served as the resource and the model for European evangelicals.[104] In 1971 the bible school of the Belgian Gospel Mission in Brussels, founded in 1919, with 30 students who mostly trained for service in their own organization, merged with the three schools of the Greater Europe Mission, the GEM. This move confirmed the European scope of evangelical education.[105] The Bibelschule Bergstrasse in Bensheim was founded by the GEM in 1955, and inspired the Freie Theologische Akademie in Seeheim in 1974. This academy moved to Giessen seven years later.[106]

102 Bauer, *Evangelikale Bewegung*, 668 and 673. It is ironic that she defines the evangelical protest as the sign of the vitality of the Church.

103 Sébastien Fath, "Evangelical Protestantism in France: An Example of Denominational Recomposition?" *Sociology of Religion* 66.4 (2005): 399-418.

104 They institutionalized their European accreditation agency in 1979.

105 Dossier fusie Belgische Evangelische Zending en Greater Europe Mission (1969-1972), KADOC, Archief Belgische Evangelische Zending (1900 (c)-2009), 870.

106 Helge Stadelmann, ed., 1998. The school in Bensheim moved to Seeheim, had internal problems and in 1959 moved to Kalkar and on in 1962 to Brake. The GEM wanted to train church planters, the original founders wanted to train for missions.

In the winter of 1964 German fundamentalist bible school president, Heinrich Jochums, welcomed eleven bible schools from Germany, one from Switzerland, and one from the Netherlands to consult about policies. They decided to meet annually, growing to 24 schools in 1977 and 36 in 1997. This association stressed the inerrancy of the bible, and was defensive towards the ecumenist liberal movement, dressing itself in fundamentalist concepts and language. The group of bible schools in Germany felt a bond to the fundamentalist ICCC.[107]

This response created two factions: the "bible-believing" and the historical-critical groups of ministers.[108] The conservative response in Germany against "a rampant humanism" was applauded by *United Evangelical Action* and utilized as a warning for American evangelicals that they should rally in support of the "fundamentals of the historic Christian faith."[109]

European Media Discover the Evangelicals

The evangelical surge did not go unnoticed in Europe. In the second half of the 1960s European journalists discovered the new force in Protestantism and its American sponsorship. Graham's initiative to organize a global conference on evangelism in Berlin in 1966 exposed the strength of this "evangelical orthodox" group.[110] Dutch reporters, for instance, noticed that this group was much better organized than the ecumenists and was able to reach a broad circle of believers outside the United States. They discovered that *Christianity Today* had a large international group of contributors and a much better international distribution than *Christian Century*. They recognized the American origins of this movement, not only because of the presence of Billy Graham and the American funds allowing a large section of the 1,250 participants to join the Berlin conference, but also because the efficient use of a great variety of modern communication was a signature American trait. They spotted hundreds of delegates equipped with a bag showing the conference logo and that of corporate sponsor PanAm.[111]

107 Ott, *Beyond Fragmentation*, 60-62.

108 Bauer, *Evangelikale Bewegung*, 360-389. Landeskirche were not always against the initiatives, e.g. the Bibelschule Bergstrasse, as many young people from the churches attended the schools and were active in the congregations with children and youth (372-373). Yet, in the 1960s they wanted to discourage attending these schools as the bible schools did not meet the theological standards of the church. In the mid-1980s they recognized the schools as part of a pluralistic spectrum (380). Moreover, evangelical students attended state schools where they founded their own evangelical support groups.

109 James S. Kiefer, "Our State in the New German Evangelical Tension," *United Evangelical Action*, April 1966, 7.

110 *Nieuwe Leidsche Courant*, 1 June 1966.

111 *Algemeen Handelsblad*, 10 November 1966.

Once these journalists had raised public awareness of the evangelicals, they continued to write about the technological innovations, such as the TV connection to other cities, tested during Billy Graham's Earls Court Crusade in London, 1967. They emphasized that such TV coverage offered an alternative to having to accommodate ever larger audiences in any particular venue.[112] Graham's campaign headquarters was fully aware of these positive European responses, and kept a collection of numerous press clippings.[113]

The movement towards the mainstream was most visible in Billy Graham's use of the new communication technology and the subsequent endeavor to train evangelists worldwide in the American techniques of evangelism. The next step of the BGEA was to simultaneously transmit a rally in Dortmund to thirty-six other European cities from April 5-12, 1970.[114] Apart from this daring technology, the evangelicals impressed the media with their streamlined organization and their integrated public relations' campaign including showings of the first Billy Graham film "The Restless Ones" (1965), and translations of his books, such as *The Challenge*.[115] A spokesperson from Philips Eindhoven, the producer of these devices, believed that Billy had shown that technology could be used to touch a European-wide audience in the heart.[116]

The organizers themselves realized, however, that reproducing Graham on numerous TV-screens was not as good as having him there in person, but there was a reason why they continued to invest in this type of communication. By the late 1960s and early 1970s Billy Graham had lost his faith in the willingness and ability of the churches to spread the gospel. This conclusion increased the need to find a new means of mass mobilization by specialized organizations and the use of communication technology. His 1966 campaign in London invested more effort into the care of converts by sending them to informal groups. While Graham did not want to offend the churches, who offered their volunteers, he believed that for new believers to easily join a traditional church was a step too far. In Berlin in 1966 he justified the need for the conference saying the established churches neglected spreading the gospel.[117]

The second effect of this abandonment of the European churches was that Graham then extended his reach by taking into his own hands the practical training of an army of new evangelists. In the 1970s, the BGEA increased its efforts to empower and train new evangelists apart from organizing mass

112 *Rotterdammer*, 18 February 1967.

113 See Collection 360, "Billy Graham Evangelistic Association Clippings File", BGCA.

114 An interview with Bronek Wlochacz on 28 January 2010 confirmed the high expectations of new technology, which led to the launch of the Dutch Evangelical Broadcasting Company (Evangelische Omroep). William Martin, *A Prophet with Honor*, 379-381; John Pollock, *Billy Graham: Evangelist to the World* (New York: Harper and Row, 1979).

115 *Provinciale Zeeuwse Courant*, 18 March 1970; *Friesch Dagblad*, 1 April 1970.

116 *Philips Koerier*, 18 April 1970. The idea that entire Western Europe, including Yugoslavia, was connected to the same event drew European evangelicals closer together.

117 *Dordts Dagblad*, 3 June 1966 and many other Dutch newspaper clippings in 8 June 1966.

evangelism events. Amsterdam would become the most important venue thanks to its efficient airport connections, conference facilities, and the easy visa policy of the Dutch authorities. At the end of August 1971 Graham spoke to 1,200 Europeans on evangelism in the Dutch capital. There he spoke of evangelism not as a project of the church, but as a mindset for all believers. Again he blamed the churches for neglecting this task and reproached the liberal theologians for breaking down religion and replacing it by political action. He concluded that the European church had become a target for evangelism instead of a source. European decline contrasted sharply with the vitality of religion in the United States, he said, especially when compared to the Jesus Revolution happening in California.[118]

The growth of evangelical missionary activities worldwide and the realization that Europe had become a mission field proved Graham's point. The evangelicals had tipped the balance in the missionary enterprise in terms of numbers of staff and they had strengthened their position to become serious contenders for the leadership of American Protestantism. Between 1935 and 1952 evangelicals increased their share in foreign missions from 40 to more than 50 percent, and by the 1980s evangelicals outnumbered the staff of denominational missions three to one.[119]

Intertwining Evangelical Networks

In the 1960s the various evangelical agencies found a solution for their small numbers and fragmentation. They would begin using each other's specialties. The Portuguese Baptists trained for mass evangelism at the Billy Graham campaigns in London, and a Youth for Christ team of musicians came to play at Portuguese outreach meetings. This combination of national growth and international support stimulated the missionaries to prepare for a national campaign in Portugal, supported by most evangelical churches and agencies. Paid for by the Graham organization, seven Portuguese evangelicals participated in Graham's June 1966 London Crusade. In London they were preparing their own outreach campaign and hoping to lure Graham to Portugal. The Portuguese used the opportunity of Brazilian evangelists who attended the Berlin Conference to stage a crusade in July.[120] In France the Conservative Baptist missionaries cooperated with Operation Mobilization, youth camps of Young Life, and students from the Greater Europe Mission's Bible School in Lamorlaye.

118 *Nieuwsblad van het noorden*, 30 August 1971; *Nieuwe Apeldoornse Courant*, 4 September 1971.

119 Joel A. Carpenter, *Revive Us Again: The Reawakening of American Fundamentalism* (New York: Oxford University Press, 1993), 185.

120 Faircloth Newsletter, September 1966, BGCA col. 658.

The Conservative Baptists had come to France in 1962 with the purpose of planting new churches in the communist suburbs of Paris and cooperating with existing Baptist churches. Their approach was to let a team of students go door to door for two weeks and collect 200 addresses of people who were interested in the gospel. The Baptists would then send four missionaries to the homes, and invite the people to weekly bible study groups. The students had impressed the French "by the friendliness, zeal, and freshness of character" that they displayed in their work and dedication. This activity resulted in the end in 30 people showing an interest. The missionaries strongly believed this team-approach-with-immediate-follow-up was the best method to sow and reap. They expected "thinking Catholics" to be interested in the gospel. What they had underestimated, however, was the tension that would be created by the requirement of adult baptism since most of the interested parties had been baptized as children.[121]

Another example of newfound cooperation was the arrival of Gospel Recordings to Europe in 1965. In the Netherlands, former Youth for Christ worker Dick Lugthart welcomed this organization to the Netherlands. They connected with the representative of Trans World Radio and distributed 60,000 gospel records in the port city of Rotterdam. In Amsterdam they linked up with the Bible Club Movement.[122]

At the end of the 1960s, the associations connected with the EFMA had stationed 327 missionaries in Europe, most in Italy (57), France (55), Germany (36), and Spain (31). The largest groups were the Assemblies of God (68), and Child Evangelism Fellowship (39), while the Conservative Baptists (38) concentrated on Portugal, Italy and France.[123] In total more than a thousand chapters of North American agencies were active in Europe and since their arrival in postwar Europe the number of missionaries had doubled each decade.

In the 1960s, the evangelical network became truly international and the American contingent became a leading player, especially in Europe. Evangelicals took over the majority position in the total numbers of American missions and were recognized as a strong factor in the American religious presence in the world. Their dominance was due to their inner drive, and partly due to the mobilizing phase in the mission cycle, which went for evangelical missions

121 Report CBFMS "France Annual Report 1966" in file "Missions Situation Europe," Wheaton College Archives, spec. col. 113, box 9.

122 Marlène Muhr, *Along Unfamiliar Paths: Proclaiming God's Light in Man's Night, the Story of Gospel Recordings Europe* (Los Angeles: Gospel Recordings; Pasadena, CA: Printed by Geddes Press, 1982), 12-13, 17.

123 EFMA Annual Missionary Statistical Report 1 January 1969, BGCA col. 165 box 8 file 26.

as it had for the mainline churches.[124] The mission experience strengthened American evangelicals' sense of universal applicability of their approaches, and reinforced their feelings of superiority over Europe. A result of this infusion was that Continental Europeans came to terms with American evangelical agenda's, broadened these to include social issues, and in doing so emerged as a viable branch in the evangelical family.

At the same time, the European relationship with American mainline churches withered as ethnic churches shifted their aid programs to other continents and Europe expanded its own social welfare programs making relief from the new homeland of the immigrants superfluous. Efforts to tie churches in Europe and the United States to the European Union stayed in tiny circles of experts and remained invisible.

124 More research is needed to assess the effect of the experiences of these tens of thousands missionaries at home. Did they support the political involvement of their coreligionists and if so, in which direction? Charles E. Van Engen, "A Broadening Vision: Forty Years of Evangelical Theology of Mission, 1946-1986," in Joel Carpenter and Wilbert R. Shenk, eds., *Earthen Vessels: American Evangelicals and Foreign Missions, 1880-1980* (Eugene, OR: Wipf and Stock Publishers, 2012), 206-211, believes evangelicals in mission areas had grown politically sensitive, but offers no evidence.

LET GO!

INTEGRATION IN THE 1970S

Reflection and Diversification

By the 1960s, the evangelical movement in the United States had matured and pollsters calculated that self-identified evangelicals had become par in size with the mainstream churches, each representing about 25 per cent of the population. Gradually, the older denominational boundaries demarcating the two had been replaced by a liberal-conservative divide. Like Joseph McCarthy's bitter attacks on liberalism in the 1950s, a similar split again carved up the political landscape. During the 1970s and 1980s religiosity and conservatism became lumped together and this association gave the impression that the force of religion was growing. In fact, it was only one specific profile that had gained greater visibility – the more theatrical aspects of (conservative) American Protestantism. And it was this highly energized American religious configuration that not only played an important role in evangelism's initial spread in Europe, but also ultimately limited its influence.[1]

The perception in Europe that interest in religion was on the upswing, was facilitated by the intense involvement of American evangelicals in supporting overseas missions and working in Europe as missionaries, for long and short-term periods of time. While grassroots activism was strong in both progressive and traditional religious subcultures – in civil rights, poverty, women's rights, pro-life, or evangelism – the most visible and explicit reli-

1 Marc Chaves, *American Religion: Contemporary Trends* (Princeton: Princeton University Press, 2011), 86, 106.

gious expression came from traditionalist circles. Building on the fundamentalist media experiences of the 1940s, evangelicals were trained in crafting religious messages for their consumers. And once evangelicals abandoned their isolation by increasingly emphasizing broad cooperation, they were successful in building first, a US national, and soon an international string of communications networks.[2] This is not to say that liberal ideas were absent from the media. Far from it. They had all the opportunities provided by the secular press. Still, they didn't manage to build an international community, and in fact actively tried to restrict the airwaves to nonsectarian broadcasts, which excluded evangelical initiatives. In the words of media historian Quentin J. Schultze, mainline Protestants acted as a tribe with an anti-tribal agenda. Their promotion of nonsectarian religion was a hard-sell abroad because it had no specific content to offer. Meanwhile, traditional denominational groups and umbrella organizations in the evangelical subculture attached a high priority to persuasion and instruction and saw these as the main tasks of media communication. Because it was harder to enter the nationalized airwaves in Europe, the creation of training facilities such as local bible schools grew in importance. Their priorities dictated that feet-on-the-ground were a crucial factor in spreading the news.[3]

It was time to consider the result of these investments. Newly gained acceptability along with power and influence at home and abroad in the 1960s, gave the evangelicals reason to take stock of their original objective of advancing a global revival. As a consequence, they had to refine their strategy. In the previous twenty-five years, American evangelicals had successfully pioneered in mainland Europe and it now belonged in the international evangelical orbit. In the United States, evangelicals responded to the radical cultural upheaval of the 1960s by turning to politics, utilizing the many institutions and ties with government and civic organizations they had built in the postwar decades. The New Christian Right welded their engagement with culture and expressive individualism to a countercultural approach in order to preserve

2 James D. Hunter, *To Change the World: The Irony, Tragedy, and Possibility of Christianity in the Late Modern World* (New York: Oxford University Press, 2010), 111-166. Hunter and many others correctly distinguish the subgroup of the liberal evangelicals as a potential bridge, but this group was hardly visible outside the US.

3 Quentin J. Schultze, *Christianity and the Mass Media in America: Toward a Democratic Accommodation* (East Lansing: Michigan State University Press, 2003), 89-174; Robert S. Fortner, "Internationalizing Evangelical Media," in Quentin J. Schultze and Robert H. Woods Jr., eds., *Understanding Evangelical Media: The Changing Face of Christian Communication* (Downers Grove, IL: IVP Academic, 2008), 20 (tribe) and 239-251; Robert S. Fortner, "Media," in Philip Goff, ed., *The Blackwell Companion to Religion in America* (Malden, MA: Wiley, 2010), 206-214; Timothy Stoneman, "Creating The Protestant Voice of Europe, 1945-1970" unpublished paper, Roosevelt Study Center, Middelburg, the Netherlands, 15 July 2015; Timothy Stoneman, "Global Radio Broadcasting and the Dynamics of American Evangelicalism," *Journal of American Studies* 51 (November 2017): 1139-1170.

traditional religion, which advocated old-style capitalism against a growing state influence. As historian Hugh McLeod has argued, this combination of cooperation with – and opposition to – the state, was a complex endeavor that contrasted with the European trend of abandoning traditional institutional religion, while embracing the welfare state.[4] This process of reorientation in the United States had strategic implications for missions as well. Despite fresh openings to new partners, older, more negative sentiments against the established churches in Europe continued to shape evangelical expectations and to put limits on close cooperation with non-evangelicals.

Christianity Today endorsed integrating the ideas and practices of corporate marketing to attain the goals of global missions. Media scholar Quentin Schulze has observed that the rhetoric of conversion-as-a-choice justified the uncritical acceptance of consumerist media expressions. John Micklethwait, the editor-in-chief of *The Economist*, argues in *God is Back* that American multinationals exported a demand for faith by undermining traditional religion, even as American evangelicals arrived in Europe with their supply of faith traditions.[5] Scholars have pointed out that in the 1970s, as economic globalization accelerated, older, more stable international political and economic systems such as exchange rates, were abandoned for more flexible and insecure ones.[6] Protestants had to respond to these new conditions, which were most keenly felt in the former European colonies. Seeking approval from European authorities was redundant, new states were often critical of their colonizers. As a result of the decolonization process and growth of NGOs, a shift took place in mainstream churches' missionary activities. They moved from founding churches to providing development services. This was especially true in Africa, where native believers assumed leadership roles. The di-

4 David A. Hollinger, *After Cloven Tongues of Fire: Protestant Liberalism and Modern America* (Princeton: Princeton University Press, 2013), 18-81; Darren Dochuk, *From Bible Belt to Sunbelt: Plain-Folk Religion, Grassroots Politics, and the Rise of Evangelical Conservatism* (New York: Norton, 2010); Axel Schaefer, *Countercultural Conservatives: American Evangelicalism from the Postwar Revival to the New Christian Right* (Madison: University of Wisconsin Press, 2011); Andrew Hartman, *A War for the Soul of America: A History of the Culture Wars* (Chicago: University of Chicago Press, 2015), 70-101; Hugh McLeod, "The 1960s and 1970s as a Period of Basic Change," in Katharina Kunter and Jens Holger Schjørring, eds., *Europäisches und globales Christentum: Herausforderungen und Transformationen im 20. Jahrhundert: Challenges and Transformations in the 20th Century* (Göttingen: Vandenhoeck & Ruprecht, 2011), 42-61; David Hempton and Hugh McLeod, eds., *Secularization and Religious Innovation in the North Atlantic World* (New York: Oxford University Press, 2017), 329-350.

5 Schultze, *Christianity and the Mass Media*, 128-29; John Micklethwait and Adrian Wooldridge, *God is Back: How the Global Revival of Faith is Changing the World* (New York: Penguin, 2009), 244-247.

6 Daniel J. Sargent, "The United States and Globalization in the 1970s," in Niall Ferguson, Charles S. Maier, Erez Manela, Daniel J. Sargent, eds., *The Shock of the Global: The 1970s in Perspective* (Cambridge: The Belknap Press of Harvard University, 2010), 49-64.

versity in denominational missions and churches in Africa insured distance between church and state, whether the government were a colonial one or independent.[7] New states fostered national churches, and mainline Protestant missionaries engaged with them, advocating for unity, and discouraging independent or denominational organizations. Again, American evangelicals feared they were being locked out by this drive for unity in the new countries. These global developments shaped the framework for American religious relations with Europe.

These concerns triggered the Evangelical Foreign Missions Association (EFMA) to conduct a survey among mission agencies. A think tank and service organization, EFMA worked to assess how evangelicals perceived the ecumenical pressures, and how they planned to ease them. In many mission areas the feedback from the survey gave no cause for alarm. In Sierra Leone, for example, a bible college, a bookstore, and meetings organized by the national Evangelical Fellowship won the respect of the United Church of Christ (UCC). The United Brethren Church Board of Missions in the United States that sympathized with evangelical missions felt uncomfortable with the presence of outspoken liberals in the UCC, but continued to be part of it.[8] Money was an important instrument to secure loyalty. All three factions within American Protestantism, hoping to increase their influence, promised funds to strengthen nascent educational institutions in non-Western regions. Even the small fundamentalist organization ICCC offered money to mission groups in India to gain their support against any competitors. But nowhere did these financial schemes cause a polarization as strong as they did in the United States.[9]

In general, the relations between Protestant groups in South East Asia proved cordial. The EFMA reported that there was little evidence of specific pressure in most places, and that only the evangelical agencies in the Congo and Taiwan felt the World Council of Churches had applied pressure to force unity, a situation often encouraged by national governments trying to prevent ethnic or tribal fragmentation.[10] In retrospect, some evangelicals in the mainline churches in the 1940s and 1950s had hoped that the WCC would support the younger churches without alienating them from traditional evangelism.

7 John Stuart, *British Missionaries and the End of Empire: East, Central and Southern Africa, 1939–64* (Grand Rapids, MI: Eerdmans, 2011), 184-202; David Maxwell, "Decolonization," in Norman Etherington, *Missions and Empire* (Oxford: Oxford University Press, 2005), 285-306.

8 "Ecumenical Pressures," BGCA col. 216 box 8 file 26. Many letters in this file from Poland, Japan, Hong Kong, Ecuador, Guatemala, Haiti, Pakistan, said they felt no pressure from WCC, but reports on Congo and Taiwan did.

9 Frank J. Kline to Clyde Taylor, 28 February 1964 and Taylor to Charles Pitts, 20 March 1964, BGCA col. 165 box 6 file 10; Emmett D. Cox to Clyde Taylor, 3 December 1970, BGCA col. 165 box 8 file 26.

10 Clyde Taylor, "Can Evangelicals Ease Ecumenical Pressures?" [1971], BGCA col. 165 box 8 file 29.

But with the affiliation of the Russian Orthodox churches and other members from Communist countries with the World Council of Churches, the attention shifted from personal to systemic problems. Mainline agencies moved from faith, mission, and evangelism to social issues. This shift opened up the possibility of financing Marxist guerrillas against capitalist or dictatorial suppression. The very thought of using church money to advance violent resistance appalled evangelicals and their cooperative hope evaporated in the 1960s. Their overall response was to strengthen their own evangelical networks and seek closer cooperation among themselves. The complexity involved in the growing national independence movements meant that some Asian countries could not agree on a person to lead their regional board of the World Evangelical Fellowship, and they ceded leadership roles to Europeans or Americans.[11]

These initiatives were more important than their cautious outcomes as it meant that mission agencies had to reposition themselves vis-à-vis established churches and also the Roman Catholic Church. The Evangelical Alliance Mission's (TEAM) advisory committee was commissioned to draft recommendations in regard to its position towards the Catholic Church. Their report confirmed the standard approach of "aggressive evangelism" meant to draw converts out of the Catholic Church. The report also opposed ecumenical dialogue, explaining that it would require giving up basic doctrines and diluting the truth. It saw the changes in the Catholic Church as both positive, because of increased opportunities to witness to Catholics, but also negative, because of the church's condoning of liberalism, relativism, and universalism.[12] The British Evangelical Alliance declined an official Roman Catholic invitation to discuss theological issues, but left open the prospect that individual board members could participate in these exchanges and they even offered them secretarial support.[13] The German Evangelical Alliance expressed a heartfelt recognition of individual Catholics, but not of their institutional church, thereby discouraging joint church services. They did not, however, reject joint action in the humanitarian, cultural, social, and political domains.[14]

The changing evangelical perceptions of the other religious players on the European mission field were fed by reflections on their own accomplishments. After the pioneer phase of American evangelical missions in Europe, the coordinators of the missions reviewed their position. With regard to the established churches in Europe, they realized that Europeans belonging to a

11 Letter Taylor to Stanley Mooneyham (World Vision International), 2 January 1973, BGCA col. 352 box 67 file 4. WEF.

12 Advisory Committee Findings 1970, BGCA col. 352 IFMA, TEAM 1970-71, box 28 file 4.

13 EAUK, Minutes of the meeting of the executive council of the Evangelical Alliance, 14-15 January 1970.

14 Peter Schneider, "Verhältnis der Evangelischen Allianz zur römisch-katholischen Kirche. Stellungnahme des Hauptvorstandes der DEA vom 2 December 1976," Archives Allianzhaus Bad Blankenburg, Germany.

foreign-based mission would be subject to alienation from their natural environment.[15] More and more, missionaries argued in favor of collaboration with existing churches since that would remove the stain of being an American proselytizer in the style of the Jehovah's Witnesses. The perks of gaining acceptability were numerous. Formal acceptance advanced legal protection, reduced isolation for new converts, encouraged an enriched two-way communication, strengthened religious unity and church responsibility for missions, and provided continuity for young believers. Slowly the conviction grew that staying separate culturally would hinder, not help, the missionary cause.

Once this strategic hurdle was cleared, however, it was hard to find a European church that shared the basic ideas of American evangelicals. A survey of key issues confirmed a transatlantic divide. Even traditional churches in Europe rejected the American concept of the verbal inspiration of the bible, and they strongly adhered to baptismal regeneration without a necessary explicit conversion experience. Most Protestants responded to the Catholic's horrifying description of hell by bending towards universalism, the comforting idea that everyone will eventually be saved. This idea robbed European churches of a sense of stewardship or urgency since they ignored the signs of the end-times. Moreover, American missionaries could offer no material benefits. Evangelical mission executives concluded, "With socialism rather widespread, the American missionary in Europe will learn that we cannot equate our interpretation of democracy with the gospel."[16]

The sobering conclusion was that finding European partners was an almost impossible task. The goal of collaboration was hindered by the low prestige of American missions. They ranked well below the majority churches either Catholic or Protestant, and below the free churches, meaning that even an affiliation with a free church would not much improve their social acceptability. As well, these free churches had a great variety within their own ranks. Some had joined the WCC in order to survive as a tiny Protestant minority in Catholic areas, such as the Waldensians in Italy, others resolutely rejected these ties and followed American separatist sentiments. The dominant American narrative of separation and opposition held by the evangelicals burdened each attempt to find European partners outside their own circles. Even if partners were found, identification with them was sure to lead to alienation from their constituency at home, as European toleration of the use of alcohol and tobacco went against evangelical taboos.[17]

The mission executives did not put all the blame on Europe. In the spirit of self-criticism, the report suggested that American impatience with the

15 Edwin E. Jacques (overseas secretary of the CBFMS), "EFMA Mission Executives Retreat. Europe Section, September 26, 1972," BGCA col. 218, Pulse Europe, box 8 folder 4.

16 Ibid., 3-4.

17 Ibid.

survival strategy of European churches was a major obstacle to fruitful cooperation. What Americans considered a lack of spirit and vitality, Europeans saw as a respectable effort to survive centuries of pressure in perceived and real minority situations. However, these mitigating circumstances did not lead to new options. As far as the evangelicals were concerned, European church bodies that allowed theological and political differences or that were affiliated with non-evangelical organizations, did not qualify as potential partners. Only after agreement of the essential issues had been reached could flexibility be granted. And even then, the pace of affiliation was slow, taking much time to build trust. Too often European pastors felt attacked by American missionaries and their need for quick successes. If a partner denomination were found, the American missionary should cooperate within the existing mission bodies of that church and identify with its responsibilities and tasks. Americans prepared for this phase of loosening transatlantic connection. The report revealed that evangelical missions to Europe had entered a new phase of reflection and calibration, and that slowly they had been forced to realize that Europe would not easily reconvert.

Though it was not made explicit in the report, an additional source of tension arose from the contradictory messages the missionaries gave to audiences in the United States and in Europe. American constituencies received the message that Europe was doomed, disabled by the structural mortgage of state-church relations, and that only an emphasis on a clear conversion experience, concentration on the bible, and a new eschatological urge could rescue the continent from drifting into full paganism. In Europe, these messages were substantially toned down to show patience and respect. They offered support. The alarmist tone that was needed to muster support in the United States was changed to a reassuring tone in the mission field. To complicate things further, American agencies constantly had to show their donors that Europe was worth their dollars invested there, by listing the number of converts and touting successful programs. The British newsletter for the Belgian Gospel Mission explained: "Evangelizing Europe from the outside demands teams of experienced, fully committed people – willing to work with small, understaffed, insufficiently taught groups of believers – teaching them God's Word and setting an example in patient personal work."[18] In contrast the American mouthpiece of the same organization highlighted their contrast with Europe, "... in this day of high culture and technology, rapidly rising standards of living, abounding education and religious activity, there exists in modern Europe a city of 25,000 people without a single Protestant church of any kind, and to our knowledge, not even a single believer. That is St. Truiden; that is why the Belgian Gos-

18 Brian Russell-Jones, "Men and Methods for Reaching Europeans," *Belgian Beacon* (Autumn 1974), 8 (newsletter for the United Kingdom).

pel Mission was there last summer... . Their prayers were answered! People came... Twelve people professed faith in Christ."[19]

The *Greater Europe Report*, the newsletter of Greater Europe Mission, struggled with this issue and asked aloud whether the time of the foreign (American) national in Europe was past. While it entertained this question as a serious one, it could not support the conclusion that foreign nationals had no role. Rather, the editors thought that Europe needed foreign engagement, citing the numerous cities without an evangelical presence and only a few nationals with the ability and correct fundamentals to fill teaching positions in the churches. They considered that the process had just begun and acknowledged a strong belief in training nationals for leadership positions. At its eight bible schools in 1978, 500 Europeans trained in evangelistic work.[20] Even in the United Kingdom, American involvement was needed to finance the buildings and staff, to provide experts, and to improve practical programs. They felt the Americans often had a clear design that was lacking in England.[21] GEM celebrated its twenty-fifth anniversary in 1974 with a palpable sense of urgency caused by growing enrollment figures and requests for money to facilitate expansion. Far from seeing its mission as coming to an end, speaker Leighton Ford, representing the Billy Graham Evangelistic Association, singled out Europe as the greatest mission field, an area that still trailed other continents when it came to opening up for evangelical missions.[22]

In the same period, American evangelical standards entered the European market of ideas through the translation of English-language religious books into European languages. General audiences in Germany and the Netherlands, for example, became familiar with translations of the work by Tim laHaye and Francis Schaeffer. Hal Lindsey's *The Late Great Planet Earth* was especially popular and was reprinted ten times during that decade. These publications spread American evangelical concerns in Europe. On both sides of the Atlantic, the infrastructure of evangelical publishers greatly improved and grew to handle the increasing number of publications as well as negotiations for translations. Books and ideas from European (mostly British) evangelicals such as John Stott's were well-received on both sides of the Atlantic. Americans organized the Evangelical Christian Publishers Association in 1974, a group that professionalized the business, launched annual evangelical book fairs, and soon expanded to include other nationalities. New evangeli-

19 American newsletter *Belgian Gospel Mission, Inc.* 1 October 1970.

20 Don Brugman, "Has the Day of the Missionary Passed?" *Greater Europe Report* 7.5 (September-October 1977) 3, 7; *Greater Europe Report* 8.1 (January-February 1978), 8-9.

21 *Greater Europe Report* 4.4 (July-August 1974).

22 Ibid. 4.6 (November-December 1974), 1, 5.

cal presses were founded in Europe, while existing ones were organized with greater efficiency.[23]

Perhaps the clearest sign of American influence was the adoption of exclusivist rhetoric by some European evangelicals. In 1970, during the period of repositioning, German Lutheran missiologists Peter Beyerhaus and Georg Vicedom formulated the Frankfurt Declaration – an uncompromising statement of faith against the ecumenical agenda. Among German evangelicals there were those who explicitly rejected the World Council as a false organization and called for separation (as in the 1974 Berlin Declaration). They were mostly premillennialists who expected the kingdom of God in the future and continued to underscore the two-kingdoms view of Luther, thus precluding social action from taking center stage. Others embraced a more positive, inviting tone.[24]

Apart from its theological contents, the Frankfurt Declaration challenged the monopoly of theological state education. It recommended that the bible schools needed to professionalize in order to confer a recognized degree and to act as an alternative to the state universities, the programs had to be accredited. Once again American contacts helped European schools to complete this process. They worked either indirectly through accreditation from the European Evangelical Accrediting Association, which was founded in 1979 and modeled after the American organization, or directly by affiliating to an American institution. In either case, the schools compared European requirements with American ones, even when their students enrolled in long-distance courses at American institutions. Many schools adopted the specializations offered in American curricula.[25] New American missionary methods, based on a social science approach and endorsed by church growth promoter Donald A.

23 Allan Fisher, "Evangelical-Christian Publishing. Where it's Been and Where it is Going," *Publishing Research Quarterly* 14.3 (1998): 3-11. A similar efficiency operation among evangelical publishing firms took place in the 1970s in Germany, see Jung, *Deutsche Evangelikale Bewegung*, 74; John P. Ferré, "Searching for the Great Commission: Evangelical Book Publishing since the 1970s," in Quentin J. Schultze, ed., *American Evangelicals and the Mass Media: Perspectives on the Relationship Between American Evangelicals and the Mass Media* (Grand Rapids, MI: Zondervan Academie Books, 1990), 99-117.

24 Bernhard Ott, *Beyond Fragmentation: Integrating Mission and Theological Education: A Critical Assessment of Some Recent Developments in Evangelical Theological Education* (Oxford: Regnum, 2001), 71, 76-79, 182, 188, 254. For a positive American endorsement of the Frankfurt Declaration see Harold Lindsell, "A Background to the Frankfort Declaration," in *Reports of the 19th Annual Mission Executives Retreat, September 28-October 1, 1970, Winona Lake, Indiana* (Washington: EFMA, n.y.), 44-47. Surprising enough Lindsell assumed that Beyerhaus was unfamiliar with the situation in the US that also pitched liberals versus evangelicals, and he advocated support for this new ally.

25 Ott, *Beyond Fragmentation*, 84 and 87, 254.

McGavran, were applied to the European situation. It was a variation on the theme of missions supported by management.[26]

In postwar bible school circles, American models guided European processes. In Germany they added a third stream with a strong American orientation between the state schools (and the pietist element in them) and the free schools. One of the reasons for the strength of these bilateral contacts was the international isolation of German institutions due to the legacy of the war and the goodwill resulting from the American liberation.

"Taking Time:" Lausanne and the Relation to the older European Churches

The EFMA report revealed that it was perhaps more an impatience with the lack of action than a fear of liberalism that distanced American evangelicals from the established churches in Europe. Lack of progress in European churches disappointed Billy Graham too, and he decided to take matters into his own hands. In contrast to the new revival in the US, in the shape of the Jesus Movement, European churches failed to take the gospel outside their sanctuaries. While the number of American evangelical missionaries swelled worldwide, the number of evangelical missionaries from Europe lagged behind. In preparation for an even larger explosion in global missions, Graham organized huge international training conferences in Europe. In late August 1971, he held the first of these in Amsterdam where he told 1,200 Europeans from 35 countries that the next decade would focus on the youth. He argued that evangelism was not a project of the church, as the Jesus Revolution in California had shown, but an attitude of each believer.

The meeting was held under the auspices of the European Evangelical Alliance and was heavily sponsored by the Billy Graham Evangelistic Association. Its targets were young, native born Europeans. The leaders stipulated that half of the delegates must be under 40, and three quarters of each delegation had to be made up of nationals and not foreign missionaries. Staging Cliff Richard was a sign of the importance they placed on trying to reach youth. One of the conference's conclusions was that global cooperation among evangelical groups was necessary and that the stagnant churches were part of the problem. The old 1910 dream to reach the entire world with the gospel was as

26 Ott, *Beyond Fragmentation*, 158-161, 169; George Harinck, "Opnieuw bezocht met het evangelie. De vermenging van het Amerikaans evangelicalisme met het Nederlands protestantisme," in George Harinck and Hans Krabbendam, eds., *A Spiritual Invasion? Amerikaanse invloeden op het Nederlandse christendom* (Barneveld: De Vuurbaak, 2010), 23-53.

alive as ever.[27] Another sign of change was adding to the program the idea that Christians should be concerned about social problems, especially drug addiction.[28] Europeans were awed by the Americans' skills, but also increasingly wary of their priorities. German participants did, however, note with gratitude that the Americans had borne the largest share of the cost.[29] Nevertheless, the next year, the German evangelicals decided that they should bear their own financial burden and not depend on American money.[30]

The money issue was a way to express the concerns the European evangelicals had with regard to questions of self-worth. Some of them raised the issue of the one-way nature of American input. Art historian Hans Rookmaaker from the Protestant Free University in Amsterdam, for example, doubted that American methods had dug deep enough into European conditions, "I feel that the American way of evangelism is not quite up to the European situation. It often passes by the real issues... there is not quite the understanding that I should like to have in analysing first the youth's real predicament and situation."[31] He acknowledged the need for personal evangelism in Europe, but found that the intellectual approach, so prevalent in Holland, was missing among the Americans. "But what they [Americans] lacked is exactly what we have. And so I feel that bringing together the two traditions is maybe the best thing we can do in the future."[32] He set out to do exactly that. He became a major influence on Francis Schaeffer, who introduced an appreciation of art history to American evangelicals as a way to reflect on western culture and broaden their cultural horizon.[33]

The German minister in the Freie Evangelische Gemeinde, Fritz Laubach, drew German parallels to the new evangelicals in the United States and emphasized that the many features that characterized American evangelicalism were present in Germany's pietism, which developed more gradually than evangelicalism had in the United States. Laubach was grateful for the evangel-

27 BGCA col. 141- BGEA: Press report 1971; Larry Eskridge, *God's Forever Family: The Jesus People Movement in America* (New York: Oxford University Press, 2013).

28 EAUK, "Minutes of the meeting of the executive council of the Evangelical Alliance, May 19 and November 19, 1970."

29 "Europäischer Kongress für Evangelisation in Amsterdam 28. August bis 4. September 1971," *Evangelisches Allianzblatt* 74 (11 November 1971), 209-210, 214-216.

30 Protokoll der Migliederversammlung der Deutschen Evangelischen Allianz, September 8, 1972, 5, Archives Allianzhaus Bad Blankenburg, Germany.

31 Collection 141- BGEA: Oral History Project, The Netherlands 29-24, Interview J.J. van Capelleveen with the Dutch art historian Hendrik Rookmaaker, August 1971. [His full name was Henderik Roelof, but he was called Hans]. Rookmaaker inspired Schaeffer to add an intellectual and artistic part to evangelism in Switzerland, but back in the US, Schaeffer became the champion of the anti-abortion coalition. His turn to the right contradicted the initial feeling that Lausanne supported the left evangelicals.

32 Ibid.

33 See Barry Hankins, *Francis Schaeffer and the Shaping of Evangelical America* (Grand Rapids, MI: Eerdmans, 2008), 124.

ical spark he saw coming from Graham's campaigns but noted that since 1960, the German Evangelical Alliance had been solely responsible for the spread and adoption of evangelicalism in Germany. Germany resumed its continental role in 1970 when Graham's campaign in Dortmund was broadcast all over Europe. This media breakthrough triggered a string of organizational initiatives aimed at assisting and furthering the responses of the viewers: study groups, an information service, and new international evangelical cooperation culminating in a call for the European evangelism conference in Amsterdam in 1971.[34]

At the same time, the older American agencies began to reconsider the wisdom of their separation from the established churches.[35] At a retreat for mission executives of its European section organized by the Evangelical Foreign Missions Association (EFMA) in September 1972, the number of arguments underscoring the need for collaboration with existing churches was overwhelming. The executives argued in detail that cooperation with European churches would remove prejudices among native populations, help smooth the path to civil authorities, and avoid believers' alienation from their natural habitat. They put forward the view that cooperation would also prevent cultural arrogance, reduce fragmentation, assist in creating the stability of new churches giving them vitality, and would increase the efficiency of the support organizations.

A feeling of being colonized by the Americans, and the haste with which this was all taking place frustrated fruitful communication, however. The number-one grievance among the European partners was what they perceived as the combination of American ignorance and arrogance. Americans gave expression to this with their attitude of, "... nobody over there is doing anything worthwhile and we're going over and show them how it's done."[36] EFMA's September 1972 meeting identified four theological and five practical obstacles. They specifically aimed at theological differences including a more open definition of the divine inspiration of the bible, child baptism, concern about the eternal security of the believer, and the lack of eschatology. They felt these things "... may influence or inhibit mission collaboration."[37] The practical obstacles they outlined were the acceptance of socialism or even communism, denominational loyalties and connections to liberal bodies, cultural codes,

34 Fritz Laubach, *Aufbruch der Evangelikalen* (Wuppertal: R. Brockhaus Verlag, 1972), 78-86. The German Evangelical Alliance depended on American support to pay for the DM 300.000 deficit of Euro 70. See "Protokoll der Sitzung des Hauptverstandes der Deutschen Evangelischen Allianz, September 11, 1970," Archives Allianzhaus Bad Blankenburg, Germany.

35 Edwin E. Jacques (overseas secretary of the CBFMS), "Can Our Missions Collaborate with European Church Bodies?" 26 September 1972, BGCA col. 218 Pulse Europe, box 8, file 4.

36 Ibid., quoting Frank Norton, "The Right Kind of Men," *His*, January 1968, 10-14.

37 Jacques, "Can Our Missions," 3.

and a lack of energy. The meeting recommended that the mission agencies look at churches that shared their doctrinal bias, and then take the necessary time to develop trust, while freely allowing non-essential differences to exist. "European pastors have been disillusioned with their [American missionaries] grandiose plans, their desire for instant results and their sometimes superficial accomplishments."[38]

In a similar vein, in April 1971, Walter Frank of the Greater Europe Mission offered a new justification for missionary activity in traditionally "Christian countries" in Europe. He took a longer European perspective, "There is the steeple, but where is the church?" he asked, recommending that when churches are weak and in an "apostatized anemic condition," they needed American reinforcements.[39] The quadrupling of staff to 1,600 missionaries in the quarter century after World War II looked impressive, but the agenda to reach a quarter of a million towns and cities without an evangelical Protestant church was truly daunting if not overwhelming. Frank thought the relationship with the established churches was inevitable given that they had only achieved meagre results after decades of investment. American missionaries faced a dilemma with the new converts: keep them in separate churches, which would isolate them from their national culture, or channel them into existing churches at the risk of them being absorbed without a trace. To Frank, the only solution was to get them out of what he considered the harmful identification of "religion with a large stone edifice for generations and that from generation to generation each new baby was automatically ushered into the church on the assembly line of infant baptism followed by the right of confirmation."[40]

The TEAM leadership reached the same conclusion. It affirmed the need to take believers out of their old churches. Paradoxically however, TEAM also acknowledged the opening up in the Roman Catholic Church that was creating space for individuals. Some delegates at the TEAM retreat were willing to reconsider their rejection of older churches, while other speakers emphasized that no compromise could be permitted. They were open to having conversations with Catholics and other Protestants, but only if they could stay separate. If dialogue meant that both sides had to abandon their position in order to merge into a new synthesis, that was unacceptable.[41] This was a firm stance; nevertheless positions were shifting.

The focal point of evangelical reflection on their relationship to established churches came at the landmark 1974 conference in Lausanne, Switzerland, which is attributed with the same kind of crucial significance as Vatican II

38 Ibid., 6.

39 Walter Frank, "IFMA Missions and Church Planting in Areas Where Old Churches are Established," BGCA col. 352 IFMA box 27 f4 GEM 1970-71.

40 Ibid., 4.

41 "Advisory Committee Findings 1970," BGCA col. 352, IFMA TEAM 1970-71, box 28, file 4.

is for the Roman Catholic Church and its relationships. The conference hosted 2,500 representatives from 150 countries, and 1,300 additional observers and consultants, to discuss their main mission to the world. They arrived with great expectations, stimulated by Billy Graham's opening address confirming their optimism: "The Harvest is Ripe."[42] Afterwards, amidst much criticism that women and non-Western speakers had been noticeably underrepresented, it was nevertheless concluded that the organizers had been more diverse and inclusive than ever and had offered the podium to many members of mainline churches and missions. At the conclusion of the conference the participants left for home reenergized. They committed themselves to a new missionary élan in the world under the motto "let the earth hear his voice."

The Lausanne movement meant to set a new agenda for evangelicals and it did. They succeeded in raising an international podium and made themselves visible as a third global force to be reckoned with alongside the Roman Catholic Church and the World Council of Churches. The conference broadened the social and political scope of the evangelicals, set the stage for indigenization, and opened up American evangelicalism to global influences.[43] After the first cautious explorations into cooperation in the 1960s, it was a logical next step for American evangelicals to broaden their scope of action in the 1970s, and part of the process was to expand the horizon for possible future cooperation with liberals, albeit reluctantly. The event was widely covered in the international press, where it was framed as the symbol of the new evangelical power.[44]

Lausanne was also important for a second reason. The delegates carefully drafted a doctrinal document to create cohesion as the basis for future cooperation. In discussions of this document, recommendations that did not make it into the final draft included a proposal from the so-called radical evangelicals, whose growing momentum opened channels to mainstream America, both in terms of convergent agendas and a plan to cooperate for gradual change.[45] The statement underwrote main evangelical concerns such as that followers should proclaim the Gospel, submit to the authority of the bible, and commit to calling people to repent. It added a significant purpose in its resolution "... to identify in him [= God] with the oppressed and work for the liberation of all

42 Billy Graham, "Why Lausanne?" in J.D. Douglas, ed., *Let the Earth Hear His Voice* (Minneapolis: World Wide Publications, 1975), 35.

43 Melani McAlister, "The Global Conscience of American Evangelicalism: Internationalism and Social Concern in the 1970s and Beyond," *Journal of American Studies* 51 (November 2017): 1197-1220.

44 Timothy Dudley-Smith, *John Stott: A Global Ministry: A Biography The Later Years* (Downers Grove, IL: InterVarsity Press, 2001), 209-210.

45 David Swartz, "The Evangelical Left and the Move from Personal to Social Responsibility," in Axel Schaefer, ed., *American Evangelicals and the 1960s* (Madison: University of Wisconsin Press, 2013), 211-230.

men and women in his name."[46] This final phrase was not standard evangelical fare. It could have been taken from a World Council of Churches document, of which the evangelicals had been and were so critical. Yet, its presence on the agenda revealed that evangelicals were ready to embrace social issues and not let resistance to these issues define their identity. This landmark meeting had important consequences for the position of American evangelicals at home in the United States and for European-American religious relations.

Maturing American-European Evangelical Relations

Mission historians have drawn attention to the major change in the scope of religious outreach among American evangelicals in the mid-1970s, but they rarely connect these trends to the social and political domestic agenda in the United States or to Europe. Historian Steven Miller offers a clue to the otherwise surprising inclusive turn that American evangelicals made in the 1970s. He argues that the impact American evangelicals had, spread beyond the reach of their membership. Even though evangelicals had separate institutions, their influence extended widely into the majority culture and not as a separate subculture, but as one with many connections to the mainstream. Their "born-again culture" (calling for a radical change) explained their political appeal beyond the card-carrying evangelical membership.[47] The culminating point of American evangelical exposure abroad at Lausanne in 1974 carried this resonant evangelical culture outside the United States. However, the ease with which it was received in the United States was mostly absent in Europe. Western Europeans were simply not the receptive mass constituency needed for successful growth, nor did they need developmental aid.

Evangelicals entered the international arena via three interlocking and simultaneous initiatives they had taken twenty years to develop. First they led efforts to create a global evangelical association leading to the World Evangelical Fellowship (WEF). At the same time they coordinated evangelical foreign mission associations. Both institutions gravitated towards the international network created by Billy Graham's outreach.

These steps helped shape a global evangelical operation, which was orchestrated by central institutions with an interlocking leadership. In 1971 Clyde Taylor, the Executive Secretary of EFMA, also became acting General Secretary of WEF. Milton G. Baker was president of EFMA and also Overseas Secretary of the Conservative Baptist Foreign Mission Society. It was Baker who sent out

46 "Theological Implications of Radical Discipleship," in Douglas, *Let the Earth Hear His Voice*, 1296.

47 See Steven P. Miller, *The Age of Evangelicalism: American Born-Again Years* (New York: Oxford University Press, 2013), 7-8 and 9-59.

the confidential survey aimed at finding out whether cooperation among missionary groups would benefit from an international evangelical fellowship, whether the WEF should be that link, and how open it should be. A unification effort earlier that year had failed. Harold Ockenga, a founding father of the National Association of Evangelicals (NAE), had advocated for a merger of NAE with the fundamentalist ACCC and big denominations of Southern Baptists and Missouri Synod Lutherans. But his attempt proved unrealistic when these groups insisted that they preferred to remain independent.[48]

These evangelical leaders worked on an international level of prominence and they sought a broader appeal, albeit one marked by confessional boundaries. At Lausanne it became clear that the evangelical family consisted of a great variety of members from widely dispersed geographical concentrations. On the American side there were the neo-evangelicals, fundamentalists, and Pentecostals, in Europe the confessionals, in Africa the ecumenical evangelicals, and in Latin America-Asia the radical evangelicals. Some Americans tried to define the core organization by emphasizing inerrancy, the Great Commission, and personal morality, and by narrowing acceptable partners to those who accepted these beliefs. But joint actions proved a strong incentive for forging inclusion that trumped institutionalization.[49]

A Dutch evangelist echoed this mood in his characterization of the religious situation in Western Europe in the 1970s as "The Church is out, the Bible is in."[50] In this quote, he was alluding to the suspicion of institutionalized religion and the vitality of grass-roots religious activity. He contrasted the decline in the number of clergy to the growth in informal bible study groups and applauded the growing American influence, as could be expected from a 1951 Moody Bible Institute graduate. Most Europeans showed more restraint and responded coolly to the American plans to host the Lausanne Conference and contributed only minimally to its funding. Barely half of the number of European invitees accepted the invitation to attend. Apparently, European expectations from American solutions were qualified. A general decline of America's prestige caused by the American war in Vietnam and the Watergate scandal, coupled with a reluctance to take a second-rate position vis à vis the Americans, dampened down expectations. The geopolitical tides were turning in the evangelical world. At international conferences the share of majority-world representation increased to 40% in 1974, up from 33% in 1966. Representatives from Latin American and Africa were added to the leadership, and they pressed for alternative perspectives on social and political issues, calling for reduced dependence on western assistance. This had already happened in

48 Letter Milton Baker, general letter, 14 July 1972, BGCA col. 352, box 67 file 4. WEF.

49 Friedhelm Jung, *Die deutsche Evangelikale Bewegung: Grundlinien ihrer Geschichte und Theologie* (Frankfurt: Lang, 1992), 68-69. This is Beyerhaus' categorization.

50 Jan van Capelleveen, "Western Europe in the Seventies," in *Let the Earth Hear his Voice*, 151.

the periodic assemblies of the World Council of Churches.[51] Simultaneously, four practical factors and a new missionary concept unraveled the tight transatlantic bonds in evangelical missions.

Growing European Independence

At least four developments distanced the United States from Europe: the decline of emigration from Europe, the inevitable phase of indigenization, the growing awareness of the European cultural context, and the loss in value of the US dollar.

The immediate postwar missionary drive in Europe had been heavily supported by European immigrant communities in the United States. But this support dwindled as Asians and Latin Americans replace Europeans as the main emigration in the 1960s.[52] The widespread sense of millennial urgency in evangelical America encouraged full time Christian service, especially prodding students to become missionaries regardless of their ethnic ties. The professionalization of the training and the intensification of expectations further weakened the earlier transnational relations.[53] As a sign of this gradual drifting apart, Moody Bible Institute offered seminars for missionaries specifically targeting Europe between 1969 and 1974, as it didn't take such knowledge for granted. At the end of the decade Europe was the destination of ten percent of all Moody graduates going overseas, but ethnic ties were rare.[54]

The second trend that strengthened the European side was the end of the pioneering phase when the first generation of missionaries passed on their responsibilities to European nationals in the late sixties and early seventies. This pattern followed the stages of their predecessors from the mainline denominations. They moved from pioneering with a growing staff, to consoli-

51 Stanley, *Global Diffusion*, 164, 158-169.

52 Carpenter, *Revive,* 141. In 1970, the general director of the Greater Europe Mission, Walter Frank, indicated that the incentive for the re-evangelizing of Europe came from European immigrants who had joined free churches in the USA and favorably compared their newfound allegiance with the situation of religious oppression and persecution in countries with a state church. They had taken up the challenge to reach their native soil "glowing with zeal to preach revival and establish groups of believers." Walter Frank, "IFMA Missions and Church Planting in Areas Where Old Churches are Established," BGCA col. 352 IFMA box 27 f4 GEM 1970-71. It seems that this is especially true for late nineteenth-century Scandinavian immigrants. Susan F. Martin, *A Nation of Immigrants* (Cambridge: Cambridge University Press, 2010), 6.

53 See for an analysis of the Dutch case, Hans Krabbendam, "They Came to Stay: The Weak Transnational Relations of the Dutch in America," in Henk Aay, Janny Venema, and Dennis N. Voskuil, eds., *Sharing Pasts: Dutch Americans Through Four Centuries* (Holland, MI: Van Raalte Press, 2017), 3-23.

54 MBI Foreign Missionary Reports, 1970 and 1979. This number corresponded with the overall proportion of American missionaries stationed in Europe.

dation and the gradual transfer of the projects to nationals. Most independent evangelical organizations and fundamentalist agencies were new on the missionary scene in Europe and their growing numbers invited a triumphalist tone. This was especially true when a large share of their mainline colleagues dropped out whenever responsibilities were transferred to the nationals. The commitment of the mainline churches remained, however, as was evidenced in the budgets. Until the 1970s, mission activities sponsored by American churches with ties to the World Council greatly outspent the evangelicals.[55] The budgets of the respective umbrella organizations were distinctly off-kilter. The 1977 WEF budget of $150,000 paled by comparison to the $18 million spent by the WCC, and was barely sufficient to keep the boat afloat. American money, in particular, a $25,000 donation from the Billy Graham organization, was necessary to keep the WEF in business as a global organization.[56]

The older evangelical mission agencies active in Europe entered the phase of indigenization in the 1960s and 1970s.[57] Youth for Christ in the Netherlands, for instance, replaced American style public rallies with smaller gatherings

55 Edward R. Dayton, ed., *Mission Handbook: North American Protestant Ministries Overseas* (11th ed., New York: Billy Graham Center, 1976). Between 1960 and 1980 fundamentalist groups replaced the evangelicals as the group with the largest growth in staff, larger than the population growth rate. Ecumenical groups focussed more on humanitarian causes and sent less staff and more money. Seventy per cent of the DOM had relief as its primary task and since Europe could take care of its own, the involvement with that continent was minimized. Samuel Wilson, "Current Trends in North American Protestant Ministries Overseas," *International Bulletin of Missionary Research* 5.2 (1981): 74-75; Paul E. Pierson, "Lessons in Mission from the Twentieth Century: Conciliar Missions," in Jonathan J. Bonk, ed., *Between Past and Future: Evangelical Mission Entering the Twenty-first Century* (Pasadena, CA: William Carey Library, 2003), 67-84. Statistics on income in Edward R. Dayton, "Current Trends in North American Protestant Ministries Overseas," *Occasional Bulletin of Missionary Research* (April 1977): 4. Between 1968 and 1976 the percentage of the NCC related associations dropped from 53 to 22%, or from $ 149.2 million to $137.4 million. In 1973 the IFMA/EFMA income was estimated at $ 135 million, see Milton Baker, "How Can Evangelicals Relate Effectively on a National, Area-Wide and Worldwide Basis," 14, BGCA col. 218 EMIS box 3 file 16.

56 Waldron Scott, "Report to the WEF Executive Council, January 1, 1978," BGCA col. 352, box 67 file 6; *New York Times*, 10 January 1979. American churches contributed a third to the WCC budget, and German churches 40%. Two thirds of the WEF funds came from the U.S. and one third from Europe (also mainly from Germany) and Australia. Waldron Byron Scott, "Double Helix: A Missionary's Odyssey," 672 <http://www.waldronscott.net/doublehelix/id12.html> visited 16 February 2012. Later this website was discontinued.

57 Edward R. Dayton, ed., *Mission Handbook: North American Protestant Ministries Overseas* (11th ed., New York: Billy Graham Center, 1976), Belgium (69 nationals to 158 missionaries), France (588 to 416), Germany (462 to 445), Greece (30 to 186), Italy (520 to 190), the Netherlands (209 to 151), Portugal (314 to 53), Spain (111 to 228), Sweden (33 to 34), Switzerland (118 to 79), United Kingdom (357 to 170). The high numbers of nationals was predominantly caused by Assemblies of God staff (except for the United Kingdom, where Christian Literature Crusade, Mission to Europe's Millions, and Navigators' staffers were mostly natives).

in informal coffee shops run by young adults. They produced Dutch-language magazines and organized music festivals in growing partnership with the main Protestant churches.[58] This transition forced the American agencies to reflect, to be self-critical, and to openly discuss the relationship between testimony and social action. Whereas earlier evangelicals had verbally denounced social work as at best, an auxiliary instrument to fulfil the Great Commission, they had done this to emphasize their differences with the liberals. But the success of their missionary operations and their investments in educational facilities to train other nations, eventually led to nationals taking over the missions. This phase put the native missionary on an equal intellectual level, whereas their social-economic status remained, sometimes astoundingly, unequal.

This process of indigenization potentially gave evangelicals in the receiving (European) countries a stronger voice in the global family. Since evangelicals valued their independence, they did not establish a strong official center anyhow, and most initiatives in that direction was left to the Americans, considered the most professional organizers. It was Billy Graham who launched the idea of a series of conferences that would line up and equip evangelicals around the globe for enduring evangelism. These impressive international gatherings completed the building of a global evangelical network and helped the evangelicals to shed their sectarian stigma.

The impetus for Lausanne was to advance missions by promoting a new mission concept that underscored reaching communities and not nations. Adhering to this new concept, usually known as the church growth ministry, took Europe out of the *avant garde* of evangelical missions. The concept had been developed by American missiologists Donald McGavran and Ralph D. Winter at the Fuller Seminary, an evangelical center in California. It was born out of a concern for the, sometimes, minimal growth taking place in many mission fields. Basing themselves on extensive data collection and borrowing freely from social science theory and anthropology to back up a rather static interpretation of culture, they reached the conclusion that missionaries should change from focusing on nations untouched by the Christian gospel to engaging with much smaller and more coherent cultural communities. This drew criticism. Europe was seen as having a less urgent need for mission work than those communities that were culturally very different, because the old continent had a sufficient concentration of Christians and a cultural affinity with the mass of white western missionaries. Moreover, this new strategy gave priority to people groups that proved receptive, and it encouraged new believers to remain part of their communities.[59] Nonetheless, this new concept did

58 Interview by author of two former directors of YFC-Holland, Arnold van Heusden and Edward de Kam, Driebergen, 13 December 2007.

59 Donald McGavran, "The Dimensions of World Evangelism," and Ralph D. Winter, "The Highest Priority: Cross-Cultural Evangelism," in *Let the Earth Hear His Voice*, 108-115 and 226-241.

not stall the flow of American missionaries to Western Europe. The growth of missionaries continued until the end of the 1980s and reached about 3,500 missionaries or ten percent in the 1990s, followed by a new growth spurt in Eastern Europe after the fall of the Berlin Wall and work among new immigrants in Western Europe.[60] In the late 1970s the evangelicals added immigrants from Muslim countries as a target group in Europe.[61] For example, TEAM began work among single men from Turkey and Greece working in Germany and Austria.[62] This new activity broadened Europe's missionary horizon, and offered an alternative to the original goal of the mission agencies.

The new concept entered the missionary overviews in the 1980s by adding a new column listing the number of people groups in a given country. Though the reporting was far from accurate (bilingual Belgium was listed with only one people group), the general pattern was clear. Northern European countries were considered homogeneous, but southern European nations significantly diverse. American mission agencies reported 73 people groups in France, 56 in Portugal, 54 in Spain, against 0 in Denmark, 1 in Switzerland, 3 in each of Norway and Sweden, and 4 in the Netherlands. Some countries were reported as having a midsize range of people groups such as Greece with 13, Italy 14, West Germany 14, the United Kingdom 18, and Austria with 20.[63] For Western Europe, renewal was sufficient because the cultural distance was insignificant. For the other parts of the world, cross-cultural work was necessary since the cultural differences were large, and according to the missiologists, the number of cross-cultural workers was relatively inadequate.[64]

Because the cultural differences between Europe and North-America were perceived as small there continued to be a preference to work in Europe among North American missionaries, despite the new missionary concept. It seemed the easiest option. The cultural advantage did not result in mass conversions, however. The agencies found it necessary to change their strategies. TEAM France, for example, adapted its approach according to the church growth

60 Martin, *A Prophet with Honor*, 444-447; Gary L. McIntosh, "Donald A. McGavran: Life, Influence and Legacy in Mission," in Charles E. Van Engen, ed., *The State of Missiology Today: Global Innovations in Christian Witness* (Downers Grove, IL: IVP Academic, 2016), 19-37; George M. Marsden, *Reforming Fundamentalism: Fuller Seminary and the New Evangelicalism* (Grand Rapids, MI: Eerdmans, 1987), 237-244; " 'The Harvest is Ripe': American Evangelicals in European Missions 1950-1980," in Axel Schäfer, ed., *American Evangelicalism and the 1960s* (Madison: University of Wisconsin Press, 2013), 239.

61 By 1978 the first conferences on Christian-Muslim relations were organized. See letter Warren Webster (CBFMS) to Wade Coggins (EFMA), 5 January 1978, BGCA col. 352, box 67 file 6.

62 Vernon Mortenson, *God Made it Grow: Historical Sketches of TEAM's Church Planting Work* (Pasadena, CA: William Carey Library, 1994), 816-817.

63 Samuel Wilson and John Siewert, eds., *Mission Handbook: North American Protestant Ministries Overseas* (13th ed., Monrovia, CA: Missions Advanced Research and Communication Center, 1986), 586-591.

64 See the explanations by McGavran and Winter in *Let the Earth Hear His Voice*, 213-225.

movement.[65] Instead of randomly starting new congregations, they planted a number of churches around a nucleus so that the new churches would strengthen each other. Though TEAM considered the 1970s as the decade of the breakthrough, the results remained miniscule.[66] In 1973 the denomination of l'Alliance des Eglises Evangéliques Indépendantes (AEEI) with six French churches (214 members) founded by TEAM, elected their first French president. This had been the intention from the beginning. In its 25th year in 1977, a team of 27 American career missionaries were needed to support the TEAM-work in France. In the following year, the organization listed church growth as its mission, right alongside the stalwart principles such as separation from the ecumenical movement, baptism by immersion, and aggressive evangelism.[67]

Of course, it was not only missiological ideas that changed the scene; the student revolts altered the mood in Europe and pushed ideological issues to the fore. Evangelicals entered these debates and in so doing were confronted with questions of contextualization that asked for a different approach. This opened American eyes to see Europe in its own historical context, and not so much from American standards of religious vitality. After the Paris student uprising, for example, Youth for Christ adapted its mode of communication by publishing a magazine called *Punch* with articles explaining Christian concepts specifically to young people, instead of distributing tracts or books explaining the core message of Christianity.[68]

Also, the material side of the missions helped make Europe less dependent on the United States. When the possibility of converting dollars into gold ended in 1971, fluctuating currency rates caused financial strain. Higher costs due to the Oil Crisis fanned inflation and increased financial insecurity. Henry Kissinger declared 1973 as the Year of Europe in an effort to reshape the Atlantic partnership. These efforts came on the heels of détente, the growth of the

65 Robert J. Vajko, "A History and Analysis of the Church-Planting Ministry of The Evangelical Alliance Mission in France 1952-1975" (MA Thesis Trinity Evangelical Divinity School, Deerfield IL, June 1975), 114; Interview by author of Dr. Robert J. Vajko on September 24, 2012, Carol Stream, IL, and e-mail interview by author with Sarah Page, 25 February, 20 March and 2 April 2013; A. Scott Moreau, "Putting the Survey in Perspective," in Linda J. Weber and Dotsey Welliver, eds., *Mission Handbook: U.S. and Canadian Protestant Ministries Overseas* (20th ed., Weathon IL: Billy Graham Center, 2007), 30.

66 "Annual Report France Field Chairman to the 1979 27th Anniversary Annual Conference," 2, TEAM archives Carol Stream, IL.

67 Memo from Richard Winchell to Vernon Mortenson, July 16, 1974; "Annual Report France Field Chairman to the 1977 25th Anniversary Annual Conference," TEAM archives Carol Stream; Robert Vajko, "AEEI – Strengths and Weaknesses as a Union of Churches, TEAM Semi-annual Conference January 30-31, 1978," 3, Carol Stream.

68 BGCA, YFC col. 48, box 16 file 51 Prayer Letters, December 1967-October 1972: Newsletter Ron and Carole Wilson, October 1968; Patrick Pasture, eds., *The Transformation of the Christian Churches in Western Europe: 1945-2000*; Patrick Pasture, "Christendom and the Legacy of the Sixties: Between the Secular City and the Age of Aquarius," *Revue d'Histoire Ecclésiastique* 99.1 (2004): 82-117.

European community and its economic protectionism, and the U.S. military defeat in Vietnam. The American pressure on Europe to pay more for U.S. military protection increased. On the American side, isolationist sentiments became stronger. Funds collected in the United States for missionaries in Germany lost 7.5 per cent of their value in 1971 and would lose even more in the next few years. Agencies suffered from the increasing costs and adapted to this by reducing their staff abroad. Due to the devaluation of the dollar, the operating costs for printing in America and distributing literature abroad became too high. As a result, indigenization was partly driven by monetary necessity.[69]

Broadening Horizons towards Global Evangelicalism

The evangelical debate about the need for social action partnered with a proclamation of the gospel entered a new phase in the early 1970s. In 1970 Ralph D. Winter, the evangelical missiologist at the Fuller Seminary who was responsible for introducing the new missionary concept, looked back on the conflict between word and deed, preaching and social action. He claimed that the spread of the word had always been accompanied by deeds. But now that the missionary field had begun to recognize that, there were structures in need of being transformed, since the pace of change was accelerating. Winter's assessment was that missionaries believed that personal transformation came out of structural social change but they forgot that personal transformation also caused social change. This latter insight was easily lost in the shuffle. Hence, Winter's plea for proclaiming the gospel.[70]

Deliberations on this process had been in the works since the mid-1960s. The Wheaton Declaration of 1966, which came out of a broad consultation on the missions, had devoted four of its five statements to the idea of preventing the missionary effort from giving social change a place of importance superior to preaching. But behind these protective fences it also urged evangelicals "to stand openly and firmly for racial equality, human freedom, and all forms of social justice throughout the world."[71] This process of reflection put the evangelicals in the middle between liberals who still found evangelicals too exclusivist, and fundamentalists who withdrew in growing numbers from denominations into unaffiliated organizations with conservative leanings, whose sole mission was to evangelize.[72]

69 Enns, "Saving Germany," 243; Letter Billy Graham to Peter Schneider, 3 April 1973, File Billy Graham, 1960-1987, Archives Allianzhaus Bad Blankenburg, Germany.

70 Ralph D. Winter, *The Twenty-Five Unbelievable Years 1945-1969* (South Pasadena: William Carey Library, 1970), 60.

71 Yri, *Quest*, 269.

72 *Mission Handbook* 11th ed. (1976), 61.

The visibility of Billy Graham as the standard bearer for American evangelicalism in Europe provoked the identification of tensions between European and American priorities. While Graham developed his technique for mobilizing others to become evangelists in the 1970s, the Anglican theologian John Stott developed ideas to broaden the evangelical intellectual horizon, without losing sight of its biblical anchor. Fortunately for the evangelical family, Graham the preacher and Stott the thinker got along well. The final statement of the 1974 Lausanne Covenant confirmed the need for proclamation, but also put social action on the agenda. It apologized for its neglect in fighting for justice, liberation, and reconciliation – activities that evangelicals often looked on as competing with evangelism. The document repeated the idea that social action was not identical to evangelism, but affirmed nevertheless "that evangelism and socio-political involvement are both part of our Christian duty... The salvation we claim should be transforming us in the totality of our personal and social responsibilities. Faith without works is dead."[73] The radical evangelicals' statement quoted above was perhaps a bit provocative, but definitely within the newly articulated boundary lines.

The mostly Latin-American radical evangelicals and some Europeans wanted to maintain this momentum, but the American delegation under Graham's leadership resisted efforts for a continuation committee. Graham wanted to concentrate on his primary task and felt that the social aspects should be left to others. Stott believed that this separation would be a betrayal of the fundamental character of the agreement.[74] Their difference in priorities was a result of the diverging perceptions of the role of the church. Graham's side of American evangelism saw the church organization as the problem and voluntary association as the solution. European evangelicals in the main churches defended having a comprehensive church embracing a broad social agenda.[75]

While Stott believed that at the conference he had successfully rescued both the primary task of spreading the gospel and its social consequences, American historian David Wells has concluded that the Lausanne Covenant marked the high point, but also the demise of confessional evangelicalism, which Stott represented. Wells uses the term "confessional" to encompass not only adherence to a clearly circumscribed body of doctrine, but also to incorporate the basic belief that cognitive ideas guided the lives of Christians. Wells saw a movement towards transconfessionality, a shift in emphasis from doctrine to action and experience and considered it a strategy that could unite

73 Yri, *Quest*, 313.
74 Dudley-Smith, *John Stott*, 220-221.
75 Ibid., 222.

different strands within evangelicalism. This trend paved the way for the inclusion of charismatics in the evangelical fold.[76]

This perspective was confirmed by the explosion of evangelical initiatives in the 1980s. While the European impulse for reflection broadened the social horizon and the social agenda of the majority world, the evangelical family gained ground at Lausanne, and the Americans continued to set the practical agenda of proclamation. The American evangelicals use of new media technology enabled them to reach Europe as one market, and through these channels, individual Christians could enter religious networks that were an alternative to mainstream churches.[77] Historian Brian Stanley has asserted that Lausanne was actually a European success, since the British and German leaders' original reservations about the scale, costs, American domination, and ascendency of inspirational message over strategic planning were pushed aside at the end of the conference. Also, conservative Americans could leave satisfied that evangelism had maintained center stage, and two out of three of Graham's objectives were accomplished: the younger generation was well represented at the conference and so were non-Western participants. This was in spite of the fact that 90 per cent of the attendees were clergy or religious professionals.[78]

Eventually, however, historians drew opposing conclusions about Lausanne. Some believed that Stott's mediation between Americans and outsiders strengthened evangelical unity thanks to his careful drafting of the closing statement. Others claimed that both wings simply disengaged and went their separate ways. Successive international conferences, however, have revealed a shift towards action and lived experience at the cost of knowledge and tradition. The growing diversity of nations in the evangelical fold has diversified the agenda. Graham's evangelism conferences in Amsterdam in 1983 and 1986 confirmed the ongoing dominance of American methods of mass mobilization and instruction.[79] And while criticism of the United States was somehow inevitable, as the partner most in evidence is always likely to hear complaints about domination from those who want to change things, the broader horizon and self-confidence within evangelicalism were signs of maturity. The dis-

76 David Wells, "On being Evangelical: Some Theological Differences and Similarities," in Mark A. Noll, David W. Bebbington, George A. Rawlyk, eds., *Evangelicalism: Comparative Studies of Popular Protestantism in North America, the British Isles and Beyond, 1700-1990* (New York: Oxford University Press, 1994), 389-410; Billy Graham, *Just as I am: The Autobiography of Billy Graham* (New York: HarperCollins/Zondervan, 1997), 567-583.

77 Walter Frank, "IFMA Missions and Church Planting in Areas Where Old Churches are Established," BGCA col. 352 IFMA box 27 f4 GEM 1970-71.

78 Brian Stanley, *The Global Diffusion of Evangelicalism: The Age of Billy Graham and John Stott* (Nottingham: Inter-Varsity Press, 2013), 160-179.

79 Noll, Bebbington, Rawlyk, *Evangelicalism*, "Afterword," 413.

agreements that surfaced could now be embraced and managed within the rising mood of expectation.[80]

In a way it was immaterial as to who was the true victor of "Lausanne." Its strongest impulse was to be a movement. Things were different, however, in the more formal institution, the World Evangelical Fellowship. This was a representative body that aimed to be a mouthpiece for global evangelicals. The expansion of the WEF meant that by 1975, the majority of its members came from the Third World and they exhibited the same concerns as the World Council of Churches had a generation earlier. A quarter of the 1980 Pattaya (Thailand) participants, for example, wanted the organization to pursue a more progressive course and they resisted the transplantation of American dominance in their country. The WEF moved further away from the Western world and as a result, altered the American missionary curricula. A sign of things to come was the development of a cross-cultural studies program in 1975 at Fuller Theological Seminary in California. This innovation made it one of the leading evangelical missionary institutions, even though the quantitative methods developed there were often dismissed as a typical American preoccupation.[81]

This new approach needed new leadership. Waldron Scott ("Scotty") became the new chief executive of the WEF based on his service as the Middle East Director for the Navigators. In that position he had redefined the course of the organization, moving it from making disciples to taking on a comprehensive strategy to advance God's Kingdom. Scott had enrolled at the Thunderbird Graduate School of International Management hoping it would enhance his managerial skills, but quickly found that many evangelical mission organizations already knew and practiced sophisticated methods of international management. At the Fuller Theological Seminary School of World Mission in Pasadena, California, he was inspired by the church growth movement, which he saw as a new way to expand the reach of Christianity. As the global strategist for the Navigators, Scott became disenchanted. He found that the organization was unwilling to expand its horizon, instead it turned to a short-term incremental strategy that he associated with a European approach. For Scott, the WEF offered an instrument to achieve a larger global vision and he

80 Martin Klauber, *The Great Commission: Evangelicals and the History of World Missions* (Nashville, Tenn.: B & H Publishing Group, 2008); John Stott, "The Significance of Lausanne," in Paul Wesley Chilcote, Laceye C. Warner, eds., *The Study of Evangelism: Exploring a Missional Practice of the Church* (Grand Rapids: Eerdmans, 2008), 305-312 (orig. article in *International Review of Missions* 64.3 (1975): 288-294); John Stott, *Christian Mission in the Modern World*, 1975.

81 See George Marsden, *Reforming Fundamentalism: Fuller Seminary and the New Evangelicalism* (Grand Rapids: Eerdmans, 1987), 238-244 on the church growth movement and 275 on the move to practicality.

succeeded Clyde Taylor as general secretary of WEF after the 1974 Lausanne Conference.[82]

The growth of the WEF made it less Western and especially less Anglo-Saxon, and it invited more variation in organizational positions. It also accepted different opinions about the WCC and did not demand its partners sever all ties to WCC bodies. Secretary-general Scott wrote to a friend in South Africa saying that the international leaders wished to make WEF "an open space where evangelicals in all their cultural diversity and historical developments can come together and get to know one another and understand one another, so as to be able to appreciate and hopefully trust one another, so as to be able to work together more effectively. I do not believe this can be achieved by making WEF into an exclusive 'club.'"[83]

The WEF board also realized that despite the growth of its network, there were still more evangelicals within the WCC community and outside the WEF (Southern Baptists and Missouri Synod Lutherans) than concentrated within it. The WEF sought their fellowship and therefore avoided emphasizing its differences with the WCC.

Maturation Phase in Europe

On the ground in Europe, Greater Europe Mission (GEM), the mission agency that had designated the continent as its core target, rephrased its plans after pausing in 1974 to reflect on a quarter century of service. The agency proudly reported on having trained two thousand students, but director Bob Evans did not conclude that this meant the mission had approached its completion. On the contrary, he noted that missions in Europe in 1975 were too relaxed.[84] In 1977, his executive director, Don Brugman, responded to the suggestion that, since many functions had been handed over to Europeans, it was time for foreign missionaries to go home. He urged, "... Europe is still at the pioneer stage of missions compared with many parts of the world. The need for missionaries is more critical than ever."[85] Yet, there were promising signs. In his 1979 overview of the agency's activities, Wayne Detzler, associate director for Northern

82 Waldron Byron Scott, "Double Helix: A Missionary's Odyssey," 624, 631 <http://www.waldronscott.net/doublehelix/id12.html> visited 16 February 2012. Since then, the digital version of this autobiography has been removed from the site. A partial print is in the possession of the author.

83 General Secretary of WEF Waldron Scott to Rev. Hugh Wetmore, General Secretary of Association of Evangelicals of South Africa, 20 August 1980, BGCA col. 338, box 6 file 5, WCC relations, 1964-1980.

84 Robert P. Evans, "As I see it this month," *Together: A Family Newsletter* 19.3 (April 1975): 1, BGCA col. 352 IFMA, box 34, file 9.

85 *Greater Europe Report*, September-October 1977, 7.

Europe, announced that a new generation of European evangelical leaders had emerged, and that "The Church in Europe [is] Coming Alive."[86] He was in a festive mood, "During the fifteen years under study, there has been a steady, almost spectacular emergence of an evangelical minority in Europe. From the Lutheran north to the Roman Catholic South, evangelicals have become more vocal and virile in the expression of their faith. Ecclesiastical authorities have been compelled to sit up and take notice. Fragmented for decades, the evangelicals now have discovered their unity and commenced to speak out with one voice."[87]

GEM's director, Evans, wanted to keep his workers from fully integrating in European churches: "... we do not believe that the foreign missionary's role is best played when he independently joins the national church structure itself. He then is in the same position as a national pastor or Christian worker. He loses the very uniqueness inherent in the nature of the missionary task." Actually, he saw that true believers would inevitably have to leave their church because they were "trapped in a less than adequate group where (they) cannot grow." Moreover, any foreign missionary who joined a national church would lose advantages that Evens described as, "a different viewpoint, an optimistic outlook born of experience in a more active evangelical environment [read: America], mobility, knowledge of worldwide methods, the prayerful backing of expectant donors, biblical oversight and accountability, and many others."[88] He pleaded for a separation of roles, cautioning the foreigner to remain at some distance to let the national churches be themselves. In actuality he was still applying the principle of organizational separation.

The Brit A. Morgan Derham, president of the European Evangelical Alliance, summarized the new position of strength and confidence of evangelicals at the end of the 1970s. They owed this progress to their access to mass communication channels which demanded a clear coherent self-definition that put them on the religious map. Even in cases where such access was denied, other modes of art have been employed, that increased their repertoire. According to him, the founding of the Fellowship of European Evangelical Theologians in 1977, marked the moment of intellectual maturity for academic practitioners and made the accreditation of bible colleges in Europe possible. He noted that the practice of periodic "raids" by evangelists had been abandoned for more structured national programs in broad church coalitions. Derham saw that young people flocked to the new missionary initiatives and that relief organizations boomed. He credited all of this to the Lausanne event, where he said, the broad international representation helped to open up new

86 *Greater Europe Report*, July-August 1979, 1.

87 Wayne A. Detzler, *The Changing Church in Europe* (Grand Rapids, MI: Zondervan, 1979), 41.

88 Robert P. Evans, "Our responsibility: disciple the weaker brother," *Greater Europe Report*, May-June 1980, 3.

horizons of understanding. Still, he counseled, the denominational structure proved highly problematic because it united and separated true believers and clear church boundaries remained impossible to draw. Derham hoped for a revival that would transcend the divisions and liberate the flow of new religious energy.[89]

Peter Schneider, the closest friend and co-worker of Billy Graham in Germany, agreed that during the 1970s evangelicals had become a respected, sometimes feared sector in Germany and in the German press.[90] American observers confirmed this self-confident opinion. Bruce Shelley, church historian at the Conservative Baptist Theological Seminary in Denver, wrote in *United Evangelical Action* in response to the Lausanne conference, that the mood was changing: "Evangelicals are no longer merely reacting; they are attempting to seize the initiative."[91] The old polarization paradigm proved tenacious, however, even though evangelicals presented themselves as positive partners rather than as mere antidotes to the WCC. This trust grew very slowly. In Germany a rumor circulated that Graham had secretly struck a deal with the World Council of Churches leadership not to attack them publicly at the Lausanne Conference. The rumor spurred conservative evangelicals in Europe to press for clear separation. The balance of opening up proved precarious but still it tilted toward more dialog.[92]

Concern about the lack of church growth spurred Walther Olsen, missionary for the Conservative Baptists in France, to investigate the process of conversions. While the method of sending out multi-question surveys was criticized as too American, Olsen's findings were useful and his results were confirmed by his fellow missionaries. He concluded that most conversions occurred due to personal relations and not to typical missionary activities such as campaigns, radio broadcasts, and camps, and that missionaries should become better aware of the socio-psychological circumstances that give rise to conversion.[93]

Some American evangelicals believed that the British were resentful of America for taking over their global imperial role and that this translated into a resistance to the "evangelical takeover." But allergy to hierarchy when faced with a centralized executive power like the American evangelicals, rather than some conceivable resentment about lost status and past glory, more likely

89 "Evangelical perspectives in Western Europe," Compendium/ Morgan Derham, N.d [1980], BGCA col. 338, Box 101 f 11.

90 Peter Schneider to Billy Graham, 31 May 1979, File Billy Graham, 1960-1987, Archives Allianzhaus Bad Blankenburg, Germany.

91 Travelog Dr. Baker [1974] 5, BGCA col. 352, box 67 file 4, WEF; Bruce Shelley, "Evangelicals Together: The Biblical and Historical Basis for Cooperation Today," *United Evangelical Action* (Winter 1975): 12.

92 Peter Schneider to Billy Graham, 10 December 1974, File Billy Graham, 1960-1987, Archives Allianzhaus Bad Blankenburg, Germany.

93 *Europe Pulse* 9.1 (September 1978).

shaped their attitude. Churches founded by European evangelical missionaries abroad tended to remain within the mainline bodies, while those founded by American evangelicals often opted for a separate existence.[94]

Slow Change Through Reconsideration of Gender Roles

A clear expression of the subtle change in attitude of American missionaries can be found in the postwar generation of evangelical women that became active in mission work. This group was more often unmarried and the target of increasing tension within the gender hierarchy that limited their work. Gender policy at bible schools had confined their education to a supportive role, where men were prepared for all kinds of situations. Though the women received equal pay in the mission field, their tasks were far from equal. The main obstacle standing in their way was the conviction that women should not exert authority over men. This served to curtail what tasks they could do in church planting work. When the TEAM leadership decided to intensify its focus on establishing churches, the space for women's involvement shrank.[95] Married women suffered less from this limitation since their contribution focused on allowing their families to function as a showcase for the missionary cause. Thus, their achievements were given more importance than those of single women. Furthermore, the role for single women was only made clear to them after they reached the mission field.[96]

The story of Sarah Page reveals these changes. Page, a single woman, joined TEAM France in the revolutionary year in 1968 when the team had reached a professional level of operation. After her initiation, she discovered that the abilities of single women remained underused because they were directed by "cultural based sex roles or arbitrary assignments."[97] Her male

94 Waldron Byron Scott, "Double Helix: A Missionary's Odyssey," 665, 670, 697 <http://www.waldronscott.net/doublehelix/id12.html> visited 16 February 2012.

95 Glenn F. Arnold, "A Comparative Study of the Present Doctrinal Positions and Christian Conduct Codes of Selected Alumni of Moody Bible Institute: 1945-1971" (PhD dissertation, New York University, 1977), 95; *Policy Book Conservative Baptist Foreign Mission Society* (1962-64), 11, 12A, 34, 74A.

96 Dana L. Robert, "The 'Christian Home' as a Cornerstone of Anglo-American Missionary Thought and Practice," in Dana L. Robert, ed., *Converting Colonialism: Visions and Realities in Mission History, 1706-1914* (Grand Rapids, MI: Eerdmans, 2008), 158-65. See for instance, the memoirs of two American missionary families in France: Ken and Lois Beach, *In the Shadow of the Almighty: The Autobiography of Ken and Lois Beach* (n.p. privately printed, December 2010); Ivan (Pete) and Donelda Peterson, *"Tears and Triumphs:" Fifty Years of Overseas Ministry* (n.p. Xulonpress, 2009).

97 Sarah Page, "A Profile of Single Women Missionaries in France" (M.A. Thesis, Wheaton College, 1979), 3. For more detailed information see Hans Krabbendam, "Full Members of the TEAM? Evangelical Women in the European Mission, 1945-1980," *Journal of American Studies* 51.4 (2017): 1095-1116.

French women listen to a speaker at a tea organized by the Christian Women's Club in Versailles, 1980. [Used with permission from Sarah Page]

colleagues realized the same thing, but their response was to recommended to TEAM headquarters that they discourage single women from applying to France. Page did not think that women's contributions could be so easily dismissed and she decided to explore this unseemly proposal.[98] Her investigations traced the root of the problem back to the instructions for planting churches. These guidelines only addressed men, whereas historically it had been single women who played the crucial role in mission evangelism and church-planting in the Third World. This memory had apparently evaporated. Page surveyed the experience of fifty single female missionaries active in France and analyzed the results for her Master's Project at Wheaton College.[99]

She found that these young women were far from feminists and did indeed accept the idea of submissive behavior. They even expected it. Yet, they felt a tension arise when the expectation of bowing to male authority bumped up against the expectation of being assertive and active in order to do an effective job. Many respondents confirmed Page's impression that even though their capabilities were overlooked, they carved out their own space and engaged in direct evangelism and personal discipleship. They organized

98 Page, "Profile of Single Women," 3; Interview Sarah Page with author, 2 April 2013.

99 Page, "Profile of Single Women"; Interviews Sarah Page with author, 30 March and 2 April 2013. Simultaneously women in the Division for World Mission and Ecumenism of the Lutheran Church in America discussed the neglect of women in mission in their conferences. See Joyce M. Bowers, "Roles of Married Women Missionaries: A Case Study," *International Bulletin of Missionary Research* 8 (January 1984), 4-6. A survey among 53 couples was held and a heated debate followed between proponents of quick and radical change and those who were satisfied with the situation. The majority of women complained about the lack of job descriptions. Also in this mainline organization (female) staff hesitated about claiming their rights. The result was the appointment of advisors for couples and opportunity for dual pay, but not (yet) opening leadership positions.

Retreat banners in English and French at a CWC retreat. The American speaker is at the left, the translator at the right, June 1980.
[Used with permission from Sarah Page]

children's clubs, women's bible discussion groups, and church events. Nevertheless, they found that access to positions of authority over men remained blocked.[100]

And not just a matter of being offended by a lack of appreciation and unequal treatment, Page noted that these gender codes were actually counterproductive to the mission of reaching secular Europeans. Most of her French colleagues had no objection to women teaching mixed classes of men and women, leading worship, participating in church services by reading the bible or praying, and even serving on church boards.[101] Page was convinced that single women missionaries were in fact a distinct asset, for they were more easily invited into French homes than married couples who were often busy attending to their families. She concluded from her data that women were often more resourceful than men in finding creative solutions to organizational dead-ends.[102]

Page's initiative did not radically change the unequal gender policies of the governing boards, but it did achieve its primary goal of lifting the ban on single women's applications. Moreover, she collected factual evidence that objectified this source of tension as serious. In the end she circulated the concerns, and most importantly, took charge of finding creative solutions that confirmed the skills of women.[103]

100 Page, "Profile of Single Women," 32; Interview author with Sarah Page, 25 February and 2 April 2013.
101 Hans Finzel, ed., *Partners Together: 50 Years of Global Impact - The CBFMS Story* (Wheaton, IL: Conservative Baptist Foreign Mission Society, 1993).
102 Interview Page, 2 April 2013.
103 Interview Page, 2 April 2013.

One of Page's innovative initiatives was the founding of the first European chapter of the Christian Women's Club in Paris in 1970. It hosted ladies-only evangelistic teas, bible studies, lectures, seminars, and retreats. This example of ministries for women, as well as evangelistic outreach to mixed audiences, was adopted by other evangelical churches across France. Once again, a woman's organization offered training in leadership to women and ultimately the agency's long-term perspective to hand over the churches to the "natives" broadened the scope of activities for women. This helped to ease tensions, even if they were not entirely resolved.[104]

Growing Exchange Between Liberals and Evangelicals

The leadership of the World Council of Churches had not abandoned the hope of drawing conservative Christians to their network. In 1976 this desire for rapprochement with conservatives resulted in initiatives for a joint missiology conference involving evangelical, conciliar, Roman Catholic, and Orthodox circles. Thanks to preparatory informal exchanges in the 1960s, American evangelical leaders recognized that, despite theological differences, they had created common ground with the World Council that could serve the evangelicals' aims. The evangelical reach across the aisle was reinforced by a renewed historical awareness. WEF Secretary Waldron Scott expressed this in 1976, "… this business of evangelical cooperation is always relative to the past and the future and is therefore evolutionary in character. I must keep this in mind. I am eager for broader evangelical cooperation… ."[105] The broadening of cooperation was in full swing when representatives from the majority world quickly took over a Western leadership role. With this expansion, Pentecostal and Charismatic Christians entered the network, some of whom maintained close contact with members of the Roman Catholic Church.[106]

While Secretary Scott welcomed contacts with numerous evangelicals in mainline churches and organizations, other American evangelical leaders, such as Milton Baker, were not so certain that the intensification of contact with the WCC would benefit evangelicals. Old modes of hostile perception and fear of cooptation persisted. But even Baker could envision a strategic dialog

104 Dana L. Robert, *American Women in Mission: A Social History of Their Thought and Practice* (Macon, GA: Mercer University Press, 1996), 216. For tightening of control see Allen V. Koop, "American Evangelical Missionaries in France, 1945-1975," in Joel A. Carpenter and Wilbert R. Shenk, eds., *Earthen Vessels: American Evangelicals and Foreign Missions, 1880-1980* (Grand Rapids, MI: Eerdmans, 1990), 180-202.

105 Baker to Waldron Scott, 12 May 1976, and Waldron Scott to Milton Baker, 14 May 1976, BGCA col. 352, box 67 file 6.

106 David Howard, *The Dream That Would Not Die*, 116-124. The serious consideration to move the office to Beirut was only abandoned due to the country's civil war.

in which the services of the World Council aimed at its evangelical constituency, could be massaged to weaken loyalty to the WCC.[107]

The WCC leadership went out of its way to insure that a representative of the WEF attended its periodic assembly in Nairobi in 1975, and in addition, it arranged other, more informal meetings on neutral territory. The WCC identified the American WEF leadership, Secretary Scott and President Hudson T. Armerding, as representing the widest possible conservative evangelical network that had the full confidence of its constituency. Yet, the rapprochement effort proved sensitive, which made the World Council want to meet the evangelicals in private, out of the glare of publicity.[108]

Despite this caution, these moves alarmed European evangelicals, who reiterated the key weaknesses of the ecumenical movement and noted their painful lack of liberal unity. The English-language German evangelical newsletter ran articles on the internal disagreements at the Fifth WCC Assembly, held in Nairobi, Kenya in late 1975. The articles noted that the assembly had adopted reports that deviated from the traditional atonement doctrine, and had rejected the WCC's exclusive condemnation of apartheid as an injustice without mentioning communist violations of human rights. The bulletin contrasted the allegedly harmonious evangelical Lausanne conference from mid-July 1974, to the internal divisions of the ecumenical Nairobi assembly, even though both meetings presented a colorful display of different cultures. Apparently unaware of the fierce debates about social issues that had ensued at Lausanne, the author exaggerated the distance between the two bodies by defining the World Council as problem oriented, and Lausanne as source (i.e. bible) oriented. Even the token appreciation of evangelicals in Nairobi, symbolized by the presence of John Stott and the inclusion of evangelicals in programs and at dinners, did not indicate to the author that real change was in the wind. Quite the opposite, the German newsletter emphasized divergence and saw Lausanne as the answer to the previous World Council mission conference in Bangkok in 1972, which was seen as abandoning evangelism. The efforts to welcome evangelicals by inviting one evangelical speaker did not impress. In fact, it proved moot as the scheduled plenary debate on missionary responsibilities at the World Council Assembly was canceled due to lack of time. This decision was seen as regretful since John Stott, who advocated for the evangelical position, had gained enough support that a number of dele-

107 Baker to Waldron Scott, 22 June 1976, BGCA col. 352, box 67 file 6. He still sensed a patronizing tone in WCC approaches and expected that evangelicals were drawn into the WCC circle, without the effect that it became more evangelical. See the exchange of letters between Milton Baker and Donald McGavran, 1975 in BGCA col. 352, box 58, file 1.

108 Konrad Raiser, deputy general secretary of the WCC to Hudson T. Armerding, president WEF, 14 October 1975 and John F. Robinson to John Mbiti, 11 September 1975, BGCA Col. 338 WEF, Box 41 f 7-8 WCC WEF, files on observer status of Waldron Scott in 1974 and 1975.

gates had put the issue of world evangelization on the agenda.[109] Yet, despite this confirmation of incompatibility after the two global conferences, even European reservations could not block the continuing ecumenist-evangelical dialog about the interpretation of the bible.[110]

It was ironic that while European evangelicals expressed this verdict, ecumenists acted upon a conclusion that had been drawn by evangelicals decades earlier: Europe had become a mission land.[111] In the 1970s, the WCC sent out international ("third world") visitation teams to assess the local mission situation in Europe and North America. The three to four-week long visits led to soul-searching in church communities. They recognized a common problem in the established churches in the West; the church was seen as an "introvert" that neglected fringe groups. Furthermore, the factfinders were perplexed by the contradiction between material wealth and unhappiness, and endured a gap between the gospel and everyday life. The conclusion of the reports could have directly walked out of a Billy Graham admonition: "The church in itself is a mission field."[112] The core question was what is the next step? The commission advised re-education that went beyond reflection as a necessary condition for rediscovering a lived-out faith in the present.

A New Crusade

While the leaders of global Protestant organizations learned to trust each other, a new grass-roots organization resorted to familiar strategies. It was ironic that just when American evangelists in Europe were reconsidering their methods, a fundamentalist section of the evangelicals in America were reviving the idea of a missionary blitz campaign in Europe and beyond. The conservative evangelicals organized in Campus Crusade for Christ (CCC) once again embraced the universalist ideology that hoisted American interests as the standard for global missionary intervention.[113]

While some American mission agencies gradually adapted their operations to align with Europe's more persistent structures and slower pace of

109 IDEA, 52/75, 4 December 1975, Special edition.

110 Letter Bruce J. Nicholls to Emilio Castro in Geneva, April 15, 1976, and to Waldron Scott, May 7, 1976, BGCA Col. 338 WEF, Box 41 f 8 WCC WEF.

111 W. A. Visser 't Hooft, "Evangelism among Europe's Neo-Pagans," *International Review of Mission* 66 (October 1977), 349-360.

112 *International Review of Mission* 67 (January 1978), 43. This special issue is filled with reports of the international team that explored the situation of Mission in the Netherlands and Sweden.

113 Andrew Preston, "Universal Nationalism: Christian America's Response to the Years of Upheaval," in Niall Ferguson, Charles S. Maier, Erez Manela, Daniel J. Sargent, eds., *The Shock of the Global: The 1970s in Perspective* (Cambridge: the Belknap Press of Harvard University, 2010), 306-318.

change, and even came to terms with the fact that it took less American control to achieve their ends, a new generation of American missionary activists launched exactly the opposite strategy. They put in place more American leadership to secure an acceleration of the conversion of the globe. The conservative evangelical student organization Campus Crusade for Christ entered Europe in 1967 by canvassing British and German universities and the 1968 Winter Olympics in Grenoble. The Dutch evangelism team was bankrolled by a Dutch-American couple, as the earlier wave in the 1940s had been financed through ethnic links.[114]

After these surveys, the strategists of Campus Crusade went full speed ahead in the early 1970s. They included Europe in their ambitious plans to (once again) spread the gospel around the entire world in a decade. Campus Crusade's founder, Bill Bright, harbored a sense of great urgency and little patience with older institutions that responded too timidly. His response matched the noise made by New Left activists, whose grave concern for the future triggered other alarmist strategies. Both movements wanted to replace petrified institutional obstacles with their own action-driven institutions.[115] Campus Crusade's growth was part of the skyrocketing number of evangelical parachurch organizations that energized a huge overlapping constituency in the 1950s and 1960s. Bill Bright's biographer explained the principles that created the enormous potential for growth, "Through their willingness to retain only a small number of theological essentials and continually adapt themselves to modern culture, evangelicals have kept their gospel an attractive product in the marketplace of American religions."[116] Campus Crusade was the most pronounced proponent of this flexible approach and created the most elaborate infrastructure for its ambitious national and eventually, international programs. At home in America, Bright effectively raised the level of urgency by hammering on the fact that communism and secular humanism were acute threats to American society, saying that they eroded the family first and Christian values next.

His organization's quick spread can be attributed to his perfecting a "gospel in a nutshell" – four spiritual laws, which could be easily memorized by young recruits and conveyed to non-believers. These formulas, which scores of evangelistic organizations adopted, condensed the gospel down to four propositions: God had a plan for everyone, human rebellion against Him caused them to lose track of this plan, Jesus' atonement restored the knowledge of this plan, and a personal acceptance of Jesus opened up the future. By presenting these propositions as laws, Bright suggested certainty and predictabil-

114 Bram Krol, *Het verhaal van Agapè (voorheen Instituut voor Evangelisatie)* (Doorn: Stichting Agapé, 1994).

115 John G. Turner, *Bill Bright and Campus Crusade for Christ: The Renewal of Evangelicalism in Postwar America* (Chapel Hill: The University of North Carolina Press, 2008), 120-131.

116 Turner, *Bill Bright*, 12.

ity. An astute organizer, Bright perfected the flow of money to his and other parachurch organizations (without enriching himself), which funded his rapidly expanding activities. Bright promised a quick spiritual return on financial investments and even calculated the cost of one conversion. "Campus Crusade Turns Dollars Into Converts," was the headline of an American newspaper.[117] His success inspired other groups to adopt his methods. The motor of his organizational growth was the emphasis on multiplication – disciples making disciples. This combination of means that could be repeated and ends that were clear, enabled the group to confidently execute a very ambitious plan.[118]

In 1968, using methodical reasoning, Bright defined his target as reaching everyone in the United States with the Gospel by 1976, and encompassing the world within four years.[119] Explo, a training conference held in 1972 in Dallas Texas, drew close to the eighty-five thousand young people who were there to train for this purpose. Bright used the expertise and reputation of the Billy Graham Evangelistic Association to make the Dallas event a success. This in turn, encouraged Campus Crusade to repeat this blueprint in the rest of the world. Beginning in Korea in 1958, by 1970, Campus Crusade had reached 45 countries with a staff of 500, and by the time of Explo 1972, it could already envision reaching all 210 countries by 1976.[120] Bright justified this geographical order as a logical strategy. The organization calculated that since only one out of 1,750 world citizens had been reached by the gospel and the United States owned 54 per cent of the world's wealth but had only six per cent of its population, the United States would need to provide the "Manpower for the World."[121] Based on growth numbers in the United States, the Campus Crusade's leadership prepared its organization for international expansion. Underlying this plan of course, was the assumption that American approaches could easily be duplicated anywhere.

For the Western Europe campaign, the leadership made the following calculation: In total 1,200 full time ministers and 790 supporting staff were needed to train 100 students each. The target was to reach the four million students already in university. In order to complete the job by 1980, they needed effective recruitment of students in Europe, with standardized training cur-

117 *Eugene Register (Oregon)*, 21 June 1980.

118 See "Essential Characteristics of Campus Crusade for Christ," 3 pages, copy in author's possession, courtesy collection John G. Turner.

119 Turner, *Bill Bright*, 139.

120 "Presentation of Campus Crusade for Christ International Ministries," (Campus Crusade, n.d. [anticipating the Explo in June 1972]), "European Training Ministry Plan, Submitted 23 February 1973," Courtesy Turner.

121 Gordon Klenck, "Collection of major motions which were passed at the International Advisory Council in Korea, August 20-25, 1974," Courtesy Turner.

ricula, computerized reporting systems, and estimates of attrition.[122] An expected ten per cent would respond favorably to the call for conversion, and 20 per cent of those would become disciples. If a minimum of 50,000 students witnessed twice a week for a year (40 weeks), the four million students could be reached. As long as the name made clear that this was a movement for students and laymen who supported "a positive, aggressive operation, and commitment" it would be good.[123]

In order to proceed quickly, the organization drafted rules, regulations, and recommendations. It dealt in detail with how to settle the expenses when staff moved to other countries. It established a clear chain of command and reporting requirements, and it organized exploratory trips abroad by Campus Crusade staff. To prepare for other Explo conferences abroad, it devoted priority to training women, and gave specific parameters for intercultural marriages. The instructions warned against disregard of local culture, but also cautioned against having too much esteem for the field assignment. They considered the possibility of too much admiration of other cultures as the larger threat. Their lack of trust was illustrated when the American staff twice rejected a translation of the Four Spiritual Laws into Dutch because they concluded that the translator had added words to the formula, when there were a larger number of words in the text after the translator was done.[124]

The mathematical idea of multiplication was basic to the expectation of accomplishing these ambitious goals. Finding more staff with personal experience in this multiplying ministry was crucial. In February 1975, Campus Crusade held its first International Advisory Council in Munich Germany.[125] The trainers presented international delegates with a number of examples aimed at teaching how to multiply or accelerate the momentum of conversions. They taught that the best way forward was to build models to reach specialized groups, such as high school or university students, military personnel, or minorities, and then to form model churches all the while being sure to gain exposure in the mass media. Each phase of gospel penetration, concentration, and saturation in Europe had to happen within two to three years. Subsequent to that, the lay ministry would take over responsibility from the professional clergy.

During the execution phase, however, it once again became clear that this American model was not so easily applied to European countries. At an

122 "European Training Ministry Plan, Submitted 23 February 1973," See also the one-page "Weaknesses in Campus Crusade for Christ- [Summary of Q. sent to staff in Gr. Lks. Region. By F. Kifer, 1971]" nr. 34 ("What happens in 1980? Do we hang up our hats and go into business or are there plans to keep on fulfilling the Great Commission?"), Courtesy Turner.

123 Memo from Mass Media Committee to the International Advisory Council, February 1, 1973, Courtesy Turner.

124 Krol, *Het verhaal van Agapè*, 28.

125 "International Advisory Council Minutes, February 18-22, 1975, Munich Germany," 22-23, Courtesy G. Turner.

early stage Dan Reeves, who had worked among European university students for several years, observed that it was more difficult than anticipated to find qualified national leaders. Moreover, the trainers in America had tried to duplicate the American experience without acknowledging cultural differences. Whereas Campus Crusade had established training centers in other parts of the world, doing so in Europe took more time. This European experience made Reeves realize, "We need to begin looking at the world at large, not as an extension of the U.S. 'model' but as a many differing cultures all needing Christ."[126] He proposed that staff needed at least a year of language training and a year of experience in the field. Reeves warned the organization that Europeans were not waiting to be mobilized; they were a critical audience that only accepted changes after direct observation of the results.

When the United States celebrated its Bicentennial in 1976, Bright once again announced his ambition to reach the entire world. He said this goal required a one-billion-dollar budget. This prerequisite threw the organization into the arms of wealthy backers, caused its fundraising to become more aggressive, and eventually led to the Campus Crusade's concentration on the majority world. The European willingness to change had once again proven disappointing.[127]

The 1970s: The Confirmation of Europe's Place in the Global Evangelical Community

By the mid-1970s, Europe was established as a recipient of structured American missionary attention, but it had also found its own evangelical voice in a multidimensional religious concern. As Europeans contested American methods and influence, and as work shifted to the majority world, the dominant American framework that opposed and competed with liberal Christians, found an alternative way to deal with others.

In a cultural sense, this alternative matched the détente framework found in the foreign policy of Nixon's Republicans. His administration moved away from confrontation to negotiation and cooperation (as progressive and conservative Christians just had tried), employing real and symbolic moves, from extending trade relations to surprising everyone with state visits such as Nixon's trip to China.[128] A second similarity was to figure out how to engage in the balancing act between pursuing a practical or realistic policy and giving

126 Dan Reeves, "Will the world be reached by 1980 with our present strategy? A re-examination of our present use of resources from a European perspective, June 30, 1972," 2, Courtesy Turner.

127 Turner, *Bill Bright*, 175-181.

128 Andrew Preston, *Sword of the Spirit, Shield of Faith: Religion in American War and Diplomacy* (New York: Alfred A. Knopf, 2012), 539-558.

in to the popular pressure that pushed for a moral policy. Among those applying pressure were conservative Christians. In U.S. foreign policy, the practical attitude prevailed until the late 1970s, but even the more obviously moral encouragement of human rights under the Carter administration sustained a cooperative approach.

Initially, American postwar evangelicals were convinced that Europe was exhibit A for the bankruptcy of liberal Protestantism. But despite their constant criticism of religious liberals, their reflections on the meagre return from their own investments, and the continuation of a still cautious dialog, evangelical missionary thinkers recognized the phases and patterns of their work in Europe. They used time-tested democratization, indigenization, and acculturalization to blame their erstwhile liberal opponents. These historical continuities and aspirations distanced the American evangelicals further from separatist fundamentalists, who had already abandoned any ambition to win over Europe. Simultaneously, ecumenists identified the need to put evangelization of Europe back on the agenda. Their allergies slowly diminished and so did their competitiveness, both against liberals and against Catholics. Their institutional successes, principally in unifying their organizational forces in massive conferences and establishing scholarly channels, helped to mainstream evangelicals in Europe.

Meanwhile, political engagement by American evangelicals puzzled, or even scandalized Europeans, including evangelical sympathizers. The Watergate scandal and Billy Graham's public support for Richard Nixon harmed America's religious reputation in Europe. American religion would only become more problematic as Reagan invoked divine approval for his policies, and the culture wars of the 1990s pitched conservatives against liberals.[129]

Tensions and mutual frustrations did not disappear, but the joint American-European efforts to institutionalize a global evangelical network was at least a qualified success, even if it took tremendous effort to strengthen the commitment from the bottom-up. This didn't mean that the missionary flow from the United States dried up. On the contrary, the drive to mobilize and channel religious energy directed from the United States to Europe proved irrepressible. The Campus Crusade for Christ showed this beyond a doubt. To the CCC one could add Operation Mobilization, World Vision, Youth With a Mission, the Pro-Life Movement, the Promise Keepers, and Women Aglow to mention a few. Beginning in the 1970s, these initiatives added to plural expressions of lived-faith and replaced fierce opposition with increasing cooperation.

129 Manfred Siebald, "Why It Is Difficult for European Observers to Understand the Relationship between American Politics and Religion in the Twenty-First Century," in Mark A. Noll and Luke E. Harlow, eds., *Religion and American Politics: From the Colonial Period to the Present* (2nd ed.; New York: Oxford University Press, 2007), 386-392.

CONCLUSION

The story of American Protestant missionaries in Europe after the Second World War unravels hidden strands that tie the North Atlantic world together and explains the perception of a growing religious contrast. U.S. missionary initiatives resulted from the increasing attention paid in the United States during World War II to Europe's religious situation. Though the expectation of mass conversions proved to be unrealistic, these operations helped build an additional link in a global religious network.

This book makes an effort to synthesize what appears to be a handful of unconnected religious events, e.g., Billy Graham's European crusades or work in individual mission fields, into a coherent and consistent stream of interactions between Protestant believers in Europe and the United States. Though itinerant revivalists, individual missionaries, and staff of small agencies had come to Europe intermittently in the late nineteenth and early twentieth centuries, the postwar enterprise developed as part of a comprehensive global plan.

Missionary activities worked in two directions. Historian David Hollinger has persuasively shown how missionary experiences changed American's perspective on the world. Unfortunately, he dismissed Europe, concluding a bit prematurely that American Protestant missionaries in Europe "... except for influencing their own churches, ... had little impact."[1] Admittedly, the impact might have looked less dramatic since Europe was not colonized like other

1 David A. Hollinger, *Protestants Abroad: How Missionaries Tried to Change the World but Changed America* (Princeton: Princeton University Press, 2017), 4.

parts of the world and thus, was less exotic and more familiar to Americans. Nevertheless, the fact that Americans acted upon the assumption that it was necessary to save Europe, changed mutual perceptions and created new opportunities for real encounters.[2]

This research shines a light on the increasing number of American missionaries who were persuaded that Europe needed to be included in the global missionary enterprise. The impact of this decision was felt on both theoretical and practical levels. On the theoretical level, missions to Europe strengthened the idea that missions were contextual and went through various phases. Practically, Europe increasingly and successfully competed with the rest of the world for the missionaries' attention. An increasing number of candidates for the mission field chose to go to Europe, roused by shapers of the missionary imagination. Retiring missionaries returning from Europe may have been had less revolutionary perspectives than those returning from New Guinea or the Amazon, but their time in the field cannot be dismissed as having had no impact at all. Missions in Europe were a strategic part of the evangelical riposte to religious liberalism at home and around the world and missionaries confirmed the impression that their home country was exceptionally religious (and the standard to follow). Americans were less involved in social and educational work in Europe, apart from the brief postwar period, compared to other continents, and therefore emphasized spreading the Word. Their missions in Europe supported an array of imaginations about a changing religious world. Fortunately, Hollinger uses a telling European example to show that he is aware of these dynamics, even if he does not think the European impact equaled the feedback gained in the majority world. He tells the story of a missionary youth – a product of American and European (Swiss-German, Bulgarian, Greek, and Turkish) cultures – who coined the term "multicultural" in 1941.[3]

This book, however, is not about American missionaries' changed conceptions about America after a tour of duty in Europe, even if it does claim that many Americans were alerted to Europe's secularity, and more aware than ever of America's religiosity. What this book does is elaborate on the new framework that transcends the widespread idea that Europe and the United States are moving in opposite religious directions. A group of historians under the supervision of David Hempton and Hugh McLeod have recently re-examined the transatlantic religious dynamics of secularization and religious innovation in the North Atlantic region. They looked at this phenomenon not as two separate trajectories, but as variations on small and large processes of

2 Charles Taylor, *A Secular Age* (Cambridge: Harvard University Press, 2007), 529-535.
3 Hollinger, *Protestants Abroad*, 22.

change in religious life in modern times. This book shows which forces and agents directly connected the two sides.[4]

Paradoxically, at the same time that these missionaries were establishing ties across the Atlantic they were also widening the gap by broadcasting the idea that Europe was rapidly losing faith, while America was opening up to it. The unprecedented atrocities of World War II had raised serious concerns among American Protestant elites about the religious and political future of their forebears' continent. They realized that Europe had proved to be morally incapable of resisting totalitarian attacks. This realization came as a shock, as up till then most Americans and Europeans believed that the transatlantic religious ventures were built on a strong common bond. Similar to war-time planning for relief, collective security, economic reform, and political stability, religious reconstruction became a shared global ideal. While American Protestant leaders were united in their concern for Europe's predicament, they greatly differed on how to order priorities to effect it. This disagreement created a second incentive for putting intense attention on religious Europe. The ecumenical movement, heavily sponsored by mainstream American Protestants, emphasized unity. Meanwhile, the new and growing formation of evangelicals feared marginalization and exclusion from the mission fields in Europe's colonies. These evangelicals also feared the separatist impulse flowing from the purity claims of fundamentalists; they were concerned that the fundamentalists would suck the blood out of the global revival that they anticipated. And in turn, the ecumenical leadership feared fragmentation, competition, and American religious hegemony on a large scale. What evangelicals and fundamentalists did share, was the conviction that an explicit proclamation of the traditional gospel would regenerate Europe. This they considered their most urgent business. Hence postwar Europe became the spiritual battleground for various American ideals.

As harmful as these internal divisions were for effectively healing the wounds of the war, they also spurred the different factions to get boots on the ground in Europe as quickly as possible. This meant engaging partners and building parallel international networks, as soon as the initial humanitarian aid had relieved the most pressing needs and established new channels of communication. These efforts marked a shift in the religious balance of power from a European advantage to an American one, similar to the shift in military, economic, and political relationships.

The American ecumenical community had begun preparing its agenda after World War I and was preoccupied with launching the World Council of Churches as a representative organization. Once World War II ended, its staff drafted basic theological statements, launched study groups, and coordinated

4 David Hempton and Hugh McLeod, eds., *Secularization and Religious Innovation in the North Atlantic World* (New York: Oxford University Press, 2017), 1-21.

relief operations with numerous international partners. Meanwhile, American evangelicals were still in the pioneering phase of defining themselves. Nevertheless, they were as eager to change the world, and were driven by high expectations of an imminent global revival, including in Europe. They concentrated their efforts on the practice of proclaiming the traditional gospel in every-day language and showing that the divine had immediate relevance.

This pioneering phase generated a wave of religious energy among American evangelicals that overwhelmed any sense of the perils of idealism that had heretofore handicapped all Christian traditions in America seeking to change the world. The evangelicals simplified the idea how culture works by cutting it loose from historical development. They underestimated the overlapping institutional network that characterizes how culture is organized, and they ignored the dynamic exchange between ideas and institutions. They overlooked the fact that culture exerts power in itself, and that it works mostly from the center to the margins. Therefore, as James Hunter has argued, most American Christian's expectation of change was unwarrantedly optimistic.[5]

The scramble for Europe by American evangelicals to establish networks for their global agenda prevented careful reflection on this potential hubris; the issue was simply too urgent. They first had to parry fundamentalist allegations of sleeping with the enemy, which they managed to do by the mid-1950s when they successfully disengaged from their accusers. American fundamentalism proved a hard sell to Europeans as they were put off by its blatant patriotism and paralyzing isolation. There was a growing European distrust of fundamentalism caused by its strict separatism and energy lost to fruitless polemical attacks and self-justifications. In contrast, evangelicals could showcase full stadiums and countless conversions.

The wide publicity for evangelical events in Europe was the result of the strategy to set-up shop outside the established religious institutions (though with support from local churches). American evangelicals convinced Europeans that they could stage impressive and massive religious spectacles using tested corporate methods to raise funds, recruit staff, and generate publicity. In these endeavors, they made robust use of modern media for instruction, channeling converts, and claiming results.

In contrast, those were things that American ecumenists could not do particularly well. Their strength lay in the decades of experience and training they had undergone to understand intercultural settings. They knew enough to be sensitive to the harmful implications of a structural power imbalance. They understood that in Europe, religious identity formation resulted from people characterizing themselves as belonging to a larger entity, often defined as "the nation" or "the culture". Self-identification with a religious tradition

5 James D. Hunter, *To Change the World: The Irony, Tragedy, and Possibility of Christianity in the Late Modern World* (New York: Oxford University Press, 2010), 26-27.

did not necessarily mean that a person engaged in (institutionalized) religious practices.[6] American evangelicals had a narrow definition of a true Christian that problematized nominal Christians. Fundamentalists, meanwhile, restricted their definition even further to the very few who would identify with all their ideas. Meanwhile ecumenists approached the various denominations in Europe on their own terms, even if they could not avoid designing a hierarchy of preferred and pliable partners, and even if they failed to create a viable transatlantic religious agenda that channelled American ideas to European issues, or vice versa.

Behind the many differences and the public rhetoric of mutual dislike and suspicion, evangelicals and ecumenists had shared concerns. In the 1940s and 1950s, they were both distressed by the lack of religious freedom in communist countries and in predominantly Catholic countries. Both called on the American diplomatic service to protect religious liberty and both institutionalized their operations in the 1950s. These religious organizations flourished and fit into the international community established by the United Nations, the World Health Organization, and the International Monetary Fund. Europe's future was secured thanks to the joint efforts of NATO and the budding European Community; Europe's speedy economic recovery restored prosperity. The religious nightmare of communist domination did not happen.

These improved conditions, however, did not automatically strengthen institutionalized religion. In fact religious crises multiplied in the 1960s. European churches faced three challenges: the implosion of membership, withdrawal from the social domain, and serious decline in authority and organization.[7] Mainline organizations responded with study groups, while the effect of the American evangelicals' response was ambiguous. On the one hand, they further undermined the authority of the established churches which they accused of inflexibility and stagnation, and they criticized the established churches' involvement in politics. On the other hand, they rejuvenated a sense of commitment by energizing the already motivated church members to recruit new members, with the plan that the newcomers would take over organizational roles after a period of training. With a focus on the young, they calculated that the next generation would continue their operations if they were sufficiently taught the established norms and ideas. Even though these activities did not fill the empty pews, they helped create a revitalization that was both innovative and familiar. Evangelicals were good at incorporating popular music, at designing specific training programs for particular sections of the population, and for sharing responsibility with lay people, especially

6 Anne-Marie Kool, "Revisiting Mission in, to and from Europe Through Contemporary Image Formation," in Charles Van Engen, ed., *The State of Missiology Today* (Downers Grove, IL: Intervarsity Press, 2016), 241-242.

the young. And if that weren't enough, they were masters in the use of mass media. These results did not go unnoticed.

During the 1960s, American evangelicals created a network parallel to the World Council of Churches and reconsidered their previous categorical rejection of social involvement. By mid-decade the term evangelical had found public recognition in Europe as a significant religious identifier. As evangelicals brought together many supporters in parachurch organizations that transcended the confinement of parish boundaries and national territories, cross-cultural activities came naturally. By this time, the ecumenical movement recognized the evangelicals as global players. Therefore, the 1960s were not only a period of polarization, but also of rapprochement; ecumenists re-discovered evangelism and evangelicals remembered the importance of social issues.

This admittedly slow trend towards convergence continued in the 1970s as evangelicals in Europe appeared poised to stay. They had secured a structural presence from which to professionalize their operations and had overcome any anxiety connected to their possible exclusion. The consolidation and accreditation of their educational institutions secured their continued presence in religious training programs. Lay people were trained in evangelism and ideas spread through international conferences and a stream of publications – all outside of the vestiges of academic theology. These structures and practices resulted in deepened transatlantic religious ties.

An American survey of the global evangelical family in 1980 revealed that Western Europe had become a full member of this clan. The chair of the European Evangelical Alliance identified Europe's greatest need as cooperation to bring about a revival that would serve as an antidote to churches entrenched in well-worn religious traditions. The proposed solution was to link local sympathizers through worship, witness, and service. Europeans realized that the Graham "raids" had only a temporary effect and they moved to find creative solutions on their own turf using new modes of art and media to contact other cultures, especially among the young. They were critical of American intervention. A European spokesperson concluded: "A great deal of damage has been done by outsiders by attempts to meet the needs of Europe without allowing for the subtle distinctions and differences which are accepted by those whose culture it is."[8] The time had arrived when Europeans needed to organize their own events.

The result of these American initiatives did not usher in the hoped-for revival that would change the religious map of Europe, nor did they stop the

7 Patrick Pasture, "Christendom and the Legacy of the Sixties: Between the Secular City and the Age of Aquarius," *Revue d'Histoire Ecclésiastique* 99.1 (2004): 82-117, esp. 83.

8 A. Morgan Derham, "Evangelical Perspectives in Western Europe," in Waldron Scott, ed., *Serving Our Generation: Evangelical Strategies for the Eighties* (Colorado Springs, CO: World Evangelical Fellowship, 1980), 87-96.

decline of church membership nor the loss in the public role of religion. What they did do was to strengthen the voluntary networks and new religious communities that had more informal structures. They helped to mainstream evangelicalism and created a new identity marker that connected believers to a global network. In doing so, this new identity transcended the boundaries of national identity within Europe as well as in North America. It also created an image of what regular American-Protestant religion entailed as a correction of the common fascination by extreme events, even if what was presented was mostly a white male, middle-class version. Most of the religious rhetoric remained masculine, martial, and managerial, even though half of the missionary staff in Europe was female. Sarah Ruble has shown in her *The Gospel of Freedom and Power: Protestant Missionaries in American Culture After World War II*, that this male identity reflected typical gender relations among American evangelicals and matched the masculine identity created by the American state to impress others with its authority. As religious groups tried to address the world with a similar authority, there was hardly any debate about men occupying what was considered the most strategic positions. Since both political and religious issues were defined by the same terms used in battle, women were encouraged to "close ranks" and submit themselves to male leadership. The attention paid to the space carved out by married and single female missionaries added another aspect of the (very slowly) growing pluralism in the mission efforts. Evangelical female missionaries were able to contribute to the purpose-driven agenda of restoring traditional Christianity in Europe. Their slow, yet serious, acceptance nevertheless proved timely, as the issues raised by second-wave feminism were being acknowledged by the churches during that epoch.[9] Further research on evangelical women in the 1980s and 1990s, will have to deal with women as indispensable agents – for that is what they were.

These insights lead to two questions: first, did the recognition of Europe as a mission field, both by American senders and European receivers, foretell the arrival of missionaries from non-Western countries, in Europe first, but also in North America? And secondly, did the European experience with the American "agents of change" encourage Americans to re-evaluate their optimistic assessment of their own agencies?

The first question can be answered affirmatively, though the link is indirect rather than direct. The return mission from North America indicated the change in status of Europe from a region sending missionaries to a continent

9 Sarah E. Ruble, *The Gospel of Freedom and Power: Protestant Missionaries in American Culture After World War II* (Chapel Hill: The University of North Carolina Press, 2014), 11.

receiving missionaries. Further explorations as to the exact process are left to others.[10]

An answer to the second question requires more systematic research on the historical reflection of the mission agencies. Reconsidering agency fits in with Jay R. Case's conclusion about the "unpredictable gospel" American missionaries in Asia and Africa experienced during the nineteenth century. Case asserts that these "missionaries were almost always lousy at converting large numbers of non-Westerners." Curiously, this was true for Westerners in twentieth-century Europe as well. Similar to the nineteenth century, however, the missionaries were able to provide ideals, instruments, and strategies for Europeans to be utilized in their own evangelism.[11] Case decided that, "evangelistic success emerged more often when missionaries operated from positions of weakness," not when they were allied with imperial powers. As well, he noted that anti-formalist missions were able to flourish because they tapped into the institutional structures and resources of formal churches and missions. One might argue that as remarkable as this postwar episode of transatlantic missions was, it, in fact, followed historical patterns.

Eventually, new cultural lenses were necessary to understand American evangelists in Europe. Their limited success rate was likely caused by the strength of other loyalties, whether national or subcultural. In Portugal, for example, it was hard for non-Catholics to be considered good citizens. In France the dispute between Catholic and anti-clerical republican subcultures required strong loyalty, and any alternative religious choice was a hard sell as it weakened one's camp. In pillarized societies like the Netherlands, chances were better. The groups were less antagonistic and more accommodating, especially among those who were tired of the militancy, internal discipline, and goals that seemed obscure. But the best opportunity for recruiting and converting people remained in pluralist societies like the United Kingdom where religious and nationalist loyalties were less compelling, and crossing lines was more acceptable.[12] But realizing where their successes lay and knowing why something succeeded could only be articulated after a round of discovery, expectation, organization, work, meeting, and letting go. Though the missionaries completed that cycle in the post war era, it is probably not the last time a sequence of the same type will be followed.

10 Stefan Paas, "Evangelistic Mission in Europe: Seven Historical Models," in Gerrit Noort, Kyriaki Avtzi, and Stefan Paas, eds., *Sharing Good News: Handbook on Evangelism in Europe* (Geneva: World Council of Churches Publications, 2017), 21-35.

11 Jay Riley Case, *An Unpredictable Gospel: American Evangelicals and World Christianity* (New York: Oxford University Press, 2012), 7-8.

12 Hugh McLeod, " 'Religious America, Secular Europe': Are They Really So Different?" in McLeod and Hempton, *Secularization*, 329-350 and Grace Davie, "Religion, Territory, and Choice: Contrasting Configurations, 1970-2015," 309-326.

ABBREVIATIONS

ACCC American Council of Christian Churches
BGCA Billy Graham Center Archives
BGEA Billy Graham Evangelical Association
CBFMS Conservative Baptist Foreign Mission Society
CCC Campus Crusade for Christ
DEA Deutsche Evangelische Allianz
EAUK Evangelical Alliance, United Kingdom
EEA European Evangelical Alliance
EFMA Evangelical Foreign Missions Association; after 1992 Evangelical Fellowship of Mission Agencies
FCC Federal Council of Churches
GEM Greater Europe Mission
ICCC International Council of Christian Churches
IFMA Interdenominational Foreign Missionary Association
IMC International Missionary Council
MBI Moody Bible Institute
NAE National Association of Evangelicals
NCC National Council of Churches
TEAM The Evangelical Alliance Mission
UCC United Church of Christ
UEA United Evangelical Action
UPC United Presbyterian Church
WCA Wheaton College Archives
WCC World Council of Churches
WEA World Evangelical Alliance
WEF World Evangelical Fellowship
YFC Youth for Christ

BIBLIOGRAPHY

Primary Sources

Amsterdam, Netherlands
Historical Documentation Center for Dutch Protestantism, Vrije Universiteit Amsterdam
Dommisse family Collection inv. 76.
T.B. van Houten Collection inv. 485.
C. Veenhof Collection inv. 296.
Municipal Archives Amsterdam
Archief van het Nederlands Billy Graham Comité, inv. 1217.
Bad Blankenburg, Germany
Deutsche Evangelische Allianz
Billy Graham Korrespondent 1954.
Billy Graham 1955.
File Billy Graham, 1960-1987.
Prot. Allianz Sitz 1960-1968.
Niederschriften von HV Sitzungen 1960-1966.
Allianz Protokolle, 1967-1979.
File Billy Graham Oct. 1966 (-1968).
WEF 1981-1989.
Carroll Stream, Illinois, USA
The Evangelical Alliance Mission archives
Annual Reports France.
Portugal field files and general files 1951-1962.
Chicago, Illinois
Moody Bible Institute Archives, Departmental Missions
MBI Archives, Annual Reports Educational Department, 1953-1955.
Culbertson Collection.
Foreign Missionary Reports, 1951, 1966, 1979.
Catalogue Moody Bible Institute, 1969, 1975-1976.
Geneva, Switzerland
World Council of Churches
Inventory 26.19.10 Miscellaneous papers, 1933-1961.
Leuven, Belgium
KADOC-KU Leuven
Evadoc Protestants-Evangelisch Archief- en Documentatiecentrum.
Archief Belgische Evangelische Zending/ Belgian Gospel Mission (1900 (c) -2009.
London, United Kingdom
Evangelical Alliance Archives
Gordon Landreth Archives
Minutes of the meeting of the executive council of the Evangelical Alliance, 1950-1960.
Minutes of the Billy Campaign, 1953-1955.
Middelburg, the Netherlands
Roosevelt Institute for American Studies
OSS/State Department Intelligence and Research Reports, Europe, 1950-1991 Supplement, Intelligence Report, Portuguese Background Series No 6180.4.
Spanish Background Series No 6098.10.
Philadelphia, Pennsylvania, USA
Presbyterian Historical Society (PHS)
RG 118 Records of the American and Foreign Christian Union
RG 480 Donald G. Barnhouse Collection
6.12 Graham, Billy, 1951, 1953, 1960.
7.28 National Association of Evangelicals, 1942-1944.
7.29 National Association of Evangelicals, 1952-1955.
7.30 National Association of Evangelicals - "Admirals and Generals" booklet, 1937-1941.

7.31 National Association of Evangelicals - Evangelical Foreign Missions Association, 1952-1962.
15.3 Barnhouse, Donald Grey - Europe, circa 1960s.
15.4 Europe and early United States ministry, 1919-1926.
15.9 Barnhouse, Donald Grey - Life in Europe and the United States, circa 1920s.
RG 360 III Personal files of Presbyterian Missionaries in Europe
Charles William and Eugenie Arbuthnot.
Katharina van Drimmelen.
Hedwig and Robert Clare Lodwick.
United Presbyterian Church
RG 139 Commission on Ecumenical Mission and Relations. Office of the General Secretary.
John C. Smith Series 4: Malone Consultations, 1962-1970.
Box 12 file 20-30 1960-70 and Papers presented at Consultation, 1962-67.
RG 209 REEL 110: 50 Evangelical Alliance Mission, 1945-1953.
RG 301.2 Box 15 file 10-12 Youth - Study on European Youth, 1967-1969.
National Council of Churches
RG 6 Division of Christian Life and Mission, 1945-1973, Series II Department of international Affairs, 1950-1972
17.4 Council on Religion and International Affairs.
18.12 Christian Study Group for European Unity, 1954-1969.
18.13 Correspondence Eleanor Roosevelt 27 May 1953.
19.19 Ecumenical Commission for European Cooperation 1951-1954.
19.23 Bilheimer, Conference of European Churches 1967-1969.
25.1 US Government-State Department.
25.2 US Government: AID; USIA; FBI; Government-Church Relations.
25.10 Van Kirk, 21 June - 30 Aug. 1952.
33.1 American Churches and International Affairs, October 1953.
36.13 Church-State Materials: Mennonite; National Association of Evangelicals.
57.1-6 Committee on Evangelism. Minutes, 1950-1962.
57.7 Executive Committee Minutes, 1951, 1954-1960; Correspondence, 1954-1957.
57.19 “A”; “B”; Bader, J.M.; Billy Graham Conf. on Evangelism.
58.13 Workshop-Consultation on Evangelism, 1957.
58.14 Workshop-Consultation on Evangelism, 1958.
58.15 Workshops on Campus Evangelism, 1957-1958.
58.6 Committee Minutes, 1937-1940.
64.20 NAE students.
RG 8 Division of Overseas Ministries Records
90-91 Europe Files, 1943-1949.
98-99 Europe, 1949-1951.
100-101 Europe, 1952.
104 Europe Files, 1955.
105 Europe Files, Scattered, 1957-1961.
113 Middle East & Europe, 1955-1971.
RG 19 International Council of Religious Education Records
7.14 Evangelical Fellowships, 1946.
18.20 National Association of Evangelicals, May 1945.
Call nr 161B (uprocessed) Presbyterian Church in the USA Board of Foreign Missions, Europe Mission and United Presbyterian Church in the USA Commission on Ecumenical Mission and Relations. Europe Mission, 1906-1972
Princeton, New Jersey USA
Princeton Theological Seminary
Carl C. McIntire Manuscript Collection (col. 222)
Box 11 files 1-7 Subseries 1:2: Correspondence Dr. J. C. Maris.
Box 19 files 23-26 Correspondence Arie Kok.
Box 22 files 20-21 Correspondence Schaeffer, Rev. Francis A.
Box 135 files 17 and 18 McIntire and Maris.
Box 165 file 44 Maris.
Box 170 file 20 Bolten, John 1944-1951.
Box 193 file 33 Schaeffer.
Box 201 files 16-19 Maris.
Box 203 file 24 Borkent.
Box 204 files 14-22 Schaeffer family 1948-1952.
Box 246 file 9 Schaeffer, Rev. Francis A. 1958.
Box 249 files 43-47 Wright, J. Elwin 1941-1947.
Box 296 files 19-26 WCC First Assembly, Amsterdam, Holland, 22 August-4 September 1948.
Box 299 files 29-30.
Box 304 file 30 Minutes of Meetings at the First Congress of the ICCC, Amsterdam, 1948.
Box 327 files 1-14.
Box 340 file 57 Europe, Middle East - Eicher/Maris.

Box 343 file 13 Commission on Lay People, Rev. Francis Schaeffer, Chairman 1950-1954.
Box 359 file 17 ACCC - European Tour.
Box 402 file 4.
Box 412 (no file No) IBPFM - Champery, Switzerland - Schaeffer, Rev. and Mrs. Francis A.
Box 546 file 18 A Testimony in Europe: Travel Letters on Missions by Carl McIntire.

Wheaton, Illinois, USA
The Billy Graham Center Archives, Wheaton College
Collection 20 Papers of Herbert J. Taylor, 1916-1979.
Collection 24 BGEA: Records of Billy Graham News Conferences, 1963-1985.
Collection 48 Records of Youth for Christ/USA, 1944-ongoing.
Collection 141 BGEA: Oral Histories and Manuscripts Project, 1970-2004.
Collection 165 Records of Evangelical Fellowship of Mission Agencies, 1937-1996.
Collection 171 Papers of Albert E. and Mary Lee Bobby, 1953-1982.
Collection 182 J. Herbert and Winnifred M. Kane, 1934-1987.
Collection 216 Oral History Interview with Horst Marquardt, 1929-1982.
Collection 218 Records of the Evangelical Missions Information Service, 1964-1981.
Collection 224 The Papers of J. Stratton Shufelt, 1930-1979.
Collection 228 Oral History Interview with Lyndon Roth Hess, 1927-1982.
Collection 285 Papers of Torrey Maynard Johnson, 1919-2001.
Collection 317 Oral History Interview with Ian H. and Ruth E. Cook, 1931-1985.
Collection 338 Records of the World Evangelical Fellowship, 1926-1992.
Collection 352 Records of the Interdenominational Foreign Mission Association (IFMA), 1934-1983.
Collection 360 Billy Graham Evangelistic Association Clippings File.
Collection 506 Decision Magazine, 1954-1987.
Collection 658 Papers of Samuel D. Faircloth, 1949-2011.

Oral histories/interviews

Cook, Ruth Witmer (missionary) by Paul Ericksen in Fort Wayne Indiana on 1 October 1985. Transcript BGCA Collection 317-T3.
Glasser Arthur F. (missionary leader) by Bob Shuster. Transcript BGCA col. CN 421, tape T8.
Page, Sarah (US missionary in France) by author, 25 February, 20 March and 2 April 2013 (by e-mail).
Rookmaaker, Hendrik (Dutch art historian), by J.J. van Capelleveen, August 1971. [His full name was Henderik Roelof, but he was called Hans]. Rookmaaker Transcript Collection 141-BGEA: Oral History Project, The Netherlands 29-24.
Schneider, Peter (German organizer for the Billy Graham campaigns, 1993) by Lois Ferm. Transcript Col 141 BGEA Oral History Project, box 62 file 13.
Vajko, Robert J. (US missionary in France) by author on 24 September 2012, Carol Stream, IL.
van Heusden, Arnold, and Edward de Kam (former directors of YFC-Holland), by author, Driebergen, the Netherlands, 13 December 2007.
Wlochacz, Bronek (program manager of the Dutch Evangelical Broadcasting Company Evangelische Omroep) by author, telephone conversation on 28 January 2010.

Periodicals

Arch (Moody's yearbook) The 1947.
Christianity and Crisis 1943.
Christianity Today 1956-1966.
Church Journal, The (New York) 1874.
Evangelisches Allianzblatt 1966-1972.
Greater Europe Report 1974-1980.
IFMA News Bulletin 1951-1963.
International Review of Missions (from April 1969 *International Review of Mission*) 1960-1980.
King's Business, The 1940-1947.
Moody Church News, The 1940-1946.
Moody Student 1948-1970.
Occasional Bulletin of Missionary Research 1960-1970.
Over There with the Churches of Christ 1940-1945.
Prophetic Word, The 1940-1950.
United Evangelical Action 1945-1948, 1966.
Youth for Christ Magazine, 1945-1953.

Published sources and literature

Ahlstrom, Sydney. *A Religious History of the American People*. New Haven, CT: Yale University Press, 1970.

Anders, Jarlert. *The Oxford Group, Group Revivalism, and the Churches in Northern Europe, 1930-1945, with Special Reference to Scandinavia and Germany*. Lund: Lund University Press, 1995.

Arnold, Glenn F. "A Comparative Study of the Present Doctrinal Positions and Christian Conduct Codes of Selected Alumni of Moody Bible Institute: 1945-1971." PhD diss., New York University, 1977.

Balbier, Uta. "Billy Graham in Berlin: German Protestantism between Americanization and Rechristianization." *Zeithistorische Forschungen / Studies in Contemporary History*, Online-Ausgabe 7 (2010) H.3. <www.zeit-historische-forschungen.de/16126041-Balbier-3-2010>.

Balbier, Uta "'Youth for Christ' in England und Deutschland: Religiöser Transnationalismus und christliche Nachkriegsordnung." *Archiv für Socialgeschichte* 51 (2011): 209-224.

Balbier, Uta A. "The World Congress on Evangelism 1966 in Berlin: US Evangelicalism, Cultural Dominance, and Global Challenges." *Journal of American Studies* 51 (2017): 1171-1196.

Bank, Jan with Lieve Gevers. *Churches and Religion in the Second World War.* Translated by Brian Doyle. London: Bloomsbury Academic, 2016.

Barton, H. Arnold. *A Folk Divided: Homeland Swedes and Swedish Americans, 1840-1940*. Carbondale, IL: Southern Illinois University Press, 1994.

Bauer, Gisa. *Evangelikale Bewegung und evangelische Kirche in der Bundesrepublik Deutschland: Geschichte eines Grundsatzkonflikts (1945 bis 1989)*. Göttingen: Vandenhoeck & Ruprecht, 2012.

Beaver, Pierce R. "Distribution of the American Protestant Foreign Missionary Force in 1952." *Occasional Bulletin from the Missionary Research Library* 4.10 (1953): 1-3.

Beaver, Pierce R. "The Expansion of American Foreign Missionary Activities Since 1945." *Occasional Bulletin from the Missionary Research Library* 5.7 (4 June 1954): 5-6.

Bebbington, David W. "Moody as a Transatlantic Evangelical." In Timothy George, ed. *Mr Moody and the Evangelical Tradition.* London: Continuum Books, 2005, 75-91.

Berg, Thomas C. "'Proclaiming Together?' Convergence and Divergence in Mainline and Evangelical Evangelism 1945-1967." *Religion and American Culture* 5 (1995): 49-76.

Berger, Peter, Grace Davie, and Effie Fokas. *Religious America, Secular Europe? A Theme and Variations*. Aldershot/Burlington VT: Ashgate, 2008.

Bergler, Thomas E. *The Juvenilization of American Christianity.* Grand Rapids, MI: Eerdmans, 2012.

Billiet, Jaak, Leo Kenis, and Patrick Pasture, eds. *The Transformation of the Christian Churches in Western Europe: 1945-2000*. Leuven: Leuven University Press, 2010.

Bjork, David E. *Unfamiliar Paths: The Challenge of Recognizing the Work of Christ in Strange Clothing: A Case Study from France*. Pasadena: William Carey Library, 1997.

Bonomi, Patricia. *Under the Cope of Heaven: Religion, Society, and Politics in Colonial America*. New York: Oxford University Press, 1986.

Boy, John D. "Blessed Disruption: Culture and Urban Space in a European Church Planting Network." Ph.D. dissertation, City University of New York, 2015.

Boyer, Paul. *When Time Shall Be No More: Prophecy Belief in Modern American Culture*. Cambridge: Harvard University Press, 1994.

Bratt, James D. "Protestant Immigrants and the Protestant Mainstream." In Jonathan Sarna, ed. *Minority Faiths and the American Protestant Mainstream*. Urbana: University of Illinois Press, 1998, 110-135.

Bratt, James D. ed. *Antirevivalism in Antebellum America: A Collection of Religious Voices*. New Brunswick, NJ: Rutgers University Press, 2006.

Brereton, Virginia Lieson. *Training God's Army: The American Bible School, 1880-1940*. Bloomington: Indiana University Press, 1990. 57-58.

Broeke, Leon van den, Hans Krabbendam, and Dirk Mouw, eds. *Transatlantic Pieties: Dutch Clergy in Colonial America*. Grand Rapids, MI: Eerdmans, 2012.

Brown, Callum G. and Michael Snape, eds. *Secularisation in the Christian World: Essays in Honour of Hugh McLeod.* Farnham, UK: Ashgate, 2010.

Buchman, Frank D. *Remaking the World.* London: Blandford Press, 1947.

Butler, Jon. *New World Faiths: Religion in Colonial America.* New York: Oxford University Press, 2008.

Callaway, Timothy Wray. "Training Disciplined Soldiers for Christ: the influence of American Fundamentalism at Prairie Bible Institute during the L.E. Maxwell Era. 1922-1980." Th.D. Dissertation, Pretoria: University of South Africa, 2010.

Calleo, David. *Europe's Future: The Grand Alternatives*. New York: Horizon, 1965.

Carpenter, Joel, ed. *The Youth for Christ Movement and Its Pioneers*. New York: Garland Publishing, 1988.

Carpenter, Joel A. *Revive Us Again: The Reawakening of American Fundamentalism*. New York: Oxford University Press, 1993.

Carpenter, Joel and Wilbert R. Shenk, eds. *Earthen Vessels: American Evangelicals and Foreign Missions, 1880-1980*. Eugene, OR: Wipf and Stock Publishers, 2012.

Case, Jay Riley. *An Unpredictable Gospel: American Evangelicals and World Christianity*. New York: Oxford University Press, 2012.

Cauthen, Baker James and Frank K. Means. *Advance to Bold Mission Trust, 1945-1980*. Foreign Mission Board of the Southern Baptist Convention, 1981.

Chard, G. R. "A history of the French Mission of the Church of Jesus Christ of Latter-day Saints, 1850-1960." M.A. thesis, Logan, Utah: Utah State University, Merrill-Cazier Library 1965.

Chaves, Marc. *American Religion: Contemporary Trends*. Princeton: Princeton University Press, 2011.

Cook, Harold R. *An Introduction to the Study of Christian Missions*. Chicago: Moody Press, 1954.

Coote, Robert T. "Finger on the Pulse: Fifty Years of Missionary Research." *The Free Library* 24.3 (1 July 2000), 98-105.

Corrigan, John and Frank Hinkelmann, eds. *Return to Sender: American Evangelical Missions in Twentieth Century Europe*. Zürich: LIT-Verlag, 2019.

Crouse, Eric R. "Popular Cold Warriors: Conservative Protestants, Communism, and Culture in Early Cold War America." *Journal of Religion and Popular Culture* 2 (Fall 2002): 1-18.

Curti, Merle. *American Philanthropy Abroad: A History*. New Brunswick, NJ: Rutgers University Press, 1988.

Curtis, Heather D. " 'God Is Not Affected by the Depression': Pentecostal Missions during the 1930s." *Church History* 80 (2011): 579-589.

Davies, Grace. "Religion, Territory, and Choice: Contrasting Configurations, 1970-2015." In David Hempton and Hugh McLeod, eds. *Secularization and Religious Innovation in the North Atlantic World*. New York: Oxford University Press, 2017, 309-326.

Dayton, Edward R., ed. *Mission Handbook: North American Protestant Ministries Overseas*. 11th ed. New York: Missions Advanced Research and Communication Center, 1976.

Decoo, Wilfried. "Mormons in Europe." In Terryl L. Givens and Philip L. Barlow, eds. *The Oxford Handbook of Mormonism*. New York: Oxford University Press, 2015, 543-557.

Dekker, Gerard. *Een moeizaam gevecht. Mijn geschiedenis met de kerk*. Hilversum: Verloren, 2005.

DePriest, Jon P. *Send the Light: TEAM and the Evangelical Mission*. Bloomington, IN: AuthorHouse, 2007.

Detzler, Wayne A. *The Changing Church in Europe*. Grand Rapids, MI: Zondervan, 1979.

Dochuk, Darren. "Evangelicalism." In Philip Goff, ed. *Blackwell Companion to Religion in America*. Chichester: Blackwell Publishing, 2010, 540-558.

Dochuk, Darren. *From Bible Belt to Sunbelt: Plain-Folk Religion, Grassroots Politics, and the Rise of Evangelical Conservatism*. New York: Norton, 2010.

Douglas, J.D., ed. *Let the Earth Hear His Voice*. Minneapolis: World Wide Publications, 1975.

Drury, Marjule Anne. "Anti-Catholicism in Germany, Britain, and the United States: A Review and Critique of Recent Scholarship." *Church History: Studies in Christianity and Culture* 70.1 (March 2001): 98-131.

Dudley-Smith, Timothy. *John Stott: A Global Ministry: A Biography the Later Years*. Downers Grove, IL: InterVarsity Press, 2001.

Ekbladh, David. *The Great American Mission: Modernization and the Construction of an American World Order*. Princeton: Princeton University Press, 2010.

Ellwood, David W. *The Shock of America: Europe and the Challenge of the Century*. Oxford, UK: Oxford University Press, 2012.

Engel, Katherine Carté. "The SPCK and the American Revolution: The Limits of International Protestantism." *Church History* 81.1 (2012): 77-103.

Enns, James. "Sustaining the Faithful and Proclaiming the Gospel in a Time of Crisis: The Voice of Popular Evangelical Periodicals During the Second World War." In L. Guenther, ed. *Historical Papers 2004*. N.p.: Canadian Society of Church History, 2004, 113-132.

Enns, James C. "Saving Germany: North American Protestants and Christian Mission to West Germany, 1945-1974." Ph.D. dissertation, Cambridge University, 2012.

Eriksen, Sidsel. "Drunken Danes and Sober Swedes? Religious Revivalism and the Temperance Movements as Keys to Danish and Swedish Folk Cultures." In Bo Strath, ed. *Language and the Construction of Class Identities: The Struggle for Discursive Power in Social Organization, Scandinavia and Germany after 1800*. Gothenburg: Gothenburg University, 1990, 55-94.

Eskridge, Larry. *God's Forever Family: The Jesus People Movement in America*. New York: Oxford University Press, 2013.

Erskine, Larry and Mark A. Noll, eds. *More Money, More Ministry: Money and Evangelicals in Recent North American History*. Grand Rapids: Eerdmans, 2000.

Espinosa, Gaston. *William J. Seymour and the Origins of Global Pentecostalism: A Biography and Documentary History*. Durham, NC: Duke University Press, 2014.

Etherington, Norman, ed. *Missions and Empire*. Oxford: Oxford University Press, 2008.

Evangelicals in the Low Countries. Special issue *Trajecta* 26.2 (2017).

Evangelist's Presbyterian Pilgrimage: Sailing per specially chartered steamer Berlin of the American line, June 26th, 1895: visiting the chief centers of Presbyterian interest in Ireland, Scotland, England, Germany, Belgium, and Holland. The [New York: The Evangelist Company, 1895].

Evans, Robert P. *Let Europe Hear: The Spiritual Plight of Europe*. Chicago: Moody Press, 1963.

Fath, Sébastien. "La reception de Billy Graham en France (1954-1986)." In Sébastien Fath, ed. *Le protestantisme* évangélique, *un christianisme de conversion: entre rupture et filiations. Actes du colloque international organisé à Paris (Iresco, EPHE Sorbonne) par le Group de Sociologie des Religions et de la Laïcité (EPHE/CNRS) du 14 au 16 mars 2002*. Turnhout: Brepols, 2004.

Fath, Sébastien. "Evangelical Protestantism in France: An Example of Denominational Recomposition?" *Sociology of Religion* 66.4 (2005): 399-418.

Ferguson, Niall, Charles S. Maier, Erez Manela, Daniel J. Sargent, eds. *The Shock of the Global: The 1970s in Perspective*. Cambridge: The Belknap Press of Harvard University, 2010.

Ferré, John P. "Searching for the Great Commission: Evangelical Book Publishing since the 1970s." In Quentin J. Schultze, ed. *American Evangelicals and the Mass Media: Perspectives on the Relationship Between American Evangelicals and the Mass Media*. Grand Rapids, MI: Zondervan Academie Books, 1990, 99-117.

Finzel, Hans, ed. *Partners Together: 50 Years of Global Impact - The CBFMS Story*. Wheaton, IL: Conservative Baptist Foreign Mission Society, 1993.

Fisher, Allan. "Evangelical-Christian Publishing. Where it's Been and Where it is Going." *Publishing Research Quarterly* 14.3 (1998): 3-11.

Fortner, Robert S. "Internationalizing Evangelical Media." In Quentin J. Schultze and Robert H. Woods Jr., eds. *Understanding Evangelical Media: The Changing Face of Christian Communication*. Downers Grove, IL: IVP Academic, 2008, 239-251.

Fortner, Robert S. "Media." In Philip Goff, ed. *The Blackwell Companion to Religion in America*. Malden, MA: Wiley, 2010, 206-214.

Frank, Walter. *North American Protestant Foreign Mission Agencies*. New York: Missionary Research Library, 1964.

Frankel, Robert P. *Observing America: The Commentary of British Visitors to the United States, 1890-1950*. Madison: University of Wisconsin Press, 2007.

Fuller, W.H. *People of the Mandate: The Story of the World Evangelical Fellowship*. Grand Rapids, MI: Baker Book House, 1996.

Gaustad, Edwin S. *Proclaim Liberty Throughout All the Land: A History of Church and State in America*. New York: Oxford University Press, 2003.

Getz, Gene A. *MBI: The Story of Moody Bible Institute*. Chicago: Moody Press, 1969.

Gjerde, Jon. "The Perils of 'Freedom' in the American Immigrant Church." In Todd Nichol, ed. *Crossings: Norwegian-American Lutheranism as Transatlantic Tradition*. Northfield, MN: Norwegian Historical Association, 2003, 3-29.

Glad, Johnnie. "Proclaiming the Message: A Comparison of Mormon Missionary Strategy with other Christian Missions." *International Journal of Mormon Studies* 2 (Spring 2009): 142-168.

Gloege, Timothy. *Guaranteed Pure: The Moody Bible Institute, Business, and the Making of Modern Evangelicalism*. Chapel Hill: The University of North Carolina Press, 2015.

Goeckel, Robert F. "German and American Churches: Changes in Actors, Priorities, and Power Relations." In Detlef Junker, Philipp Gassert, Wilfried Mausbach, eds. *The United States and Germany in the Era of the Cold War, 1945-1990: A Handbook. Volume 2, 1968-1990.* New York: Cambridge University Press, 2004, 466-473.

Goodall, Norman. *Missions under the cross: addresses delivered at the enlarged Meeting of the Committee of the International missionary council at Willingen, in Germany, 1952; with statements issued by the Meeting.* London: Edinburgh House Press, 1953.

Goodall, Norman. *Christian Ambassador: A Life of A. Livingston Warnshuis.* Manhasset, NY: Channel Press, 1963.

Graham, Billy. *Just as I am: The Autobiography of Billy Graham.* New York: HarperCollins/Zondervan, 1997.

Green, Abigail and Vincent Viaene, eds. *Religious Internationals in the Modern World: Globalization and Faith Communities since 1750.* Basingstoke: Palgrave Macmillan, 2012.

Greene, Alison Collis. "The End of the 'Protestant Era'?" *Church History* 80.3 (September 2011): 600-610.

Gregory, Jeremy. "Transatlantic Anglican Networks, c.1680-c.1770: Transplanting, Translating and Transforming the Church of England." In Jeremy Gregory and Hugh McLeod, eds. *International Religious Networks.* Woodbridge: The Boydell Press/Ecclesiastical History Society, 2012, 127-142.

Gregory, Jeremy and Hugh McLeod, eds. *International Religious Networks.* Woodbridge: The Boydell Press/Ecclesiastical History Society, 2012.

Gribben, Crawford. *Evangelical Millennialism in the Trans-Atlantic World, 1500-2000.* Basingstoke: Palgrave Macmillan, 2011.

Grossman, Johannes. "Ein Europa der 'Hintergründigen': Antikommunistische christliche Organisationen, konservatieve Elitenzirkel and private Aussenpolitik in Westeuropa nach dem Zweiten Weltkrieg." In Johannes Wienand and Christiane Wienand, eds. *Die kulturelle Integration Europas.* Wiesbaden: Springer, 2010, 303-340.

Haanes, Vidar L. "Pastors for the Congregations." In Todd Nichol, ed. *Crossings: Norwegian-American Lutheranism as Transatlantic Tradition.* Northfield, MN: Norwegian Historical Association, 2003, 93-118.

Hammond, Sarah Ruth (edited by Darren Dochuk). *'God's Business Men': Entrepreneurial Evangelicals in Depression and War.* Chicago: University of Chicago Press, 2017.

Handy, Robert T. "The American Religious Depression, 1925-1935." *Church History* 29 (1960): 3-16.

Hangen, Tona. *Redeeming the Dial: Radio, Religion, and Popular Culture in America.* Chapel Hill: University of North Carolina Press, 2002.

Hankins, Barry. *Francis Schaeffer and the Shaping of Evangelical America.* Grand Rapids, MI: Eerdmans, 2008.

Harinck, George and Hans Krabbendam, eds. *A Spiritual Invasion? Amerikaanse invloeden op het Nederlandse christendom.* Barneveld: De Vuurbaak, 2010.

Harris, W. Stuart. *Eyes on Europe.* Chicago: Moody Press, 1965.

Hart, D.G. *Defending the Faith: J. Gresham Machen and the Crisis of Conservative Protestantism in Modern America.* Baltimore: Johns Hopkins University Press, 1994.

Hart, D.G. and John R. Muether. *Seeking a Better Country: 300 Years of American Presbyterianism.* Phillipsburg, NJ: P and R Publishing, 2007.

Hartman, Andrew. *A War for the Soul of America: A History of the Culture Wars.* Chicago: University of Chicago Press, 2015.

Hempton, David. *Methodism: Empire of the Spirit.* New Haven, CT: Yale University Press, 2005.

Hempton, David. "International Religious Networks: Methodism and Popular Protestantism, c.1750-1850." In Jeremy Gregory and Hugh McLeod, eds. *International Religious Networks.* Woodbridge: The Boydell Press/Ecclesiastical History Society, 2012, 143-164.

Hempton, David and Hugh McLeod, eds. *Secularization and Religious Innovation in the North Atlantic World.* New York: Oxford University Press, 2017.

Henry, Carl F.H. and W. Stanley Mooneyham, eds. *One Race One Gospel One Task. World Congress on Evangelism Berlin 1966. Official Reference volumes: Papers and Reports.* 2 vols. Minneapolis: World Wide Publications, 1967.

Herzog, Jonathan P. *The Spiritual-Industrial Complex: America's Religious Battle against Communism in the Early Cold War.* New York: Oxford University Press, 2011.

Hinkelmann, Frank. "Die Glaubensbasis der Europäischen Evangelische Allianz". Unpublished paper Theological University Apeldoorn April 2005.

Hinkelmann, Frank. *Die Evangelikale Bewegung in Österreich. Grundzüge ihrer historischen und theologischen Entwicklung 1945-1998*. Bonn: Verlag für Kultur und Wissenschaft, 2014.

Hollinger, David A. *After Cloven Tongues of Fire: Protestant Liberalism in Modern American History*. Princeton: Princeton University Press, 2013.

Hollinger, David A. *Protestants Abroad: How Missionaries Tried to Change the World but Changed America*. Princeton: Princeton University Press, 2017.

Holtrop, P.N. *Tussen Piëtisme en Réveil. Het 'Deutsche Christentumsgesellschaft' in Nederland, 1784-1833*. Amsterdam: Rodopi, 1975.

Hopewell, Wm. J. *The Missionary Emphasis of the General Association of Regular Baptist Churches*. Chicago: Regular Baptist Press, 1963.

Howard, David M. *The Dream that Would Not Die: The Birth and Growth of the World Evangelical Fellowship 1846-1985*. Exeter: Paternoster, 1986.

Howard, Thomas A. *God and the Atlantic: America, Europe, and the Religious Divide*. New York: Oxford University Press, 2011.

Huizinga, Johan. *America: A Dutch Historian's Vision, from Afar and Near*, translated, with an introd. and notes, by Herbert H. Rowen. New York: Harper & Row, 1972.

Hunter, James D. *To Change the World: The Irony, Tragedy, and Possibility of Christianity in the Late Modern World*. New York: Oxford University Press, 2010.

Hutchinson, Mark and John Wolffe. *A Short History of Global Evangelicalism*. Cambridge: Cambridge University Press, 2012.

Hutchison, William R., ed. *Between the Times: The Travail of the Protestant Establishment, 1900-1960*. Cambridge: Cambridge University Press, 1989.

International Missionary Council. *Minutes of the enlarged meeting and the committee of the International missionary council, Willingen, Germany, July 5th to 21st, 1952*. London: International Council, 1952.

Jacobsen, Douglas and William Vance Trollinger, Jr., eds. *Re-Forming the Center: American Protestantism, 1900 to the Present*. Grand Rapids: Eerdmans, 1998.

Janssens, Ruud. "I would Rather Go to Europe than go to Heaven." In Michael J. Wintle, ed. *Imagining Europe: Europe and European Civilisation as Seen from its Margins and by the Rest of the World, in the Nineteenth and Twentieth Centuries*. Brussels: Peter Lang, 2008, 123-145.

Jenkins, Philip. *Mystics and Messiahs: Cults and New Religions in American History*. New York: Oxford University Press, 2000.

Jongeneel, Jan. "European-Continental Perception and Critiques of British and American Protestant Missions." *Exchange* 30.1 (2001): 103-124.

Jung, Friedhelm. *Die deutsche Evangelikale Bewegung: Grundlinien ihrer Geschichte und Theologie*. Frankfurt: Lang, 1992.

Kee, Kevin. *Revivalists: Marketing the Gospel in English Canada, 1884-1957*. Montreal and Kingston: McGill-Queen's University Press, 2006.

Kessler Jr., J.B.A. *A Study of the Evangelical Alliance in Great Britain*. Goes: Oosterbaan en le Cointre, 1968.

Kincheloe, Samuel C. *Research Memorandum on Religion in the Depression*. New York: Social Science Research Council, 1937; repr. 1972.

Kirby, Dianne, ed. *Religion and the Cold War*. New York: Palgrave Macmillan, 2003.

Klauber, Martin. *The Great Commission: Evangelicals and the History of World Missions*. Nashville, Tenn.: B & H Publishing Group, 2008.

Klimke, Martin. *The Other Alliance: Student Protest in West Germany and the United States in the Global Sixties*. Princeton: Princeton University Press, 2010.

Kloppenberg, James T. *Uncertain Victory: Social Democracy and Progressivism in European and American Thought, 1870-1920*. New York: Oxford University Press, 1988.

Koop, Allen V. *American Evangelical Missionaries in France, 1945-1975*. Lanham, MD: University Press of America, 1986.

Kosc, Grzegorz, Clara Juncker, Sharon Monteith, Britta Waldschmidt-Nelson, eds. *The Transatlantic Sixties: Europe and the United States in the Counterculture Decade*. Bielefeld: Transcript, 2013.

Kraan, E.D. *Rapport stand geestelijk leven: Generale Synode Utrecht*. Utrecht, 1959.

Krabbendam, Hans. "Zielenverbrijzelaars en zondelozen. Reacties in de Nederlandse pers op Moody, Sankey en Pearsall Smith, 1874-1878." *Documentatieblad voor de Nederlandse Kerkgeschiedenis na 1800* 34 (May 1991): 39-55.

Krabbendam, Hans. *Freedom on the Horizon: Dutch Immigration to America, 1840-1940*. Grand Rapids: Eerdmans, 2009.

Krabbendam, Hans. "'The Harvest is Ripe': American Evangelicals in European Missions 1950-1980." In Axel Schäfer, ed. *American Evangelicalism and the 1960s*. Madison: University of Wisconsin Press, 2013, 231-254.

Krabbendam, Hans. "Opening a Market for Missions: American Evangelicals and the Re-Christianization of Europe." *Amerikastudien* 59.2 (2014): 153-175.

Krabbendam, Hans. "The Transformers: Continuity and Change in the European Campaigns of American Evangelists Frank Buchman and Billy Graham, 1920-1960." *Journal of Religion in Europe* 7 (2014): 223-245.

Krabbendam, Hans. "Three-Way Chess: Arie Kok and the Failure to Organize American Fundamentalism in Europe." *Church History and Religious Culture* 94 (2014): 227-258.

Krabbendam, Hans. "A Transatlantic Religious Alliance? American and European Protestant Encounters, 1945-1965." *Journal of Transatlantic Studies* 15.3 (2017): 1-17.

Krabbendam, Hans. "Billy Graham and American Evangelicals in Europe, 1946-1986: Building Bridges or Separating Continents?" *Trajecta* 26.1 (2017): 195-218.

Krabbendam, Hans. "Full Members of the TEAM? Evangelical Women in the European Mission, 1945-1980." *Journal of American Studies* 51.4 (2017): 1095-1116.

Krabbendam, Hans. "They Came to Stay: The Weak Transnational Relations of the Dutch in America." In Henk Aay, Janny Venema, and Dennis N. Voskuil, eds. *Sharing Pasts: Dutch Americans Through Four Centuries*. Holland, MI: Van Raalte Press, 2017, 3-23.

Krabbendam, Hans. "Introduction: American Evangelical Missions and Postwar Europe." In John Corrigan and Frank Hinkelmann, eds. *Return to Sender: American Evangelical Missions in Twentieth Century Europe*. Zürich: LIT-Verlag, 2019, 9-16.

Kraemer, Hendrik. *The Christian Message in a Non-Christian World*. New York: Harper, 1938.

Krol, Bram. *Het verhaal van Agapè (voorheen Instituut voor Evangelisatie)*. Doorn: Stichting Agapé, 1994.

Kruse, Kevin M. *One Nation Under God: How Corporate America Invented Christian America*. New York: Basic Books, 2015.

Kunter, Katharina and Jens Holger Schjørring, eds. *Europäisches und globales Christentum: Herausforderungen und Transformationen im 20. Jahrhundert: Challenges and Transformations in the 20th Century*. Göttingen: Vandenhoeck & Ruprecht, 2011.

Lammers, Alfons. *Helden van het geloof: Amerika in de greep van de dominees*. Amsterdam: Balans, 1988.

Lanzinger, Klaus. *Jason's Voyage: The Search for the Old World in American Literature: A Study of Melville, Hawthorne, Henry James, and Thomas Wolfe*. New York: Peter Lang, 1989.

Larson, Mel. *Young Man on Fire: The Story of Torrey Johnson and Youth for Christ*. Chicago: Youth Publications, 1945.

Larson, Mel. *Youth for Christ*. Grand Rapids: Zondervan, 1947.

Laubach, Fritz. *Aufbruch der Evangelikalen*. Wuppertal: R. Brockhaus Verlag, 1972.

Layman with a Notebook, The. *What is the Oxford Group?* London: Oxford University Press, 1933.

Lean, Garth. *Frank Buchman: A Life*. London: Constable, 1985.

Leiper, Henry Smith, ed. *Christianity Today: A Survey of the State of the Churches: Sponsored by the American Committee for the World Council of Churches*. New York: Morehouse-Gorham, 1947.

Levine, Harry G. "Temperance Cultures: Concern about Alcohol Problems in Nordic and English-Speaking Cultures." In Malcolm Lader, Griffith Edwards, and D. Colin Drummond, eds. *The Nature of Alcohol and Drug Related Problems*. Oxford: Oxford University Press, 1992, 15-36.

Lewis, Donald M., ed. *Christianity Reborn: The Global Expansion of Evangelicalism in the Twentieth Century*. Grand Rapids: Eerdmans, 2004.

Loveland, Anne C. *American Evangelicals and the U.S. Military, 1942-1993*. Baton Rouge: Louisiana State University Press, 1997.

Lüdke, Frank. "Von Bonifatius bis Willow Creek – eine kurze Geschichte der englisch-amerikanischen Einflüsse auf das Christentum in Deutschland." In Frank Lüdke and Norbert Schmidt, eds. *Die neue Welt und der neue Pietismus. Angloamerikanische Einflüsse*. Berlin: LIT-Verlag, 2012, 5-33.

MacSweeney, Edward. *Amerikanische Wohlfahrtshilfe für Deutschland 1945-1950*. Freiburg i.Br.: Caritas, 1950.

Mäläskä, Hilkka. *The Challenge for Evangelical Missions to Europe: A Scandinavian Case Study*. South Pasadena, CA: William Carey Library, [1970].

Marsden, George M. *Reforming Fundamentalism: Fuller Seminary and the New Evangelicalism.* Grand Rapids, MI: Eerdmans, 1987.

Marshall, David B. *Secularizing the Faith: Canadian Protestant Clergy and the Crisis of Belief, 1850-1940*. Toronto: University of Toronto Press, 1992.

Martin, David. *Pentecostalism: The World Their Parish.* Oxford: Blackwell, 2002.

Martin, David. *On Secularization: Towards a Revised General Theory*. Farnham, UK: Ashgate, 2005.

Martin, Marion F. "The Conservative Baptist Mission in Italy: Past Achievements, Future Opportunities." D. Miss. Dissertation. Deerfield, IL: Trinity Evangelical Divinity School, 1994.

Martin, R.H. "The Pan-Evangelical Impulse in Britain 1795-1830: With Special Reference to Four London Societies." PhD diss. Oxford, UK, 1974.

Martin, Suzan F. *A Nation of Immigrants*. Cambridge: Cambridge University Press, 2010.

Martin, William. *A Prophet with Honor: The Billy Graham Story.* New York: Morrow, 1991.

McAlister, Jack. *Evangelizing Europe: Heart of the World.* Studio City, CA: World Literature Crusade, 1961.

McAlister, Melani. "The Global Conscience of American Evangelicalism: Internationalism and Social Concern in the 1970s and Beyond." *Journal of American Studies* 51 (November 2017): 1197-1220.

McGavran, Donald. "Uppsala's 'Program for Mission' and Church Growth." *Church Growth Bulletin* 5.2 (November 1968): 12.

McIntire, Carl. *A Testimony in Europe: Travel Letters on Mission.* Collingswood, NJ: Christian Beacon Press, 1951.

McIntosh, Gary L. "Donald A. McGavran: Life, Influence and Legacy in Mission." In Charles E. Van Engen, ed. *The State of Missiology Today: Global Innovations in Christian Witness.* Downers Grove, IL: IVP Academic, 2016, 19-37.

McLeod, Hugh. "The 1960s and 1970s as a Period of Basic Change." In Katharina Kunter and Jens Holger Schjørring, eds. *Europäisches und globales Christentum: Herausforderungen und Transformationen im 20. Jahrhundert: Challenges and Transformations in the 20th Century.* Göttingen: Vandenhoeck & Ruprecht, 2011.

Micklethwait, John and Adrian Woolbridge. *God is Back: How the Global Revival of Faith is Changing the World.* New York: Penguin, 2009.

Miller, Steven P. *The Age of Evangelicalism: American Born-Again Years*. New York: Oxford University Press, 2013.

Moore, Walter W. *A Year in Europe*. 3rd ed., Richmond, VA: The Presbyterian Committee on Publication, 1905.

Moreau, A. Scott. "Putting the Survey in Perspective." In Linda J. Weber and Dotsey Welliver, eds. *Mission Handbook: U.S. and Canadian Protestant Ministries Overseas*. 20th ed.; Weathon IL: Billy Graham Center, 2007.

Mortenson, Vernon. *God Made it Grow: Historical Sketches of TEAM's Church Planting Work.* Pasadena, CA: William Carey Library, 1994.

Mouw, Dirk. "Dutch Clergy in Colonial North America." In Leon van den Broeke, Hans Krabbendam, and Dirk Mouw, eds. *Transatlantic Pieties: Dutch Clergy in Colonial America.* Grand Rapids, MI: Eerdmans, 2012, 1-34.

Mott, John R. *The Evangelization of the World in this Generation.* New York: Student Volunteer Movement for Foreign Missions, 1900.

Moyer, Kenyon E. "The Selection and Training of the Overseas Personnel of the Christian Church." *Occasional Bulletin* 8.8 (15 August 1957): 1-15.

Moyer, Kenyon E. *A Study of Missionary Motivation, Training, and Withdrawal (1932-1952): Based on Questionnaires Answered by 915 Missionaries Who Represent 16 North American Mission Boards.* New York: Missionary Research Library, 1957.

Muhr, Marlène. *Along Unfamiliar Paths: Proclaiming God's Light in Man's Night, the Story of Gospel Recordings Europe.* Los Angeles: Gospel Recordings; Pasadena, CA: Printed by Geddes Press, 1982.

Mulder, William. *Homeward To Zion: The Mormon Migration from Scandinavia.* Minneapolis: University of Minnesota Press, 2000.

Murray, Ian H. *David Martyn Lloyd-Jones: The Fight of Faith, 1939-1981*, vol. 2. Edinburgh: The Banner of Truth Trust, 2004.

Nichol, Todd, ed. *Crossings: Norwegian-American Lutheranism as Transatlantic Tradition.* Northfield, MN: Norwegian Historical Association, 2003.

Nolan, Mary. *The Transatlantic Century: Europe and America, 1890-2010.* Cambridge: Cambridge University Press, 2012.

Noll, Mark A. *America's God: From Jonathan Edwards to Abraham Lincoln.* New York: Oxford University Press, 2002.

Noll, Mark A. *The Old Religion in a New World: The History of North American Christianity.* Grand Rapids, MI: Eerdmans, 2002.

Noll, Mark A. *The New Shape of World Christianity: How American Experience Reflects Global Faith.* Downers Grove, IL: IVP Academic, 2009.

Noll, Mark A., David W. Bebbington, George A. Rawlyk, eds. *Evangelicalism: Comparative Studies of Popular Protestantism in North America, the British Isles and Beyond, 1700-1990.* New York: Oxford University Press, 1994.

Noll, Mark A. and Luke E. Harlow, eds. *Religion and American Politics: From the Colonial Period to the Present.* 2nd ed., New York: Oxford University Press, 2007.

North American Protestant Foreign Mission Agencies. New York: Missionary Research Library, 1962.

North American Protestant Foreign Mission Agencies. New York: Missionary Research Library, 1964.

North American Protestant Ministries Overseas. New York: Missionary Research Library, 1968.

Ott, Bernhard. *Beyond Fragmentation: Integrating Mission and Theological Education. A critical Assessment of some Recent Developments in Evangelical Theological Education.* Oxford: Regnum Books, 2001.

Overland, Orm. "Religion and Church in Early Immigrant Letters." In Todd Nichol, ed. *Crossings: Norwegian-American Lutheranism as Transatlantic Tradition.* Northfield, MN: Norwegian Historical Association, 2003. 42-43, 46

Paas, Stefan. "The Making of a Mission Field: Paradigms of Evangelistic Mission in Europe." *Exchange* 41 (2012): 44-67.

Paas, Stefan. *Church Planting in the Secular West: Learning from the European Experience.* Grand Rapids, MI: Eerdmans, 2016.

Paas, Stefan. "Evangelistic Mission in Europe: Seven Historical Models." In Gerrit Noort, Kyriaki Avtzi, and Stefan Paas, eds. *Sharing Good News: Handbook on Evangelism in Europe.* Geneva: World Council of Churches Publications, 2017, 21-35.

Pasture, Patrick. "Christendom and the Legacy of the Sixties: Between the Secular City and the Age of Aquarius." *Revue d'Histoire Ecclésiastique* 99.1 (2004): 82-117.

Pfeiffer, Joseph F. "John H. Yoder and the Secretive Malone College Consultations on Mission 1961-1967." Unpublished research paper, Associated Mennonite Biblical Seminary 2008 at www.academia.edu.

Pierson, Paul E. "Lessons in Mission from the Twentieth Century: Conciliar Missions." In Jonathan J. Bonk, ed. *Between Past and Future: Evangelical Mission Entering the Twenty-first Century.* Pasadena, CA: William Carey Library, 2003.

Pollock, John. *Billy Graham: Evangelist to the World.* New York: Harper and Row, 1979.

Porter, Andrew. *Religion Versus Empire? British Protestant Missionaries and Overseas Expansion, 1700-1914.* Manchester: Manchester University Press, 2004.

Postel, Charles. *The Populist Vision.* Oxford: Oxford University Press, 2007.

Preston, Andrew. "The Death of a Peculiar Special Relationship: Myron Taylor and the Religious Roots of America's Cold War." In John Dumbrell and Axel Schäfer, eds. *America's Special Relationships: Foreign and Domestic Aspects of the Politics of Alliance.* New York and London: Routledge, 2009, 202-216.

Preston, Andrew. *Sword of the Spirit, Shield of Faith: Religion in American War and Diplomacy.* New York: Alfred A. Knopf, 2012.

Prins, Aaldert. "The History of the Belgian Gospel Mission from 1918 to 1962." Doctoral dissertation Leuven University, 2015.

Probst, Andreas. "Billy Graham in Westdeutschland 1954/55 – Ein amerikanischer Exportschlager auf Missionierungsfeldzug." M.A. Thesis, Ruprecht-Karls-Universität Heidelberg, 2012.

Railton, Nicholas M. *No North Sea: The Anglo-German Evangelical Network in the Middle of the Nineteenth Century.* Leiden: Brill, 2000.

Randall, Ian M. "Conservative Constructionist: The Early Influence of Billy Graham in Britain." *Evangelical Quarterly* 67.4 (1995): 309-333.

Randall, Ian M. "American Influence on Evangelicals in Europe: A Comparison of the Founding of the Evangelical Alliance and the World Evangelical Fellowship." In Hans Krabbendam and Derek Rubin, eds. *Religion in America: European and American Perspectives*. Amsterdam: VU University Press, 2004, 263-274.

Randall, Ian. "Evangelicals and European Integration." *European Journal of Theology* 14.1 (2005): 17-26.

Raud, G. P. *A Life Lived for God: The Story of G.P. Raud, Founder of the Bible Christian Union*. New York: Bible Christian Union, 1955.

Rawlyk, George and Mark A. Noll, eds. *Amazing Grace: Evangelicalism in Australia, Britain, Canada, and the United States*. Grand Rapids, MI: Baker, 1993.

Reports of the 19th Annual Mission Executives Retreat, September 28-October 1, 1970, Winona Lake, Indiana. Washington: EFMA, n.y.

Rhoads, Gladys Titzck and Nancy Titzck Anderson. *McIntire: Defender of Faith and Freedom*. Maitland, FL: Xulon Press, 2012.

Roeber, A.G. "The Waters of Rebirth: The Eighteenth Century and Transoceanic Protestant Christianity." *Church History* 79.1 (2010): 40-76.

Rohrer, S. Scott. *Wandering Souls: Protestant Migrations in America, 1630-1865*. Chapel Hill, NC: The University of North Carolina Press, 2010.

Ruotsila, Markku. *The Origins of Christian Anti-Internationalism: Conservative Evangelicals and the League of Nations*. Washington DC: Georgetown University Press, 2008.

Ruotsila, Markku. "Carl McIntire and the Fundamentalist Origins of the Christian Right." *Church History* 81.2 (June 2012): 378-407.

Ruotsila, Markku. *Fighting Fundamentalist: Carl McIntire and the Politicization of American Fundamentalism*. New York: Oxford University Press, 2016.

Sack, Daniel. *Moral Re-Armament: The Reinventions of an American Religious Movement*. New York: Palgrave, 2009.

Sadler, George W. a.o. *Europe, Whither Bound? A Symposium Telling of Southern Baptist Missionary Work in Italy, Spain, and the Balkan States – Hungary and Yugoslavia*. Nashville: Broadman Press, 1951.

Sanneh, Lamin. *Translating the Message: The Missionary Impact on Culture*. Maryknoll, NY: Orbis Books, 2009.

Schaefer, Axel. *Countercultural Conservatives: American Evangelicalism from the Postwar Revival to the New Christian Right*. Madison: University of Wisconsin Press, 2011.

Schaefer, Axel, ed. *American Evangelicals and the 1960s*. Madison: University of Wisconsin Press, 2013.

Schultze, Quentin J. *Christianity and the Mass Media in America: Toward a Democratic Accommodation*. East Lansing: Michigan State University Press, 2003.

Scott, Waldron. "Double Helix: A Missionary's Odyssey." N.p., n.d. retrieved 16 February 2012.

Scripps, Jan. *Sojourner in the Promised Land: Forty Years among the Mormons*. Urbana: University of Illinois Press, 2000.

Secretariat for Evangelism of the World Council of Churches in Geneva. *Evangelism in France*. Geneva, 1951.

Sehat, David. *The Myth of American Religious Freedom*. New York: Oxford University Press, 2011.

Setran, David P. *The College 'Y': Student Religion in the Era of Secularization*. New York: Palgrave, 2007.

Shephard, Ben. *The Long Road Home: The Aftermath of the Second World War*. London: The Bodley Head, 2010.

Silk, Mark. *Spiritual Politics: Religion and America Since World War II*. New York: Simon and Schuster, 1988.

Slack, Kenneth, ed. *Hope in the Desert: The Churches' United Response to Human Need, 1944-1984*. Geneva: World Council of Churches, 1986.

Smith, Oswald. "The Miracle of Youth for Christ in Europe." *People's Magazine* 1 (1949): 10-21.

Snape, Michael. *God and Uncle Sam: Religion and America's Armed Forces in World War II*. Woodbridge, UK: Boydell Press, 2015.

Sollors, Werner. *The Temptation of Despair: Tales of the 1940s*. Cambridge, MA: The Belknap Press of Harvard University Press, 2014.

Southern Baptist Convention. *Southern Baptists in Europe*. Richmond, VA: Foreign Mission Board of the Southern Baptist Convention, 1939.

Stanley, Brian. *The Bible and the Flag: Protestant Missions and British Imperialism in the Nineteenth and Twentieth Centuries*. Leicester: Apollos, 1990.

Stanley, Brian. *The World Missionary Conference: Edinburgh 1910*. Grand Rapids: Eerdmans, 2009.

Stanley, Brian. *The Global Diffusion of Evangelicalism: The Age of Billy Graham and John Stott.* Nottingham: Inter-Varsity Press, 2013.

Stanley, Brian. "Mission to the World: Changing Perspectives in American Protestantism, 1910-2010." In Larry Eskridge and Edith L. Blumhofer, eds. *Saving the World? The Changing Terrain of American Protestant Missions, 1910 to the Present.* University of Alabama Press, forthcoming.

Stark, Rodney. "Efforts to Christianize Europe, 400-2000." *Journal of Contemporary Religion* 16:1 (2001): 105-123.

Stenning, Robert E. *Church World Service: Fifty Years of Help and Hope.* New York: Friendly Press, 1996.

Stephan, Alexander, ed. *The Americanization of Europe: Culture, Diplomacy, and Anti-Americanism after 1945.* New York: Berghahn, 2006.

Stoneman, Timothy. "Creating The Protestant Voice of Europe, 1945-1970." Unpublished paper, Roosevelt Study Center, Middelburg, the Netherlands, 15 July 2015.

Stoneman, Timothy. "Global Radio Broadcasting and the Dynamics of American Evangelicalism." *Journal of American Studies* 51 (November 2017): 1139-1170.

Stott, John. "The Significance of Lausanne." In Paul Wesley Chilcote and Laceye C. Warner, eds. *The Study of Evangelism: Exploring a Missional Practice of the Church.* Grand Rapids: Eerdmans, 2008, 305-312.

Stout, Harry S. *The New England Soul: Preaching and Religious Culture in Colonial New England.* New York: Oxford University Press, 1986.

Strom, Jonathan, Hartmut Lehmann, and James Van Horn Melton, eds. *Pietism in Germany and North-America, 1680-1820.* Farnham, UK: Ashgate, 2009.

Stuart, John. *British Missionaries and the End of Empire: East, Central and Southern Africa, 1939-64.* Grand Rapids, MI: Eerdmans, 2011.

Sunquist, Scott W. and Caroline N. Becker, eds. *A History of Presbyterian Missions 1944-2007.* Louisville, KY: Geneva Press, 2008.

Sutton, Matthew Avery. "Was FDR the Antichrist? The Birth of Fundamentalist Antiliberalism in a Global Age." *Journal of American History* 98.4 (March 2012): 1052-1074.

Sutton, Matthew Avery. *American Apocalypse: A History of Modern Evangelicalism.* Cambridge: The Belknap Press of Harvard University Press, 2014.

Swartz, David R. *Moral Minority: The Evangelical Left in an Age of Conservatism.* Philadelphia: University of Pennsylvania Press, 2012.

Szulc, Tad. *Pope John Paul II: The Biography.* New York, 1995.

Taylor, Charles. *A Secular Age.* Cambridge: The Belknap Press of Harvard University Press, 2007.

Taylor, Clyde W. *Ecumenical Strategy in Foreign Missions.* Washington, DC: Evangelical Foreign Missions Association, 1961.

Thompson, Michael G. *For God and Globe: Christian Internationalism in the United States Between the Great War and the Cold War.* Ithaca, NY: Cornell University Press, 2015.

Thompson, Phylis. *Firebrand of Flanders: The Gospel in Belgium Seen in the Life of Odilon Vansteenberghe.* Chicago: Moody Press, 1966.

Thorkildsen, Dag. "Revivalism, Emigration and Religious Networks in Nineteenth-Century Norway." In Jeremy Gregory and Hugh McLeod, eds. *International Religious Networks.* Woodbridge: The Boydell Press/Ecclesiastical History Society, 2012, 165-182.

Trollinger, William Vance. *God's Empire: William Bell Riley and Midwestern Fundamentalism.* Madison: University of Wisconsin Press, 1990.

Turner, John G. *Bill Bright and Campus Crusade for Christ: The Renewal of Evangelicalism in Postwar America.* Chapel Hill: The University of North Carolina Press, 2008.

Tyrrell, Ian. *Reforming the World: The Creation of America's Moral Empire.* Princeton: Princeton University Press, 2010.

Vajko, Robert J. "A History and Analysis of the Church-Planting Ministry of The Evangelical Alliance Mission in France 1952-1975." MA Thesis Trinity Evangelical Divinity School, Deerfield IL, June 1975.

Van Capelleveen, Jan et al. *De story van Youth for Christ.* Kampen: Kok, 1977.

van Dijk, Roelof. *"Veranderend getij": Structuurveranderingen in Nederland en hun consequenties voor het kerkelijk leven,* 3 vols. Amsterdam: Stichting Gereformeerd Sociologisch Instituut, 1961-1962.

Van Rooden, Peter. "Long-term Religious Developments in the Netherlands, ca 1750-2000." In Hugh McLeod and W. Ustorf, eds. *The Decline of Christendom in Western Europe, 1750-2000.* Cambridge: Cambridge University Press, 2002, 113-129.

Van Rooden, Peter. "The Strange Death of Dutch Christendom." In Callum G. Brown and Michael Snape, eds. *Secularisation in the Christian World: Essays in Honour of Hugh McLeod.* Farnham: Ashgate, 2010, 175-196.

Vellenga, Sipco. *Een ondernemende beweging. De groei van de evangelische beweging in Nederland.* Amsterdam: VU University Press, 1991.

Voigt, Karl Heinz. *Die Heiligungsbewegung zwischen methodistischer Kirche und landeskirchlicher Gemeinschaft: die "Triumphreise" von Robert Pearsall Smith im Jahre 1875 und ihre Auswirkungen auf die zwischenkirchlichen Beziehungen.* Wuppertal: Brockhaus, 1996.

Vought, Dale G. *Protestants in Modern Spain.* South Pasadena, CA: William Carey Library, 1973.

Wacker, Grant. *America's Pastor: Billy Graham and the Shaping of a Nation.* Cambridge, MA: Harvard University Press, 2014.

Währisch-Oblau, Claudia. *The Missionary Self-Perception of Pentecostal/Charismatic Church Leaders from the Global South in Europe: Bringing Back the Gospel.* Leiden: Brill, 2009.

Wagner, William L. *North American Protestant Missionaries in Western Europe: A Critical Appraisal.* Bonn: Verlag für Kultur und Wissenschaft, 1993.

Walls, Andrew. *The Missionary Movement in Christian History.* Maryknoll, NY: Orbis Books, 1996.

Warner, Keith C. "History of the Netherlands Mission of the Church of Jesus Christ of Latter Day Saints, 1861-1966." Master thesis, Provo, Utah, Brigham Young University, 1967.

Warnshuis, A.L. *The Church's Battle for Europe's Soul.* New York: American Committee for the World Council of Churches, 1945.

Westin, Gunnar. *The Free Church Through the Ages.* Nashville, Tennessee: Broadman Press, 1958.

"The Wheaton Declaration." *Evangelical Mission Quarterly* 2 (1966): 231-244.

Wilson, Samuel. "Current Trends in North American Protestant Ministries Overseas." *International Bulletin of Missionary Research* 5.2 (1981): 74-75.

Wilson, Samuel and John Siewert, eds. *Mission Handbook: North American Protestant Ministries Overseas.* 13th ed. Monrovia, CA: Missions Advanced Research and Communication Center, 1986.

Winter, Ralph D. *The Twenty-Five Unbelievable Years 1945-1969.* South Pasadena: William Carey Library, 1970.

Witmer, Safara Austin. *Bible College Story: Education With Dimension.* Manhasset, NY: Channel Press, 1962.

Wolffe, John. "Transatlantic Visitors and Evangelical Networks, 1829-1861." In Jeremy Gregory and Hugh McLeod, eds. *International Religious Networks.* Woodbridge: The Boydell Press/Ecclesiastical History Society, 2012, 183-193.

World Survey by the Interchurch World Movement of North America, 2 vols. New York: Interchurch Press, 1920.

Wyneken, JonDavid K. "The Western Allies, German Churches and the Emerging Cold War in Germany, 1948-1952." In Philip Muehlenbeck, ed. *Religion and the Cold War: A Global Perspective.* Nashville: Vanderbilt University Press, 2012, 18-43.

Zeilstra, Jurjen A. *European Unity in Ecumenical Thinking, 1937-1948.* Zoetermeer: Boekencentrum, 1995.

Zeilstra, Jurjen A. *Visser 't Hooft: Een leven voor de oecumene. 1900-1985.* Middelburg: Skandalon, 2018.

INDEX OF NAMES, PLACES, AND ORGANIZATIONS

COLOPHON

FINAL EDITING
Luc Vints

COPY EDITING
Lieve Claes

LAY-OUT
Alexis Vermeylen

KADOC
Documentation and Research Center on Religion, Culture and Society
Vlamingenstraat 39
B - 3000 Leuven
www.kadoc.kuleuven.be

Leuven University Press
Minderbroedersstraat 4
B - 3000 Leuven
www.lup.be